C000200198

Worship in the Spirit

Charismatic Worship in the Church of England

STUDIES IN EVANGELICAL HISTORY AND THOUGHT

A complete listing of all titles in this series
appears at the close of this book

STUDIES IN EVANGELICAL HISTORY AND THOUGHT

Worship in the Spirit

Charismatic Worship in the Church of England

James H. S. Steven

Foreword by Andrew Walker

PATERNOSTER

Copyright © James H S Steven (2002)

First published (2002) by Paternoster

Paternoster is an imprint of Authentic Media,
9 Holdom Avenue, Bletchley, Milton Keynes, MK1 1QR, U.K.
and
P.O. Box 1047, Waynesboro, GA 30830-2047, U.S.A.

08 07 06 05 04 03 02   7 6 5 4 3 2 1

British Library Cataloguing in Publication Data
A catalogue record for this book is available from the British Library

ISBN 1-84227-103-2

Typeset by the author
and printed and bound in Great Britain by
Nottingham Alpha Graphics

STUDIES IN EVANGELICAL HISTORY AND THOUGHT

Series Preface

The Evangelical movement has been marked by its union of four emphases: on the Bible, on the cross of Christ, on conversion as the entry to the Christian life and on the responsibility of the believer to be active. The present series is designed to publish scholarly studies of any aspect of this movement in Britain or overseas. Its volumes include social analysis as well as exploration of Evangelical ideas. The books in the series consider aspects of the movement shaped by the Evangelical Revival of the eighteenth century, when the impetus to mission began to turn the popular Protestantism of the British Isles and North America into a global phenomenon. The series aims to reap some of the rich harvest of academic research about those who, over the centuries, have believed that they had a gospel to tell to the nations.

Series Editors

In memory of Michael Vasey
whose teaching and inspiration
first kindled my interest in the study of Christian worship

Contents

FOREWORD

A common weakness in studies of the Charismatic Renewal is the inability to be able to grasp both the theological and social dimensions of the movement, so that we are often left feeling dissatisfied with one sided and partisan accounts. In recent years, however, a multi-disciplined and, I think, increasingly balanced approach to Charismatic Christianity has begun to emerge that seeks to overcome the either/or distinctions of theology and social science. The usual profile of a researcher in this field is a theologically trained social scientist, or conversely a scientifically competent theologian. There is no guarantee of course that such a researcher, even a very good one, will always tell Charismatics what they want to hear; Martyn Percy's study of Wimber is not exactly an endorsement of Vineyard spirituality (*Words, Wonders and Power: Understanding Contemporary Christian Fundamentalism and Revivalism*, London: SPCK, 1996). Increasingly, however, we note that this new generation of scholars write with the insights of the insider, but in a reflective manner (Anglican Mark Cartledge, is an excellent example of such a person. See his *Charismatic Glossolalia: An empirical-theological study*, Ashgate, 2001).

This present book exemplifies the new scholarly generation at its best. Its author, James Steven, writes polemically but with eirenic intent. That he had the necessary skills to apply both ethnography and theology to the study of Charismatic worship was presaged in two previous works he published nearly ten years apart. The first was a descriptive but telling study of Restorationist worship and its total rejection of mainline liturgical forms (*Worship In The Restoration Movement*, Nottingham, Grove Books, 1989). His second study, which was altogether more ambitious, was a comparison of the hymnody of early Methodism and present day Charismatic practice ('Charismatic Hymnody in the Light of Early Methodist Hymnody', *Studia Liturgica* 27 (1997) 2:217-34).

What we find in this book on Anglican Charismatic worship is that James Steven presents us not only with the marriage of the earlier different approaches but also with something altogether more mature and satisfying. Indeed everything in this study satisfies more than we might have expected. The initial historical section on the Renewal in the Church of England, for example, is a model of historiography – not merely informative but contextually informed: this is an account that participants in these events will recognize as both accurate and authentic. The methodological choice of case studies conducted by interview and participant observation is pleasing because they are easy to follow, and modest in scope (and the modest tone throughout the whole study is a distinctive and welcoming contrast to much of the bombastic and iconoclastic manner of many social scientific studies).

The ethnographic account that emerges, however, is not bland or simplistic for it is given critical bite by the application of anthropological insights into rites and ceremonies; and the sympathetic understanding – *verstehen* – of Max Weber is utilised in the cause of making sense of these ritual processes and the shared meaning of an accessible 'public horizon'. And truth to tell if we were only presented with the ethnography we would be satisfied enough, for from it we learn something we did not know before of the inner-workings and intimacy of Anglican Charismatic Worship.

But when all is said and done, what makes this study critically important not only for scholars but also for the reflective praxis of Charismatic practitioners, is James Steven's theological assessment. On the one hand he does not fall for the old chestnut of drawing improper conclusions from empirical data: there are no unwarranted extrapolations from 'is' statements to 'ought' prescriptions. On the other hand this is no arm chair theology either: it is gleaned and gathered from the labours of participant observation. And what James Steven has found on the ground is both heartening and worrisome. It is heartening because we discover that the pneumatological character of Charismatic Worship is open to the epicletic incoming and indwelling of the Holy Spirit with its concomitant sense of the presence of God. What remains worrying, however, despite the lip service to Trinitarian orthodoxy, is the apparent failure to relate Word, Spirit, and Father together in true inter-communion: not to worship the Father in the Son through the Spirit, so that we are caught-up in the life of the Trinity, is to run the risk of falling back on, and into, ourselves where too easily we mistake the natural tremors of our hearts for the divine action of the Spirit in our midst.

But as the conclusion makes clear, further research is needed to determine the spiritual and theological contours of Charismatic worship. It remains to be seen whether such worship typically promotes a Jesuology over a pneumatology, and whether the Christology underlying such an object of worship is predicated on a sentimental and docetic Jesus. If this should turn out to be so it would mean that the Incarnate Christ – the God among us who is also one of us – is unwittingly denied. On the other hand it may turn out that further research will reveal Charismatic experience and worship is indeed both anchored in a Trinitarian God and grounded in an Incarnate Christ. If this should turn out to be so it will give those of us who see ourselves rooted in the historical Christian tradition cause to rejoice.

What ever may be found, one thing is certain, James Steven has set a benchmark for future researchers with this study, for it is both sociologically rigorous and theologically perspicacious.

Professor Andrew Walker, King's College London, March 2002

Acknowledgements

In completing this book, which is a lightly revised version of my PhD thesis, I am aware of many to whom I am indebted for their help and support. I am grateful to all at St. John's Church in Welling, whose company in worship inspired and stimulated the beginnings of this work. The sustained advice and constructive criticism of Professor Andrew Walker, my supervisor, was invaluable throughout the development of the research and I am honoured that he has written the Foreword to this book. The success of the research hinged upon the generous hospitality of my case study parishes and the willingness of my good friend Richard Parrish to be an observer and fellow participant on fieldwork visits. My thanks go to them for their cooperation in what proved to be a fruitful and enjoyable fieldwork experience. I also acknowledge the practical help and support I received from the Diocese of Winchester, and in particular Dr John Cullen, and Dr Alan Chitty, former Principal of the Bournemouth and Poole College of Further Education, who encouraged me to take a term's sabbatical to write-up.

Having worked hard on the successful completion of my PhD in 1999 I am very glad that Paternoster have provided the opportunity for a wider audience to read the fruits of this research. As my work demonstrates, the story of Charismatic Renewal in the Church of England is an important strand in the late twentieth-century history of evangelicalism and so it is appropriate that this book takes its place in the series 'Studies in Evangelical History and Thought'. I am also pleased that by publishing this work Paternoster has added to its publications on the Charismatic Movement. It was in 1986 that Peter Hocken's important and seminal work, *Streams of Renewal*, was first published, providing the first and still most substantial work on the early history of the Charismatic Movement. I trust that my book will add to the understanding of a Movement that has significantly influenced the public worship of a wide range of churches, not least in my own denomination, the Church of England.

Above all, I would like to thank Rachel, my wife, for her unstinting help, encouragement and patience. Without her support this book would never have reached completion.

CHAPTER 1

Introduction

Since the 1960s there have been two significant developments in the public worship of the Church of England. The first was the liturgical revision that led to the publication in 1980 of the *Alternative Service Book* (*A.S.B.*), a major landmark in the history of Anglican worship since it was the first successful major liturgical revision since the 1662 version of Cranmer's *Book of Common Prayer*. Drawing upon the insights and inspiration of the Liturgical Movement, this revision process, which has continued with recent authorization of the *A.S.B.*'s successor, *Common Worship*, has introduced new ritual structures and liturgical language to congregational worship. The second development has been the growth of Pentecostal styles of worship associated with the Charismatic Movement. Unlike the authorized liturgical revision, this has been a grassroots development in liturgical praxis that has developed more or less independently of the official provision. Borrowing a phrase from the founding father of liturgical theology, Alexander Schmemann, through the influence of the Charismatic Movement the Church of England has absorbed a new kind of 'liturgical piety'.[1] Alongside Anglican spiritualities that focus the encounter with the Holy within the ministry of the Word (evangelical) and the Sacraments (catholic), the new liturgical piety typically locates this encounter within the Pentecostal elements of extended periods of congregational singing, inspired individual participation, and prayers for healing.

Whilst there has been plenty of documentation and commentary that has accompanied the development of the authorized liturgical provision,[2] the character and significance of worship associated with the Charismatic Movement has received comparatively little attention. Clearly, liturgical

---

[1] A. Schmemann, *Introduction to Liturgical Theology*.

[2] R.C.D. Jasper and P.F. Bradshaw, *A Companion to the Alternative Service Book*; R.C.D. Jasper, *The Development of the Anglican Liturgy 1662-1980*; C.O. Buchanan (ed.), *Modern Anglican Liturgies 1958-1968*; *Further Anglican Liturgies 1968-1975*; *Latest Anglican Liturgies 1976-1984*.

commentators and interpreters have found it easier to work with the relatively self-contained process of liturgical revision than to document changes in the public performance of parish worship, a process that demands time-consuming field research. This preference also reflects the fact that academic liturgists have inherited a scholarly discipline and methodology primarily concerned with the study of texts, rather than the full range of social and ritual processes within worship,[3] an exploration of which is essential to the attainment of a complete understanding of the more oral and less text based traditions of charismatic worship. One of the main purposes of this study is to redress this balance.

Studying Charismatic Worship

Within the Church of England, those who have written about charismatic worship fall into three categories. The first are participants who, as practitioners, have written to commend the theory, ideals, and practice of this worship to others. Notable examples are Andrew Maries in his book *One Heart, One Voice*, John Leach and his book *Liturgy and Liberty*[4], John Gunstone's *A People for His Praise* and a variety of publications associated with the Community of Celebration, for example Betty Pulkingham's *Sing God a Simple Song*. The main value of these works lies in the theory of worship they promote, allowing the reader access to the framework of a charismatic liturgical piety. However, while able to give a picture of what worship *should* look like, they do not give much information on worship as it is experienced by parishes seeking to incorporate charismatic elements into public worship.

The second are the incumbents of parishes that have been influenced by the Charismatic Movement. These accounts often include some detail on the related changes in the public worship. Examples include *Open to God*, Tom Walker's account of St. John's, Harborne in Birmingham, *When the Spirit Comes*, Colin Urquhart on St. Hugh's in Luton, and *In the Crucible*, Robert Warren on St. Thomas', Crookes in Sheffield. However, with the exception of Walker, the difficulty with these accounts is the relatively small amount of attention given to details of public worship. This limitation is compounded by the fact that only the parish priest's version of events has been recorded, thus making the accounts vulnerable to criticisms of incompleteness and partiality.

For a more impartial account I turn to the third category, those who have written as researchers of the Charismatic Movement within the Church of England. As an observer and participant in the Movement in the 1970s,

---

[3]   See L.A.Hoffman, *Beyond the Text: A Holistic Approach to Liturgy*, 1-19.

[4]   A revised and updated version of which is *Living Liturgy* (Eastbourne: Kingsway Communications, 1997).

Colin Buchanan wrote *Encountering Charismatic Worship* and a contributory essay on the same theme in *Authority and Freedom in Liturgy*. He was also the catalyst for the report presented to the General Synod of the Church of England in 1981, *The Charismatic Movement in the Church of England*, which included a section on the worship of the Movement. The other main report on the Movement in the 1980s was Josephine Bax's *The Good Wine*, which included a chapter on worship. Common to all these contributions is a reflective analysis of the main characteristics of charismatic worship. The Synod Report, for example, outlines five characteristics of the style of worship that accompany the regular charismatic practices of speaking in tongues, prophecy and healing: the varied use of the human body, new styles of music, an increased freedom for individual contributions, the phenomenon of the 'rally' (worship meetings outside the context of Sunday worship) and a new found sacramentalism (which the Report calls an 'inchoate sacramentality'). However, the work of both Buchanan and Bax, and to a degree the Synod Report, although grounded in experience and observation of worship, would not claim to be systematic in method, and thus tend to be impressionistic and anecdotal in presentation. The one example of systematic research I discovered was Hillyer's work on the effect of liturgical change upon three churches in Cambridge between 1966 and 1976.[5] One of the three churches, which she designated 'St.C', became influenced by the Charismatic Movement in 1971 through its new vicar. In documenting the development of charismatic influence upon the Low Church worship at St.C, Hillyer looked at issues of liturgical language, the use of music and liturgical space, attitudes to the body, congregational participation, and adaptations in liturgical structure.

In picking up the trail that Hillyer laid I have developed a systematic investigation of charismatic worship in a selection of Church of England parishes, concluding with a developed theological reflection. The innovative patterns of ritual and the distinct understandings of the nature of communion with God in charismatic worship have required a multi-disciplined approach, drawing upon the social sciences and theology. Details of my methodology are given in Chapter 3, but at this point it is sufficient to note that the main purpose of my approach is to provide a more detailed and systematically rigorous account of charismatic worship in the Church of England than has hitherto been available.[6]

---

[5] J.V. Hillyer, *Liturgical Change in Cambridge: Attitudes to Liturgy with Special Reference to Charismatic Gifts*.

[6] I am not aware of any substantial work that has been done on the influence of the Charismatic Movement upon the worship of other historic denominations. For a preliminary study on the charismatic worship of the house church or 'Restorationist' movement, an independent offshoot of the Charismatic Movement, see J.H.S. Steven, *Worship in the Restoration Movement*.

I also hope that this work, with its specific focus on the Church of England, will contribute to wider discussions on the role and characteristics of Pentecostal and charismatic worship. Foremost amongst recent contributors to this broader conversation is Daniel Albrecht, whose *Rites in the Spirit* marks the first sustained academic attempt by a Pentecostal to study the spirituality of Pentecostal and charismatic worship. Albrecht's approach is similar to mine in conviction, aim and method. He is convinced that ritual expressions are not peripheral actions for Pentecostals but represent fundamental elements of authentic Pentecostal spirituality. As he puts it, Pentecostal rituals 'enfold the secrets of Pentecostal spirituality'.[7] His main aim, therefore, is to understand Pentecostal and charismatic spirituality by describing, analysing and interpreting ritual. This led him to two years of ethnographic fieldwork in three Northern Californian churches, collecting observation and interview data from their Sunday worship services. The result is an impressive analysis of common core components of Pentecostal spirituality as interpreted through the lens of ritual.

There are, however, significant differences between our respective studies that are worthy of mention, and which make them potentially fruitful conversation partners. Whereas Albrecht's fieldwork focus is on congregations that stand firmly within the Pentecostal-Charismatic tradition, my interest is in investigating how this tradition has been translated within the worship of an historic denomination, the Church of England. Secondly, although our respective analyses run along similar lines, I make greater use of comparable religious and secular social contexts as a means of illuminating key features of the worship observed, and I outline the rationale for this in Chapter 3. Thirdly, my approach takes a further step than Albrecht, whose work ends with an interpretative summary, by offering a concluding theological evaluation of the liturgical piety encountered in fieldwork worship. Albrecht is a skilful exponent and interpreter of a tradition that is his own, whereas I stand within a denomination that both hosts and yet also interrogates the Pentecostal-Charismatic tradition.

My work begins with a chapter outlining the history of Charismatic Renewal in the Church of England, which provides an important historical context for the subsequent discussion of worship in the churches selected for study. Chapter 3 provides the methodological foundation to the following three chapters that describe, analyse and interpret the social and ritual realities of the worship observed in a selection of case study churches. Chapter 4 explores the liturgical characteristics of the churches in their varied strategies to render public worship hospitable to charismatic

---

[7]   D. Albrecht, *Rites in the Spirit: A Ritual Approach to Pentecostal/Charismatic Spirituality*, 150.

expression. Chapters 5 and 6 analyse the two core charismatic rites in case study worship, congregational sung worship and the public ministry of prayer. A theological appraisal of the case studies' worship forms the basis of the final main chapter, Chapter 7. However, before moving on to the main discussion, it is necessary to clarify some of the distinctive features of the Charismatic Movement, particularly in relation to its historical antecedent, classical Pentecostalism.

The Charismatic Movement and Pentecostalism

In summarizing its research on the Charismatic Movement, the 1981 Synod Report acknowledged that it was easier to describe the Movement's characteristics than offer a tidy definition. The British Council of Churches consultation on Charismatic Renewal in 1978 encountered a similar difficulty when in its early stages 'it had become apparent that there was no immediately acceptable definition for "Charismatic Renewal", either to those who felt themselves part of it or to those observing'.[8] This lack of agreement on definition is reflected in the plurality of nomenclature: 'Charismatic Renewal', 'Charismatic Movement', or simply 'Renewal' are terms used to describe the Movement that has embodied a resurgence of Pentecostal Christianity within the denominational and non-denominational churches. 'Neo-Pentecostalism' is another term that has been used, often by those who are academic commentators on the Movement rather than participants.[9] I shall use the popular terms 'Charismatic Movement' and 'Charismatic Renewal', the former with reference to the widespread influence of neo-Pentecostalism within all forms of Christianity, and the latter with reference to the particular influence of neo-Pentecostalism within the historic denominations, which includes, of course, the Church of England. I shall avoid the shortened term 'Renewal', despite its popular use amongst denominational charismatics, because it fails to distinguish charismatics from other movements that would regard themselves as legitimate movements of renewal in the church.

The term favoured by denominational charismatics, 'Charismatic Renewal', first gained titular status in 1963 when it appeared in the American Episcopalian journal *Trinity*, the journal of the first charismatic service agency, the Blessed Trinity Society. In an article entitled 'The Charismatic Renewal in the Historic Churches',[10] the editors distanced themselves from the term 'neo-Pentecostalism', favouring 'Charismatic Renewal'. This

---

[8] Quoted in *The Charismatic Movement in the Church of England*, 1.

[9] For example, C.G. Williams, *Tongues of the Spirit: A Study of Pentecostal Glossolalia and Related Phenomena*.

[10] Quoted in P. Hocken, *Streams of Renewal: The Origins and Early Development of the Charismatic Renewal in Great Britain*, 185.

avoidance of Pentecostal terminology was a deliberate attempt by the Episcopalians to distance the new Movement from its Pentecostal antecedents, lest it be discredited as a result (in general Episcopalians were suspicious of Pentecostalism, regarding it as an enthusiastic sectarian version of Christianity). In an article surveying the first twenty years of the Charismatic Movement, Andrew Walker comments that one of the major problems facing the proponents of the emerging Movement was how to demonstrate to their fellow denominationalists that they were not merely Pentecostals, and certainly not classical Pentecostals.[11]

'Charismatic Renewal' therefore was a convenient term that had descriptive power for the new Movement and avoided the connection with Pentecostalism. It also became a means by which charismatics within denominational churches were distinguished from those in the non-denominational house church movement, which became known as the 'Restorationist' movement.[12] These independent churches had little or no interest in renewing denominational church life, believing that the Spirit had been given to restore New Testament life *de novo* outside church structures and traditions.

The term 'charismatic', first coined by *Trinity* magazine in 1962, is derived from the Greek word, *charismata*, one of the words used by Paul in 1 Corinthians 12 to describe the gifts of the Spirit present among the Corinthian church.[13] The gifts that have been particularly associated with the Charismatic Movement are found in 1 Corinthians 12:8-10, most commonly, speaking in tongues and interpretation, words of knowledge, gifts of healing, and prophecy. Like the Corinthian church which Paul addresses, these gifts have typically been expressed in settings of corporate worship.

Although the term 'charismatic' had the advantage of distinguishing the emerging Movement from Pentecostalism, it cannot be denied that the relationship is a close one, as has been recognized by leading charismatics. One of Michael Harper's first books on the Charismatic Movement, *As At The Beginning*, portrayed it as a reappearance of Pentecostalism in the mainstream churches. Another influential charismatic Anglican, John Gunstone, called his book on Charismatic Renewal in the Church of England *Pentecostal Anglicans*, and defined charismatic Anglicans as those 'who are influenced by classical Pentecostal teaching and practice'.[14] The Roman Catholic commentator on the Charismatic Movement, Peter

---

[11] A. Walker, 'Pentecostal Power: The "Charismatic Renewal Movement" and the Politics of Experience' in E. Barker (ed.), *Of Gods and Men*, 89-108.
[12] This is a designation used by Andrew Walker in his study *Restoring the Kingdom: The Radical Christianity of the House Church Movement.*
[13] 1 Cor 12:4 and 31.
[14] J. Gunstone, *Pentecostal Anglicans*, 46.

Hocken, began his book on the early development of the Movement in Great Britain, *Streams of Renewal*, with a prophecy given in 1936 by Smith Wigglesworth to fellow Pentecostal David du Plessis indicating that the Pentecostal blessing would break out in the established churches.[15] Hocken comments that this prophecy suggests a possible framework for understanding the new Movement. This strong sense of Pentecostalism being an historical antecedent is reinforced in the way that the Charismatic Movement has been characterized by the central experience of baptism in the Spirit and accompanying phenomena of charismatic, or, as they are also sometimes called, 'spiritual' gifts (following the Pauline use of *pneumatikos* in 1 Cor 12:1 and 14:1), both of which were core characteristics of Pentecostalism.

However, the Charismatic Movement can be distinguished from classical Pentecostalism in a number of ways. First, sociologically, far more participants in the Charismatic Movement have been drawn from the professional and middle classes than was ever the case with the earlier Pentecostal movement. Secondly, in origin, Pentecostalism is associated with an identifiable time and place, namely Azusa Street, Los Angeles in 1906, whereas the origins of the Charismatic Movement are more diverse and diffuse. As Peter Hocken has demonstrated, the Movement grew out of different 'streams of renewal'. Thirdly, the ecclesiology of the Charismatic Movement has been inherently ecumenical in vision, with its emphasis upon the Spirit being given for the renewal of the entire church, understood in Pauline terms as the 'body of Christ'. Pentecostalism, on the other hand, has become a cluster of distinctive denominations, with limited influence upon the wider church. Early Pentecostals did not think in terms of the body of Christ, for they were convinced that the return of the Lord was so imminent that there was no time to think in terms of church renewal.[16]

Fourthly, the two movements differ in their interpretation of the shared central characteristics of baptism in the Spirit and charismatic gifts. The Pentecostal interpretation of baptism in the Spirit was based upon the account of Pentecost in Acts 2. 'Pentecost Has Come' is how the *Apostolic Faith* heralded the outpouring of the Spirit at Azusa Street, in 1906.[17] The first Pentecostals believed that the central blessing of the new movement, the baptism in the Spirit accompanied by speaking in tongues, was the recurrence in the twentieth century of the experience of the first Christians at Pentecost. These Pentecostals were heirs of the tradition of the nineteenth-century American revivalist preachers, Charles Finney, D.L Moody

---

[15] Hocken, *Streams*, 19.
[16] Hocken, *Streams*, 175.
[17] The Apostolic Faith was the newspaper of the Azusa Street church. Quoted in P. Hocken, *The Glory and the Shame: Reflections on the 20th-Century Outpouring of the Holy Spirit*, 45.

and Richard Torrey, who had taught that the baptism in the Spirit was an essential endowment of God's power, or anointing, subsequent to conversion, enabling the believer to grow in holiness and effectiveness in Christian witness. What was new in Pentecostalism was the identification of spiritual gifts, in particular speaking in tongues, with baptism in the Spirit. This was primarily due to Charles Parham, who whilst principal of the Bethel Bible School in Topeka, Kansas in the early 1900s, formulated the teaching that speaking in tongues, which he associated with the miracle of speech on the Day of Pentecost, was the proof of baptism in the Spirit. As Andrew Walker has pointed out, Parham had made the exegetical mistake of confusing the *xenolalia* (speaking in foreign languages) of Acts 2 with the ecstatic *glossolalia* mentioned by Paul in 1 Corinthians 12.[18] However, the result of this error was that the gift of tongues was viewed by early Pentecostals not only as evidence of baptism in the Spirit but also as a miracle of grace by which Christians could evangelize in the mother tongue of the nations of the world.

As argued by Peter Hocken, and more recently by John Goldingay in an article in *Theology*, baptism in the Spirit is also central to the experience of Charismatic Renewal.[19] It has also often been accompanied by speaking in tongues, but in contrast to Pentecostalism, charismatics have been unwilling to maintain that tongues were proof of baptism in the Spirit. The Anglican Michael Harper, a key figure in the development of Charismatic Renewal, wrote in 1968:

> There are some who insist that speaking in tongues is today the invariable initial evidence that a person has received or been filled with the Holy Spirit. But it is difficult to be dogmatic about this, for the only Scriptural evidence we have at our disposal is a series of incidents in the Acts, and even this slender documentation is not conclusive.[20]

Over time, charismatics related baptism in the Spirit to their received theologies of initiation, and so distanced themselves from the Pentecostal teaching that baptism in the Spirit was a second blessing following conversion. For Anglican charismatics, it was related either to initial conversion (such as in the teaching of David Watson[21]), or to the sacra-

---

[18] A.Walker, 'Pentecostalism and Charismatic Christianity' in A.E. McGrath (ed.), *Encyclopedia of Modern Christian Thought*, 428-434.

[19] Hocken, *Streams*, 163-179. J. Goldingay, 'Charismatic Spirituality - Some Theological Reflections', *Theology* XCIX (May/June 1996), 789:178-87.

[20] M. Harper, *Walk in the Spirit*, 20. Harper's own personal experience of speaking in tongues followed some months after the experience he identified as his baptism in the Spirit.

[21] T. Saunders and H. Sansom, *David Watson: A Biography*, 72-73.

mental context of Baptism and Confirmation (as illustrated in the Anglican Renewal Ministries' course *Saints' Alive*[22]). Harper's terminology in the above quotation of 'receiving' or 'being filled' with the Spirit is indicative of a trend amongst charismatics to use alternative descriptions to baptism in the Spirit which played down the initiatory, and therefore potentially divisive, emphasis implicit in the phrase. This enabled them to embrace the view that there may be a number of significant in-fillings of the Spirit in a Christian's pilgrimage.[23] The manner of reception of baptism in the Spirit also differed from Pentecostalism. The Pentecostals had traditionally 'tarried' for the baptism in the Spirit, with deep heart-searching and persistent seeking. Charismatics typically prayed over people, often by laying hands upon them, to receive the baptism in the Spirit.[24]

With regard to speaking in tongues, charismatics distanced themselves from being labelled as a 'tongues movement', and instead emphasized the importance of the rediscovery of the full variety of spiritual gifts mentioned in the New Testament, and placed these gifts in the ecclesiological context of the body of Christ, following the teaching of 1 Corinthians 12. Therefore, unlike Pentecostalism, the gift of speaking in tongues was seen primarily as a gift for the church, rather than an evangelistic gift for the nations. It is in this context that 'Renewal' became an important descriptive term for it denoted that spiritual gifts were not an end in themselves, but a means to renew the church. So Harper writes:

It is the renewal of the Church that God is principally concerned about – not that of the gifts. The gifts are for the building up of the Church – in order that it may become once more a powerful and influential force in the world. It is the recovery of New Testament Church life which is our greatest need today.[25]

Drawing this introduction to a close, and looking ahead to the main discussion of this study, I note finally that despite the important distinctions

---

[22] F. Lawson and J. Finney, *Saints Alive!*

[23] Harper himself would still argue for the importance of using the term baptism in the Spirit as a description of an event which was fundamental to Christian initiation. However, he was increasingly out of sympathy with his fellow Anglican charismatics by continuing to maintain the Pentecostal view that this event was distinct from conversion and sacramental initiation. See his short article 'The Baptism in the Holy Spirit' in *ARMLink* 31 (Winter 1987/88), 10-11.

[24] This practice was a concern to some Pentecostals who regarded the practice as minimizing the moral responsibilities of receiving the Spirit, a concern that was deeply embedded in the Holiness tradition. Desmond Cartwright, an Elim Pentecostal with considerable experience of British Pentecostalism, believed that this factor accounted for Pentecostal hesitation in welcoming the new Movement (Hocken, *Streams*, 147, n.21).

[25] Quoted in Hocken, *Streams*, 174.

outlined above, the Charismatic Movement and classical Pentecostalism share common ground when respected opinion assesses their overall significance to the wider church. Walter Hollenweger in his classic and authoritative study of Pentecostalism, *The Pentecostals*, claimed that it is in the public performance of worship 'that the Pentecostal movement seems to me to have made its most important contribution'.[26] The same claim has been made of the Charismatic Movement. Colin Buchanan writes:

> The key to the Charismatic Movement is its worship. Its influence upon the future is more significantly in the sphere of worship than elsewhere, and to relate other features of the Movement to its styles and content of worship is the best way to understand them all.[27]

Another, more recent, commentator claims that the Charismatic Movement 'was at its most profound and also at its most influential as it worshipped'.[28] If this is indeed the case, then my work will not only be a useful contribution to contemporary liturgical study but also to the study of a Movement whose *raison d'être* has been the worship of God.

---

[26] W. Hollenweger, *The Pentecostals*, 466.
[27] C.O. Buchanan, *Encountering Charismatic Worship*, 9.
[28] P. Ward, *Growing Up Evangelical: Youthwork and the Making of a Subculture*, 126.

CHAPTER 2

A History of Charismatic Renewal
in the Church of England

Early Beginnings

The first documented evidence of the influence of Pentecostalism within the Church of England was the case of the Revd Alexander Boddy, parish priest of All Saints, Monkwearmouth, in the Durham diocese. In his history of the twentieth-century Pentecostal movement, *As At The Beginning*, Michael Harper introduces Alexander Boddy as a precursor to the Charismatic Movement.[1] Through the visit of a Norwegian Methodist minister, T.B Barratt, who himself had experienced the baptism in the Spirit during a visit to Los Angeles in 1906, Boddy witnessed a Pentecostal revival amongst his congregation in the autumn of 1907. People were baptized in the Spirit and spoke in tongues, and as Harper writes, it was not long before 'this staid Anglican church became the mecca for pilgrims seeking the experience of God's Spirit'.[2] People came from all over England and Wales, including Smith Wigglesworth, who was to become an influential Pentecostal figure in England. In the years after 1907, Boddy hosted an annual Pentecostal convention at Sunderland, and also edited the Pentecostal periodical *Confidence* from 1908 to 1926. As a result, Pentecostalism became established in Britain, and following the American experience of the sectarian development of Pentecostal denominations, by the mid-1920s there had emerged three significant Pentecostal denominations: The Elim Foursquare Gospel Church, the Assemblies of God and the smaller Apostolic Church.

It was in the early 1960s that Pentecostalism re-emerged in the Church of England, this time in a form that was to take root and establish itself. To begin with, as Peter Hocken documents, there were a number of isolated incidents of Anglicans who were baptized in the Spirit but who then left the

---

[1]   For a more recent study, see G. Wakefield, *The First Pentecostal Anglican: The Life and Legacy of Alexander Boddy*.

[2]   M. Harper, *As At The Beginning: The Twentieth Century Pentecostal Revival*, 39.

Church of England.[3] Richard Bolt, a training ordinand at Clifton College, Bristol was asked to leave the College in 1959 having propagated baptism in the Spirit and speaking in tongues among his fellow students. Bolt had received baptism in the Spirit at an Assemblies of God hall in Durham in 1957, and after his expulsion from Clifton College he went on to found the Student Pentecostal Fellowship in 1961, and then the Central London Full Gospel Church in London in 1964. Bolt's ministry was to influence an Anglican vicar by the name of George Forester, who received baptism in the Spirit with speaking in tongues through visiting Bolt. By autumn 1963 fifteen members of Forester's church, St. Paul's in Beckenham, had participated in the Pentecostal experience, some of these again through Bolt's ministry. In November 1963 the *Church of England Newspaper* published an article on the events at Beckenham entitled '"Baptism of the Spirit" at Beckenham', triggering a correspondence on what the newspaper called the 'glossolalia' movement. Forester however resigned his living toward the end of 1964, unable to continue the practice of infant baptism in good conscience.

At the time that events at Beckenham were receiving national interest, there were Pentecostal stirrings elsewhere in the Church of England which were to prove decisive for the future shape of Charismatic Renewal. Hocken describes how the prayers of some Pentecostal-minded parishioners at All Souls, Langham Place for their clergy were answered in the case of Michael Harper, a curate on the All Souls staff. In September 1962, at a conference in Farnham, Surrey, Harper had an experience of the Spirit that he was later to name as his baptism in the Spirit. It was not until August 1963 that he began to speak in tongues, a gift that was facilitated by meeting Philip Smith, vicar of St. John's, Burslem in the Potteries, and the American Lutheran Larry Christenson.[4] Smith had received the baptism in the Spirit in 1962 through Pentecostal friends, and this led him to introduce charismatic prayer meetings in his Rectory and other homes in the parish.[5] Harper quickly emerged as a key spokesman for the emerging Movement in the Church of England, and beyond, a course that eventually led him to resign from his ministry at All Souls in July 1964, and form the Fountain Trust a few months later. It was through this agency that Harper exercised leadership in the developing Charismatic Movement.

In the emerging Movement, evangelicals were in the ascendancy. John Gunstone, one of the first catholic Anglicans (or 'anglo-catholics') to have been baptized in the Spirit, writes that he went to a meeting convened by Harper at Stoke Poges a few months before the Fountain Trust was founded

[3] P. Hocken, *Streams of Renewal: The Origins and Early Development of the Charismatic Renewal in Great Britain*, 71-81.
[4] Hocken, *Streams*, 88.
[5] Hocken, *Streams*, 78-81.

which drew together ministers involved or interested in the new Movement. 'Of the twenty-one people present, seventeen were clergy of the Church of England and fifteen of those were Evangelicals; Michael Meakin and I were the only Catholic Anglicans.' [6] This evangelical dominance of the emerging Movement was no doubt encouraged by the fact that Harper was himself evangelical, but probably just as influential was an editorial article by Philip Hughes in the evangelical journal *The Churchman* in 1962. A prominent evangelical scholar, Hughes wrote of his visit to American Episcopalian churches that had experienced the Pentecostal blessing, and commended what he saw.[7] Hughes' influence was not limited to the written page. Colin Buchanan writes of the occasion of the Oxford Conference of Evangelical Churchmen in 1962 where he heard 'Philip Hughes, a dyed-in-the-wool Puritan and "reformed" theologian, speaking with wonder of a new movement of the Spirit (attested by speaking in tongues) amongst – of all people – "high church" American Episcopalians'.[8] One of these Episcopalians, Dennis Bennett, subsequently made a number of visits to Britain, and was an influential early figure in encouraging charismatic life within the Church of England. There was also much in this new Movement that affirmed evangelical spirituality: through baptism in the Spirit individuals spoke of a fresh encounter with Christ, a renewed desire to read the bible, and a new confidence in witness. As one evangelical commentator wrote, 'Some touched by the Movement would appear, to this observer at least, to have had an old-fashioned evangelical conversion!'[9] There were other features of Charismatic Renewal that evangelicals found attractive because they supplemented what was lacking in the evangelical tradition. These included an emphasis on the church as the fellowship of the Spirit in the body of Christ (which led to a greater ecumenical vision amongst evangelicals), a deeper appreciation of the non-cerebral and sacramental aspects of worship, and a prayerful expectation of the dynamic work of the Holy Spirit in realizing the authority of Christ through healing and deliverance.[10] For these reasons, as Gunstone writes, 'The Charismatic Movement caught the Evangelical armada like a crosswind as it sailed towards the conquest of the Church of England.'[11]

However, it was not all plain sailing, and the early period of evangelical openness and welcome to the new Movement was effectively ended when John Stott, the Rector of All Souls in Langham Place, publicly rejected

---

[6] J. Gunstone, *Pentecost Comes to the Church: Sacraments and Spiritual Gifts*, 11.

[7] *The Churchman* 76 (September 1962), 3:131-135.

[8] C.O. Buchanan, *Encountering Charismatic Worship*, 5.

[9] D. Robinson, 'Renewal from an Evangelical "Non-Charismatic" Viewpoint', in C. Craston (ed.), *Open To The Spirit: Anglicans and the Experience of Renewal*, 84.

[10] J. Gunstone, *Pentecostal Anglicans*, 78-9.

[11] Gunstone, *Pentecostal Anglicans*, 69.

baptism in the Spirit, understood as a distinctive post-conversion experience, on exegetical grounds at the annual Islington Clerical Conference in
January 1964. Hocken comments that 'for several years after this,
evangelical parishes identifying with the new move of the Spirit ... were
suspect in the eyes of most fellow-Evangelicals in the Church of England'.[12] Charismatics and non-charismatics within the evangelical wing of
the Church of England were to remain at arms length until the Fountain
Trust and the Church of England Evangelical Council met in 1975, leading
to the publication of the joint report *Gospel and Spirit* in 1977.

1964–1970: Fountain Trust and Developments

With increasing demands upon Harper as a reputable Anglican spokesman
for the Charismatic Movement, and with his rector, John Stott, opposing a
post-conversion baptism in the Spirit, it was not surprising that Harper
resigned from All Souls in July of 1964 to devote himself to the task of
forming a service agency for the Charismatic Movement, the Fountain
Trust. In his newsletter announcing his plans, Michael Harper outlined his
ecumenical vision for the Trust:

> We feel called to serve every section of the Church, without fear or
> favour. We are seeing the Holy Spirit moving in some unlikely places
> today, and we rejoice in His power to bring men of different traditions
> together.[13]

Harper's Pentecostal experience had brought him in contact with a wide
variety of Christian leaders in Britain who had been similarly affected, from
both the main denominations and independent churches, and the formation
of the Trust crystallized this nascent ecumenical group. The vision for the
Trust was developed and clarified in an edition of *Renewal* magazine, the
Fountain Trust's publishing arm. Its stated aims were:

> 1. To encourage Christians of all churches to receive the power of the
> Holy Spirit and to glorify Christ by manifesting in their lives the fruit and
> gifts of the same Spirit, so that they may enrich their worship, strengthen
> their witness and deepen their fellowship.
> 2. To encourage local churches to experience renewal in the Holy Spirit
> and to recover the full ministry of the Holy Spirit including that of
> healing.
> 3. To encourage Christians to expect and pray for worldwide revival.[14]

---

[12] Hocken, *Streams*, 118.
[13] Quoted in Hocken, *Streams*, 125.
[14] *Renewal* 19 (1969), Editorial.

The magazine *Renewal* became one of the chief means of fulfilling the agenda of the Fountain Trust. It was edited by Harper, and first published in January 1966 and bimonthly thereafter. The content of editorials and the range of topics in the first four years of publication reflect the concerns of the emerging Movement, both within and outside denominational structures. Baptism in the Spirit was promoted as a foundational experience, and was celebrated primarily through the medium of testimony. The experience was championed as an essential endowment of spiritual power, subsequent to conversion, which enabled the church to recapture the early church's dynamism. For example, Dr Philip Hughes was reported to have said to the 1967 gathering of Evangelicals at the Keele Congress that the Charismatic Renewal was 'a symptom of the dissatisfaction with the drabness of church life, and a reminder that the way forward is not to be found in gimmicks but in the Gospel *plus* the Holy Spirit' (italics mine).[15] One editorial likened Charismatic Renewal to the Reformation in terms of being a protest against a spiritually corrupt church, which is characterized by:

(a) formalism, dullness and over-organization;
(b) ecclesiastical bureaucrats running it like a business or state department;
(c) a deadly intellectual approach of some that suggests that man is a soulless brain;
(d) the dispensationalist viewpoint that denies the reality of miracles and wonders.[16]

There were articles and letters about the gifts of the Spirit, especially the gift of tongues which was regarded as a normal, though not essential, sign of baptism in the Spirit.[17] The magazine however countered accusations that the new Movement was a 'tongues movement':

Please, please do not call this the 'Tongues Movement' ... the great majority of those who are being filled with the Holy Spirit in the churches have no desire to be a 'movement' at all. They have elected to remain in their own churches and contribute responsibly to their blessing. They also have no desire to emphasise 'tongues' to the exclusion of everything else ... we thoroughly dislike this unfortunate label.[18]

This rebuttal highlights the Fountain Trust's role as a service agency; one

---

[15] *Renewal* 9 (1967), Editorial.
[16] *Renewal* 12 (1967/68), Editorial.
[17] *Renewal* 4 (1966), 'Quest'.
[18] *Renewal* 4 (1966), Editorial.

couldn't belong to the Trust, although the Trust supported you in your life
in the local church. Harper regarded the Trust as a temporary measure, and
hoped that the day would soon come when the church at large was in full
possession of the reality that the Trust stood for, thereby making it
redundant.[19]

Renewal magazine also advertised the conferences organized by the
Fountain Trust which, like the magazine itself, played an important role in
consolidating and extending the Trust's influence. As well as providing
opportunities for teaching and meeting, these conferences gave charismatics
exposure to a developing style of corporate charismatic worship. According
to an anglo-catholic observer at the ministers' conference at High Leigh in
June 1968, there were three main ingredients. First, uninhibited periods of
congregational singing, including the phenomenon of singing in tongues,
which helped the participants unite and 'discover the freedom of the Spirit
together'.[20] Singing in tongues has been described by Tom Smail, a leading
figure in the Fountain Trust, as embodying the quintessence of charismatic
worship, which he identified as the non-rational and joyful offering of
praise by the renewed heart in a direct, spontaneous and simple manner,
enabled by the Spirit of God.[21] Secondly, there was a fresh experience of
the church as the Pauline body of Christ, where gifts could be mutually
shared and recognized. This had already been Michael Harper's experience
in the worship at the 1964 Stoke Poges conference for leaders of the
nascent Charismatic Movement. As he wrote, 'For the first time in 8½ years
of ordained ministry – and 12 years of Christian experience – I saw 1
Cor.12,13 and 14 operating exactly as we read in the scriptures. It was
thrilling.'[22] Thirdly, the concluding Communion service was an unhurried
act of worship extending to nearly three hours, with time given for spoken
individual contributions at appropriate points in the liturgy, and prayer with
laying on of hands after the administration of Communion. These extended
Eucharists continued to be a feature of Fountain Trust conferences
throughout the 1970s.[23]

There was also debate, often through published correspondence, about
the relationship between the new experience of the Spirit and ecclesiology.
The independent charismatics, such as Arthur Wallis and David Lillie,
viewed the fresh outpouring of the Spirit as the restoration of the New

---

[19] *Renewal* 19 (1969), Editorial.
[20] 'Acts of the Apostles Comes True', *Renewal* 16 (1968), 18-20.
[21] T. Smail, A. Walker, and N. Wright, *Charismatic Renewal: The Search for a Theology*, 109.
[22] 'Stoke Poges Prayer Conference 1964', a report by Michael Harper, quoted in Hocken, *Streams*, 122.
[23] Interview with Revd Graham Cray, a regular attender at Fountain Trust conferences in the 1970s (25/10/94).

Testament church of Christ, but saw the locus for this restoration outside the historic denominations. This was to lead eventually to the development of the Restorationist (or house church) movement in the 1970s.

During the remaining years in the 1960s, Charismatic Renewal contin- ued to grow in the Church of England, particularly in its evangelical wing. Various evangelicals, who were to be associated with well known charismatic parishes, became involved with the Movement during this period: John Collins (St. Mark's, Gillingham and subsequently Holy Trinity, Brompton in London), David Watson (St. Cuthbert's and St. Michael-le-Belfry in York), Tom Walker (St. John's, Harborne in Birming- ham) and John Perry (St. Andrew's, Chorleywood). However the public profile of Charismatic Renewal in wider Anglican evangelical circles was yet to develop. The first National Evangelical Anglican Congress (N.E.A.C.) at Keele in 1967 produced a 10,000-word statement without any reference to the subject. Colin Buchanan recalls going regularly to the annual national conferences of Eclectics Society (a fellowship linking together younger progressive evangelical clergy) from 1966 to 1970 where he observed that Michael Harper kept a very low, even semi-underground, profile.[24]

1970–1980: Broadening Horizons

According to John Gunstone, one of the most significant events for the Charismatic Movement at the beginning of the 1970s was the Guildford Conference in 1971, sponsored by the Fountain Trust. Seven hundred Christians from over twenty countries and several different denominations came together to explore 'The Fellowship of the Holy Spirit'. Gunstone commented that 'for the first time in history Roman Catholics, traditional Protestants and classical Pentecostals shared the same platform'.[25] The ecumenical achievement of the conference was also recognized by the internationally renowned Pentecostal teacher David du Plessis, who wrote, 'I believe the conference is the demonstration of what Holy Spirit ecumenism is ... The Holy Spirit is creating ecumenicity without organization, bringing about a unity which organization so far has failed to achieve.'[26] This ecumenical vision was to affect a number of Anglicans present. David Watson, for example, went to the conference with doctrinal worries about his first contact with Roman Catholic charismatics, but came away convinced that 'on basics we were one in Christ, though there might

---

[24] Buchanan, *Encountering*, 6 n.1.
[25] Gunstone, *Pentecostal Anglicans*, 11.
[26] Quoted in C.Williams, *Tongues of the Spirit: A Study of Pentecostal Glossolalia and Related Phenomena*, 112.

have been some differences of opinion on secondary issues'.[27] Watson's
ecumenism was to shock his fellow evangelicals at the second N.E.A.C.
conference in Nottingham in 1977 when he referred to the Reformation as a
'tragedy' on the grounds that it marked a division in the body of Christ.

Within the Church of England, the 1970s were years of growth in public
profile for the Charismatic Movement, and in the spirit of the Guildford
conference, a broadening of influence from its evangelical beginnings. A
good example of a catholic parish which experienced Charismatic Renewal
was St. Hugh's, Lewsey in Luton, where Colin Urquhart was vicar, the
story of which was popularized through Urquhart's book *When the Spirit
Comes*. One of the interesting features of the growth of charismatic life at
St. Hugh's was the fact that it began independently of the wider Charismatic Movement, a pattern that emulated the early development of the
Charismatic Movement in the 1960s which was marked by a convergence
of individual and independent 'streams' of renewal. Partly through the
popularity of his book, Urquhart was to become an influential figure in the
Fountain Trust, developing an independent itinerant ministry after the
Trust's closure in 1980.

Urquhart was not the first clergyman from the anglo-catholic wing of the
Church of England to be influenced by Charismatic Renewal. In 1963 the
anglo-catholic Michael Meakin, Rural Dean of Woburn Sands in South
Bedfordshire, received the baptism in the Spirit, followed in 1964 by John
Gunstone, priest in charge of St. Augustine's, Rush Green in Romford, who
was to become the most articulate spokesman for the charismatic anglo-
catholic wing of the Church of England. Although never as numerous as the
evangelical charismatics, the anglo-catholics grew to be an established
presence within Anglican Charismatic Renewal. Rosemary Radley, in a
brief pamphlet outlining the history of charismatic anglo-catholics, called
'Holy Spirit Renewal', writes of the small beginnings of five people
gathering for a Pentecostal Mass in 1967 at Bethnal Green, London, 'with
the intention that other Anglicans in the Catholic tradition of the Church of
England might also come to know the renewing power of the Holy Spirit'.[28]
Numbers remained small, and the group started to make an annual
pilgrimage to Walsingham in 1974. After a few years the annual pilgrimage
became so popular that the extra numbers demanded a change of venue.
Thereafter, High Leigh Conference Centre in Hertfordshire became the
venue for the annual Anglo-Catholic Charismatic Convention.

The first anglo-catholics to attend the 1960s Fountain Trust meetings
found the experience something of a culture shock, especially the worship
with its evangelical bias. However, there were encouragements for them to
believe that charismatic life could be integrated into their tradition.

---

[27] Quoted in Gunstone, *Pentecostal Anglicans*, 85.
[28] R. Radley, *Holy Spirit Renewal*.

Charismatic Renewal in the American Episcopal Church had originated from High Church parishes, including the Church of the Holy Redeemer in Houston, which was to have a large impact upon Charismatic Renewal in Britain in the 1970s. There was news in the late 1960s of the Movement having spread to the Roman Catholic Church, focused on Notre Dame in the U.S.A., and popularized in books like *Catholic Pentecostals* by Kevin and Dorothy Ranaghan. Archbishop Michael Ramsey's interest in Charismatic Renewal led him to invite John Gunstone to write the 1974 Archbishop of Canterbury's Lent Book, *Greater Things Than These*, an account of how the Charismatic Renewal had affected Gunstone's ministry as an anglo-catholic parish priest. 1973 saw the news of the first Church of England bishop to align himself directly with the Charismatic Renewal, Richard Hare, the Bishop of Pontefract. Hare was from the catholic wing of the church, and became a staunch advocate for Charismatic Renewal within the existing structures.

Like the evangelicals, the charismatic anglo-catholics engaged in adapting the Pentecostal emphases into their theology. Baptism in the Spirit became interpreted as a release of the Spirit that was already present through sacramental initiation, and spiritual gifts were understood in a sacramental context as outward signs conveying inward grace.[29] Parallels were drawn between the Oxford Movement and the Charismatic Movement. John Gunstone, for example, portrayed the Oxford Movement as inspiring community life, devotion to Jesus (through the Eucharistic sacrament), an emphasis upon the Holy Spirit's work of sanctifying grace, and a recovery of the importance of retreats and pilgrimages, all of which had their parallels in the developing charismatic spirituality.[30]

The early 1970s also saw a fresh American Episcopalian influence within Charismatic Renewal in the Church of England. In 1972, the Bishop of Coventry invited the Episcopalian Graham Pulkingham, together with some members of his church, the Church of the Holy Redeemer in Houston, to Britain. The Church of the Holy Redeemer had experienced Charismatic Renewal and had developed a strong emphasis on community life, expressed through worship, and a commitment to the under-privileged in Houston.[31] After a year in Coventry, they moved to occupy a disused convent in Berkshire, Yeldall Manor, just outside the village of Wargrave, and it was here that the community assumed the official name of The Community of Celebration. The Community made contact with charismatic churches through involvement with the Fountain Trust conferences, where they led worship and ran workshops. Their travelling teams, known as the Fisherfolk, received many invitations to parishes where they ran workshops

---

[29] Radley, *Holy Spirit Renewal*.
[30] Gunstone, *Pentecostal Anglicans*, 95-100.
[31] See G. Pulkingham, *Gathered for Power*.

on worship. Examples of clergy who made frequent use of the Fisherfolk were John Holmes in Leeds, David Watson in York, and Tom Walker in Birmingham.[32] After two years, the Community moved on from Yeldall Manor and diverged, with one team going to Post Green in Dorset where they continued to be a resource for worship in churches, and another team going to the Isle of Cumbrae.[33] The influence of the Community waned towards the end of the decade, which according to Maggie Durran, then a member of the Post Green Community, was partly due to the fact that their message had been communicated, and partly due to Fisherfolk members finding the demands of touring increasingly gruelling and impractical to combine with family commitments.[34] However, their impact upon the developing forms of worship within charismatic Anglican parishes in the 1970s was seminal. This is discussed further below.

Like those in the Community of Celebration, there were other charismatics who were drawn to community life. An example of this was Reg East, who had been involved in Charismatic Renewal since 1964 (it was East who encouraged John Gunstone to receive baptism in the Spirit that same year), and who moved from his parish ministry in Essex and set up Whatcombe House in 1971. Whatcombe was a Georgian mansion near Blandford in Dorset, and the community that East founded was called the Barnabas Fellowship. John Gunstone was invited to be chaplain of the newly formed community. There were also examples of community households that developed, such as the Watson's rectory in York, which were directly inspired by the model of community offered by the Community of Celebration.[35]

Attempts to heal the division between charismatics and non-charismatics in the evangelical Anglican community led to the publication in 1977 of the *Gospel and Spirit* report, the fruit of dialogue between the Fountain Trust and the Church of England Evangelical Council.[36] John Gunstone suggests that the measure of reconciliation achieved by *Gospel and Spirit* was reflected at N.E.A.C. in 1977: charismatics contributed to the preparatory book, *Obeying Christ in a Changing World*, and the worship was conducted very much in the style of a Fountain Trust conference.[37]

1978 saw an event that celebrated the presence of charismatic life within the wider Anglican Communion. This was the international conference for charismatic Anglicans which took place in Canterbury in July of that year,

---

[32] Interview with Maggie Durran, an ex-Fisherfolk member (8/6/94).

[33] The story of this second group is told in M. Durran, *The Wind at the Door*.

[34] Interview with Maggie Durran (8/6/94).

[35] T. Saunders and H. Sansom, *David Watson: A Biography*, Ch.16, 'Community Living and the Mustard Seed'.

[36] 'Gospel and Spirit: a joint statement', *The Churchman* 91 (1977), 2:102-105.

[37] Gunstone, *Pentecostal Anglicans*, 83-4.

two weeks before the Lambeth Conference. Michael Harper, one of the conveners of the conference, described it as 'a significant milestone in the growth of the Charismatic Renewal in the Anglican Communion'[38] and edited a report on the conference entitled *A New Canterbury Tale*. The climax was an extended Eucharist in the choir of Canterbury Cathedral, a memorable moment being Bill Burnett, then Archbishop of Cape Town, leading the bishops in a liturgical dance around the high altar. One outcome of the conference was the establishment of S.O.M.A. (Sharing of Ministries Abroad) in 1979, which became a network for the different Charismatic Renewal organizations in the Anglican Communion.

1978 also saw the General Synod of the Church of England become involved in reviewing the progress of Charismatic Renewal. Colin Buchanan, then principal of St. John's College Nottingham (an Anglican theological college which, during the 1970s, had become known for its affirmative stance towards Charismatic Renewal), presented a motion to the Synod asking for a report to be prepared. John Gunstone comments that this 'was the first time the Synod had been given the opportunity to air the topic, *sixteen years* after the appearance of the Pentecostal movement in the parishes in this country!' (italics original).[39] The report was eventually presented to Synod in 1981.[40]

The Synod report provides a helpful vantage point from which to summarize the characteristic features of the 1970s worship culture associated with Charismatic Renewal in the Church of England. The Report contained a number of personal accounts of how charismatic worship developed in parishes during the 1970s, the success of which appeared to involve a number of common factors.[41] These included a supportive and 'renewed' parish priest who could negotiate change, a mid-week prayer group as a place to foster the new charismatic style of worship, and access to the wider charismatic support network, focused on the Fountain Trust. An example of one of these parishes was St. John's, Harborne in Birmingham, the detailed story of which was told by the vicar, Tom Walker, in his book *Open to God*. The main catalyst for the growth of a charismatic style of worship was the mid-week prayer meeting called 'Open to God'. This included lengthy times of praise, using choruses and hymns, led by piano and guitars, bible teaching, intercession, periods of silence and opportunities for individuals to make contributions, which would typically include the use of charismatic gifts, or as Walker puts it, 'sharing some word, or vision, or dream, or some word of scripture, or some song which is just the *right* contribution for the

---

[38] M. Harper, 'These Stones Cry Out' in C. Craston (ed.), *Open to the Spirit: Anglicans and the Experience of Renewal*, 18.
[39] Gunstone, *Pentecostal Anglicans*, 25.
[40] *The Charismatic Movement in the Church of England.*
[41] *Charismatic Movement*, 12-29.

moment' (italics original).[42] The ethos of such meetings can be summarized as whole-hearted praise (often reflected in bodily gestures such as lifted hands), freedom for individual contribution, spontaneity (acts of worship which happened 'without human planning'[43]) and hence flexibility within the meeting structure, and listening to God (through bible teaching or silence). Tom Walker's oversight was crucial to development. Not only did he fully encourage the development of 'Open to God', but he also negotiated the sensitive introduction of some its elements into regular Sunday worship, thereby partly resolving tensions arising from the 'contrast between the free expression of prayer with ministry to one another in the midweek meeting, and more traditional worship on Sundays'.[44] Changes made to Sunday worship included the introduction of choruses during the administration of Communion and congregational extempore prayer during intercessions. Walker's contacts with the Fountain Trust and the Fisherfolk teams also facilitated the use of arts, dance and drama in worship.

As has been mentioned, the Fisherfolk teams had a seminal influence upon the development of parish charismatic worship in the 1970s. The constitutive elements of the charismatic worship style identified by the Synod Report were embodied and mediated by them. In their leading of worship at charismatic gatherings (which the Report referred to as the 'rally'), ranging from the parish level to the national Fountain Trust conferences, they modelled bodily expression: the raising of hands in song, the use of drama, mime and dance, the laying-on of hands in prayer for healing, and informal hugs during the kiss of peace. Their commitment to the use of artistic gifts in worship, such as movement, colour, artwork and banners,[45] enhanced a renewed catholic sense of the sacramental nature of worship, or 'inchoate sacramentality' as the Report called it. But their greatest influence was in the sphere of music and song where they made three main contributions. First, in their leadership of worship they modelled a community of musicians at worship, whose main aim was to facilitate congregational worship through the primary medium of folk art. This model, which was in some ways reminiscent of the church gallery bands of the eighteenth century, provided the basis for the development of 'music groups' in charismatic parishes throughout the country. For instance, Hillyer's charismatic church in Cambridge (St.C) formed a music group on the basis of contact with St. Michael-le-Belfry in York who had themselves

---

[42] T. Walker, *Open to God: A Parish in Renewal*, 14.
[43] T. Walker, *Open*, 12.
[44] T. Walker, *Open*, 12.
[45] See, for example, P. Beall and M. Keys Barker, *The Folk Arts in Renewal: Creativity in Worship, Teaching and Festivity as Developed by the Fisherfolk*.

based their musical ministry on the Fisherfolk.[46] Secondly, the Fisherfolk
inspired the first three major collections of songs which contained items
original to the Charismatic Renewal: *Sound of Living Waters*, *Fresh Sounds*
and *Cry Hosanna!* [47] There had been a previous Fountain Trust publication
in 1971, called the *Renewal Songbook*, but at that stage there were very few
songs original to the Charismatic Movement and so the Songbook was
limited to inherited material popular amongst evangelicals, such as songs
from the Church Pastoral Aid Society's publications *Youth Praise* and
various gospel hymns. Thirdly, the Fisherfolk song collections promoted
the ideals of the charismatic liturgical piety. As Pete Ward has highlighted,
the songs typically envisaged worship as an expression of the Pauline 'body
of Christ' in which everyone has something to contribute, an encounter with
God whose active presence among the worshipping assembly is celebrated
in terms of the transforming and healing power of Jesus, and a response to
the invitation to receive the life giving Spirit who fills, refreshes and
empowers the worshipper to follow the example of Jesus in sacrificial
service in a needy world.[48]

Early 1980s: Closure of the Fountain Trust

In 1980 the leaders of the Fountain Trust announced that the Trust was
closing down (the Trust officially closed on 31st December 1980, although
Renewal magazine continued to be published). Gunstone writes that
'humanly speaking this was an astonishing decision',[49] a comment that
reflects the shock of many Anglican charismatics at the loss of an agency
that had been so highly regarded. The Trust had been enormously
influential, and had remained predominantly Anglican (at the end of the
1970s three of the full-time directors were Anglicans: Tom Smail, Michael
Harper, and John Richards). However the message from those responsible
for the Trust was that they sensed its distinctive role had come to an end,
and that Charismatic Renewal was now well enough established to be taken
forward by local parishes and churches. An alternative reading of the
Trust's closure is offered by Andrew Walker who suggests that its
dissolution was a symptom both of the decline of Charismatic Renewal
since its zenith in the mid-1970s, and increasing tensions between some of

---

[46] J.V. Hillyer, *Liturgical Change in Cambridge: Attitudes to Liturgy with Special Reference to Charismatic Gifts*.

[47] Published 1974, 1976 and 1980 respectively.

[48] P. Ward, *Growing Up Evangelical: Youthwork and the Making of a Subculture*, 119-33. Ward's work concentrates on the first of the three Fisherfolk songbooks, although his analysis holds true for the content of all three songbooks.

[49] Gunstone, *Pentecostal Anglicans*, 26.

the Trust's leaders.[50]

Evidence of the fact that charismatic Anglicans were not willing to let go of the idea of a Charismatic Renewal service agency was the formation of Anglican Renewal Ministries (A.R.M.) in 1980.[51] Lawrence Hoyle resigned from his living in order to devote himself to a full-time role as co-ordinator, and there were seven others on the initial advisory committee, including Gunstone, and Michael Harper as director of S.O.M.A. Following the pattern established by the Fountain Trust, A.R.M. arranged two annual conferences at Swanwick, and published a magazine four times a year, called *Anglicans for Renewal*.[52] Education material was also produced with parochial ministry in mind. One of the first and most popular of these was *Saints Alive!*, a course that integrated prayer for the reception of (or 'baptism in') the Holy Spirit within the context of Christian initiation.[53]

Whilst Anglican charismatics were reorganizing themselves, and finding their Movement debated at General Synod,[54] the beginning of the 1980s also saw the growth of the independent Restorationist church networks. The distinctive stance of the earlier independent charismatics in relation to the Spirit and ecclesiology, referred to above, had now developed into an ecclesiology based on a commitment to the five-fold ministry of Ephesians 4:11 together with strict discipleship teaching.[55] The different networks were each led by a charismatic apostolate, and under the leadership of such men as Bryn Jones, Gerald Coates, Terry Virgo, John Noble and David Tomlinson, this became the fastest growing Christian movement in Britain. Like the denominational charismatics, they also had large conference events: the Downs Week, and the Dales and Welsh Bible Weeks. They also generated their own song collections, which were published by Kingsway in successive volumes called *Songs of Fellowship*[56] and *Songs and Hymns of Fellowship*.[57] These songs share some elements of the Fisherfolk songs, such as the celebration of God's presence within worship and the joy of

---

[50] A. Walker, 'Pentecostal Power: The "Charismatic Renewal Movement" and the Politics of Pentecostal Experience' in E. Barker (ed.), *Of Gods and Men: New Religious Movements in the West*, 89-108.

[51] Named after the charismatic 'Episcopal Renewal Ministries' in the U.S.A.

[52] Its name was changed to *ARM Link* for volumes 31–41 in the late 1980s.

[53] In my first curacy at St. John's, Welling in Kent, the course was used to prepare adults for Baptism and Confirmation.

[54] The Synod Report on the Charismatic Movement was debated in November 1981. See General Synod 'Report of Proceedings' 12, 3:1117-38.

[55] A. Walker, *Restoring the Kingdom: The Radical Christianity of the House Church Movement*, 147-91.

[56] First published in 1980, followed by an expanded version in 1981, and then successively as Book 2 (1983), Book 3 (1985), Book 4 (1989), a combined edition (1991), and Book 5 (1994).

[57] Published in 1985.

being in fellowship with others. However, as Pete Ward demonstrates, these songs reflect a different ecclesiological vision, based primarily upon the notion of a restored kingdom of God.[58] A large proportion of the songs 'exalt' or 'magnify' God as king. Jesus is praised as the ascended king, celebrated as the Book of Revelation's victorious Lamb of God, and enthroned on the praises of the redeemed, but references to the incarnate Jesus, a strong feature of Fisherfolk songs, are very few. The vision of a theocracy is also mediated by Old Testament themes of temple, land and kingship. The worshipper's approach to God is cast in cultic language from the temple, and the church's relationship to the world is defined in terms of conquest, 'claiming' alien ground for the majestic king. This again contrasts with the Fisherfolk songs where the church serves a needy world in the name of a humble Lord. Rather surprisingly, in the earlier editions of *Songs of Fellowship*, and again in contrast to the Fisherfolk collections, there are very few songs that celebrate the reality of the Spirit's ministry. Instead Jesus the king dwells with his people and empowers them for the service of his kingdom. Finally, unlike the Fisherfolk collections, which provided some songs for the authorized liturgy of parish worship, there are no liturgical items within *Songs of Fellowship*, reflecting the non-conformist origins of the Restorationist movement.

1984–1990: Wimber and 'Signs and Wonders'

Neither Anglican charismatics nor Restorationists could have predicted at the beginning of the 1980s that the Charismatic Movement was about to take a fresh turn. Repeating a pattern that we have already observed, the catalyst for change came from America, though this time the main ecclesial influence was independent Quaker-evangelical rather than Episcopalian. The visitor concerned was a Californian pastor, John Wimber, whose church had experienced a Pentecostal-style revival on Mother's Day in 1981, an event that was to launch what was to become commonly known as Wimber's 'signs and wonders' ministry. Carol Wimber, John's wife, describes how a young man who had been asked by John to preach that evening, invoked the Holy Spirit with the words 'Come Holy Spirit'. Most of the 400 young people present fell to the floor, weeping, wailing and speaking in tongues.[59] In that same year David Watson visited John Wimber's growing church, and a friendship was forged that was to provide Wimber with his introduction to the Charismatic Movement in Britain.[60] Michael Mitton, Lawrence Hoyle's successor as director of A.R.M., sums

---

[58] Ward, *Growing*, 133-40.

[59] K. Springer (ed.), *Riding the Third Wave: What Comes After Renewal*, 44-7.

[60] For the importance of the friendship to both men see Saunders and Sansom, *David Watson*, Ch. 21, 'Fuller and Wimber'.

up the significance of Watson's friendship with Wimber as follows: 'When David Watson died in 1984, one of his parting gifts to the church was to introduce us to his good friend, John Wimber, Because David was so well loved and respected, people instinctively warmed to this big-hearted Californian who has made many visits to this country.'[61]

Wimber's first large-scale conference in Britain was in October 1984 at Westminster Central Hall, which proved to be the curtain raiser to the expansion of the 'signs and wonders' ministry amongst charismatic churches in this country. Douglas McBain, a Baptist pastor who organized the event, comments that 'large sections of the charismatic church look back to 1984 as a major turning point in their growing experience'.[62] The significance of Wimber's arrival on the charismatic stage is captured by Peter Wagner's phrase 'The Third Wave', which was the title of Wimber's initial conference. Wagner was a teaching colleague of Wimber's at Fuller Theological Seminary, and he coined the term to identify what he saw as the third wave of the power of the Spirit in the twentieth century. The first wave was the Pentecostal movement that began at the turn of the century, the second was the Charismatic Movement, emerging in late 1950s and early 1960s, and the third wave began in the early 1980s, and was identified closely with the phenomenon associated with Wimber's ministry. According to Wimber, the Third Wave had a number of characteristics which distinguished it from the previous two waves. It had modified the language of charismatic experience, moving away from the term 'baptism in the Spirit' to terms like 'being filled with the Spirit', or 'empowered by the Spirit', indicating that encounters with the Holy Spirit were seen as steps in spiritual growth, rather than initiatory experiences. It was inclusive of those who did not speak in tongues, and it did not promote tongues as a prominent gift in charismatic experience. Wimber also claimed that one of its particular emphases was the equipping of all Christians to experience all the gifts for ministry, especially personal evangelism and divine healing. Hence the catchphrase of the 1984 conference, 'equipping the saints for evangelism in the power of the Holy Spirit.'[63]

Further conferences for Wimber were organized in Brighton, Wembley (the official follow-up to the 1984 conference) and Sheffield in October 1985, followed by a similar itinerary in late October and November in 1986 (Brighton, Wembley and then Harrogate). Each conference had a standard format of a period of sung worship, followed by a teaching sermon, and concluding with what was known as a 'ministry time'. The sung worship would be accompanied by a modern band, and typically consisted of a series of songs sung over an extended period of time (often over twenty

---

[61] *Anglicans for Renewal*, 45 (Summer 1991), Editorial.

[62] *ARMLink*, 35 (Winter 1988/89), 12.

[63] J. Wimber, 'Afterword', in Springer (ed.), *Third Wave*, 249-52.

minutes), with a minimum amount of vocal interjection and musically seamless as one song ran into the next. Conference delegates would follow the songs in their songsheet, which was entitled *Songs of Vineyard*, a reference to the Vineyard church network that Wimber had established in the United States since 1981. Wimber's own musical background as a secular pop musician with the Righteous Brothers was reflected in the distinctive musical genre of the Vineyard songs, which, in the period of sung worship, tended to develop from items with a Californian 'soft rock' to items with an emotionally intense ballad melody. Like the *Songs of Fellowship*, a dominant theological theme of the Vineyard songs is the kingship of God, who is worshipped as the source of all power and authority. Juxtaposed with this is the theme of the immanence of God through the Spirit, in whom the worshipper experiences an intense and intimate encounter with Jesus, represented musically in the ballad melodies, and lyrically in references to the Spirit, or Jesus, 'touching' or 'enfolding' the worshipper. These 'love songs to Jesus', as they have been popularly dubbed, are a distinctive feature of the Vineyard songs, and are typically used at the climax of the sung worship. Martyn Percy's study of the Vineyard songs identifies this juxtaposition of themes in terms of two repeated metaphors in the songs: 'you' and 'Lord'. 'You' communicates the immanence of God and the worshipper's response of loving adoration, and 'Lord' communicates God's sovereignty and power, to which the worshipper submits and as a result finds spiritual empowerment.[64]

The middle section of the Wimber conference format, the teaching sermon, was used to impart Wimber's theology. Robert Warren, vicar of St. Thomas', Crookes in Sheffield, summarizes Wimber's teaching in four points:

1. An emphasis on the fact that western Christianity had allowed itself to be squeezed into a rationalistic and mechanical worldview;
2. An emphasis on the kingdom of God as the central theme of Jesus' teaching and healing ministry, interpreted in terms of the age to come invading this present age, driving out evil, and bringing the wholeness of heaven;
3. An emphasis on Jesus proclaiming the coming of the kingdom by both words *and* deeds;
4. An emphasis on the need to follow Jesus' example of training disciples to continue this kingdom ministry.[65]

---

[64] M. Percy, *Words, Wonders and Power: Understanding Contemporary Christian Fundamentalism and Revivalism*, 73-8.

[65] Italics original. R. Warren, *In The Crucible: The Testing and Growth of a Local Church*, 206. See also Wimber's works: *Power Evangelism: Signs and Wonders Today*, *Power Healing* and *The Dynamics of Spiritual Growth*.

The teaching was followed by the 'ministry time', which as Warren's third point highlights, was a natural consequence of the sermon. The 'ministry time' was essentially a demonstration of the works of God through 'signs and wonders'. As Percy neatly summarizes, 'for Wimber, the kingdom of God is a kingdom of power – announced, then practised – which overthrows the controlling power of Satan'.[66] The following is an observer's account of what was typically experienced during a Wimber conference 'ministry time':

> We're all on our feet now in an attitude of prayer, many with hands held up and open, waiting quietly while the leader says "Come Holy Spirit". More time passes before someone starts to weep; another to sigh; the leader says some are feeling heat or vibration sensations; others have fallen under the power of the Spirit; someone else lets out a scream. The visiting ministry team are moving among all the people, laying on hands, praying deeply and thoroughly for many. Sometimes people are approached because the team sense or even see the presencing of the Holy Spirit upon a person; sometimes it's a response to a very specific word of knowledge.[67]
>
> Most of the meeting is entering into this ministry; the team leader now says that many more of us are called and even anointed to minister in this way to others – perhaps even now we're feeling tingling in our fingers and so should move out ... Some begin to share testimony of healing or deep cleansing or release. Someone reads out the first four verses of Isaiah 61 and says that once again, as in Jesus' day, it's happening among us in front of our very eyes! Well, something is certainly happening.[68]

As McBain had accurately observed, for many charismatics in the Church of England, these conferences were indeed a significant 'turning point'. 'New Power for "Bankrupt" Britain' was the title of an article in *Anglicans for Renewal* which heralded Wimber's visits as the major cause of fresh power in churches across the land, amidst a 'spiritually bankrupt Britain'.[69] Some charismatics saw this as the necessary tonic to 'gee-up' a flagging Renewal. Robert Warren writes, 'With hindsight, I see that the renewal of the 1970s was running out of steam ... we had lost a sense of direction, our first love for the Lord, and spiritual momentum. We were, in terms of

---

[66] Percy, *Words*, 18.

[67] These 'words of knowledge' would normally be given out from the conference platform, and are understood to be divinely inspired and descriptive of individuals present in the conference.

[68] G. Crocker, 'Come Holy Spirit', *ARMLink*, 33 (Summer 1988), 11-12.

[69] *Anglicans for Renewal*, 27 (Winter 1986), 32.

catching the wind of the Spirit, in the doldrums.'[70]

There were a number of reasons why Wimber was received as the answer to the perceived spiritual malaise. For evangelicals, still very much in the ascendancy in Charismatic Renewal, Wimber's teaching was welcomed because of its constant appeal to the bible. Significantly, through his 'signs and wonders' ministry, Wimber was able also to make a direct connection between contemporary experience and New Testament experience, and so, to a large degree, resolved the evangelical dilemma of reconciling the biblical account with modern understanding. This is illustrated well in the 'ministry time' described above in the participant's comment that what happened in Jesus' day was 'happening among us in front of our very eyes'. This point is also dealt with apologetically by Wimber's criticism of the Western rationalistic worldview.[71] There was also a pragmatic appeal for all charismatics in Wimber's methodology, for it held out the hope that evangelism and healing would become all the more effective if 'signs and wonders' accompanied them.

The practical consequences of the conferences were two-fold. First, many charismatic parishes set up 'ministry teams' to enhance the ministry of healing within the context of Sunday worship, modelling themselves on the 'ministry teams' at conferences. For example, after Wimber's first Westminster Conference, Michael Cole, vicar of All Saints, Woodford Wells, reported that the Parochial Church Council (P.C.C.) passed the following resolution: 'The P.C.C. endorses the healing ministry within the church and seeks to call out and help to equip members of the congregation to share in that ministry'. Steps were then taken to form a regular team to minister after Sunday worship.[72] Graham Dow, vicar of a Coventry parish church, reported that he had a 30-strong healing team, and at least half of the 200 strong congregation had indicated that they had received some degree of healing.[73]

Secondly, a number of parishes became centres for teaching and models for practice of the new Wimber gospel. St. Thomas', Crookes in Sheffield followed up the 1985 Sheffield conference with interdenominational 'signs and wonders follow up days' on a quarterly basis for leaders from all over the north of England. St. Andrew's, Chorleywood and Holy Trinity, Brompton became important centres for the south of England. At Chorley-wood, for example, under the leadership of David Pytches, parish 'Faith Sharing Teams', became vehicles for the new 'signs and wonders' ministry

---

[70] Warren, *Crucible*, 191.

[71] For example, Wimber in *Power Evangelism*, Ch. 5, 'Signs and Wonders and Worldviews'.

[72] M. Cole, 'We Learned Much From John Wimber', *Anglicans for Renewal*, 21 (Spring 1985), 5-6.

[73] *Anglicans for Renewal*, 27 (Winter 1986), 32.

to spread to other parishes.[74] In 1987, St. Andrew's also began convening an annual summer holiday week at Shepton Mallet, called 'New Wine', the aim of which was to bring spiritual refreshment and training for leaders and parties from all denominations, and experience of the Wimber style 'ministry in the power of the Spirit'.[75]

At the time when charismatics across denominational and non-denominational churches were welcoming Wimber, a fresh perspective on the place of Charismatic Renewal in the Church of England was offered by Josephine Bax in her book *The Good Wine*, published in 1986. This was the result of a year's research, at the Board of Mission and Unity's request, to review the place of spiritual renewal in the Church of England.[76] Alongside the Charismatic Renewal, she considered the Cursillo movement and other contemplative movements, and placed them in a broader context of the search for meaning and belonging in society at large. She wrote that although the Charismatic Movement within the Church of England may have peaked in the 1970s, by the mid-1980s it appeared to be growing and merging with other spiritual movements in the church. She acknowledged the important influence of Wimber, particularly in encouraging the healing ministry as a means to evangelism. She observed charismatics becoming involved in the Meditation Movement, and being drawn into greater contemplation (encouraged by figures such as Joyce Huggett, and her writings such as the book *Open to God*). She also discerned a new breed of charismatic 'radicals' who were taking an interest in political issues, and involving themselves in local social issues. An example of this was St. Peter's, Conisbrough, in South Yorkshire, highlighted in *Anglicans for Renewal* magazine as an example of a parish that had been both influenced by Wimber's ministry and also learnt to relate creatively to the great social needs in the parish.[77] Bax also saw charismatics involved in the Church Growth movement, as was witnessed by the developing enthusiasm for 'church planting' in the late 1980s. For example, Holy Trinity, Brompton, which had planted congregations in London, hosted a conference on church planting in May 1991, at which the Archbishop of Canterbury gave the opening address.

By the end of the 1980s, the signs were that the yeast of Charismatic Renewal was now well mixed in the dough of parochial life across the Church of England. An indication of this was the beginning of a series in *Anglicans for Renewal* called 'The Face of my Parish', which began in

---

[74] D. Pytches, 'Fully Anglican, Fully Renewed' in Springer (ed.), *Third Wave*, 164-76.

[75] H. Saunders, 'New Wine' in *Anglicans for Renewal*, 44 (Spring 1991), 9.

[76] For a summary of Bax's research conclusions see her article 'The Charismatic Movement', *ARMLink*, 31 (Winter 1987/88), 30.

[77] *ARMLink*, 'The Face of my Parish' 41 (Summer 1990), 10-3.

spring 1988. There had been occasional reports on parishes affected by Charismatic Renewal in previous issues, but now it became a regular feature. There were also aspects of the Movement, most notably its songs, which had also influenced non-charismatic parishes. One reason for this was the popularity of successive editions of the hymnbook *Mission Praise*, which had been initially published in connection with Billy Graham's 'Mission England' in 1984. This book combined the various strands of charismatic hymnody (Fisherfolk, *Songs of Fellowship* and the Vineyard songs) and made them available to the wider church. Its popularity is confirmed by a survey accomplished in 1988 by the Archbishops' Commission on Church Music, in which it was found that, in a random sample of 524 Church of England parishes, *Mission Praise* and the accompanying children's book, *Junior Praise*, were used in 36% of the churches represented, the highest proportion for any of the wide range of hymnbooks listed in the questionnaire.[78] Another means by which the songs of the Charismatic Movement were spread more widely to non-charismatics was through large inter-church gatherings. Both Spring Harvest and 'Make Way' marches for Jesus, for instance, attracted evangelicals and others with no particular charismatic loyalty. The Easter holiday Christian festival Spring Harvest had begun in 1979, become increasingly popular in the 1980s and by the 1990s it could boast some 80,000 residents at different venues across Britain.[79] Since 1987 the 'Make Way' open-air musical processions had popularized the songs of Graham Kendrick and aimed to combine a witness to the gospel, prayer for the nation and a demonstration of Christian unity.[80] Cassettes and songbooks from these events have also enhanced the popularization of charismatic hymnody.

1990s: Post-Wimber and the 'Toronto Blessing'

In 1990 it was announced that George Carey, the Bishop of Bath and Wells, was to be the new Archbishop of Canterbury. *Anglicans for Renewal* magazine offered congratulations to Carey, describing him as 'a good friend of Anglican Renewal Ministries ever since it began'.[81] The appointment of Carey as a known supporter of Charismatic Renewal had the effect of validating charismatics as a *bona fide* tradition within the Church of England, alongside the well established anglo-catholic, liberal and evangelical traditions.

However, despite the 'feather in the cap' of Carey's appointment, leaders

---

[78] J. Cooper, *Music in Parish Worship*.

[79] A. Walker, 'Pentecostalism and Charismatic Christianity' in A.E. McGrath (ed.), *Encyclopedia of Modern Christian Thought*, 428-434.

[80] J.H.S. Steven, 'Praise Marches', *News of Liturgy*, 179 (Nov. 1989).

[81] *Anglicans for Renewal*, 42 (Autumn 1990), Editorial.

in A.R.M. were beginning to make known their disquiet about the direction of the Charismatic Movement. Taking an unprecedented step, they sent Volume 44 of *Anglicans for Renewal*, without charge, to all bishops and clergy in the Church of England, with the front cover headline 'Crisis Time For Renewal'. In the following edition, Michael Mitton asked in the editorial, 'Are we seeing the beginning of a post-Wimber Britain?' Mitton was openly critical of Wimber's recent association with Paul Cain and the Kansas City Prophets, whom Walker describes as 'a throw-back to the earlier Pentecostal Holiness movements and the circle of followers connected with Pentecostalism's most controversial figure, William Branham'.[82] Wimber's association with the Kansas prophets went back to the mid-1980s, but this became publicly evident in Britain during 1990 when Wimber shared conference platforms with them, at Holy Trinity, Brompton in July, followed in October by a large London Docklands conference, and by a 'Church in the Nineties' Conference in Harrogate. Mitton had serious reservations about what he identified as the strongly revivalist nature of these conferences. He had observed that this had made the Wimber 'we knew and loved' less accessible: 'many in Anglican Charismatic Renewal have depended a lot on the lead that John Wimber has given, but I sense that the revivalism espoused by Wimber has distanced him from some'.[83]

This perceived crisis led leading figures within A.R.M. to consider alternative 'roots' for Charismatic Renewal. At the 1994 A.R.M. National Conference, David Gillett, then principal of Trinity College Bristol (and previously successor to Colin Urquhart at St. Hugh's, Lewsey) presented the fourth century Desert Fathers as a model for Renewal, identifying a charismatic element in the Fathers who 'shared words of knowledge, words of wisdom and words of prophecy with the people for whom they were responsible'.[84] Earlier that year in March, A.R.M. had convened a symposium on Celtic spirituality in which it emerged that the leaders of A.R.M. were engaged deeply and seriously with the Celtic tradition.[85] In presenting the Celtic saints as 'Spirit-led' prophets, healers, visionaries and evangelists, the symposium speakers encouraged participants to view them as inspirational models for contemporary charismatics. One person's report on the symposium indicated that it had met a need:

[82] A. Walker, 'Pentecostalism and Charismatic Christianity', 433.
[83] *Anglicans for Renewal*, 45 (Summer 1991), Editorial.
[84] D. Gillett, 'A Spirituality for Evangelism', *Anglicans for Renewal*, 56 (Spring 1994), 10.
[85] 'Roots for Renewal: A Symposium on Celtic Christianity and Charismatic Renewal', 8–10th March, 1994. I attended this conference.

We were challenged from the outset as to whether Celtic Christianity was the next piece of entertainment for bored Charismatics. Speaking as a bored Charismatic, I came yearning for something deeper, more integrated, more connected to life; and came away with a desire to pursue the Celtic understanding of life, work, prayer, and rest: a spirituality of wholeness.[86]

Whilst charismatics in the Church of England were searching for new inspirational roots, there unfolded a new and unexpected twist in the story of the Charismatic Movement, the 'Toronto Blessing'. This phenomenon had its origins in a Vineyard church in Toronto, the Toronto Airport Vineyard Fellowship. On 20th January 1994, the Fellowship began a four-night series of meetings. The senior pastor, John Arnott, and the leadership team were overwhelmed when on the first night, following the speaker's address (Randy Clarke, another Vineyard pastor), the whole congregation responded to an invitation to receive prayer. They understood the ecstatic behaviour that followed, and on successive evenings, as a powerful move of the Holy Spirit. This included falling to the ground and lying on the floor (called 'resting in the Spirit'), shaking, trembling and jerking, laughing, weeping and wailing, apparent drunkenness and intense physical activity such as running on the spot and animal sounds. There were also mystical experiences, such as the receiving and proclaiming of prophetic insights, and visions.

After January 1994 the Toronto Fellowship continued to hold nightly revival meetings that drew visitors from different parts of the world. In May 1994, one of those visitors was Eleanor Mumford, the wife of the leader of the local South West London Vineyard church. She returned to England and on Sunday May 22nd spoke to her own congregation and after invoking the Spirit, the same phenomena occurred. The following Sunday she was invited to speak at Holy Trinity, Brompton, when there was a similar outburst of the Toronto phenomena. This prompted a number of leading charismatic Anglicans to visit Toronto immediately, among them Sandy Millar (vicar of Holy Trinity, Brompton), Bishop David Pytches, John Hughes (vicar of St. John's, Harborne in Birmingham) and Bishop Graham Dow (Bishop of Willesden, and previously vicar of Holy Trinity, Coventry). On their return, Bishop David Pytches and Sandy Millar organized meetings in June and July at Holy Trinity, Brompton for clergy and church leaders who wanted to experience the 'Blessing' in their own churches. Later that summer the Toronto phenomena were witnessed at 'New Wine', and Bishop David Pytches and Eleanor Mumford both led seminars on the subject.

The arrival of this new wave of charismatic phenomena caught national

---

[86] J. Searle, 'Celtic Connections', *Anglicans for Renewal*, 57 (Summer 1994), 13.

press attention, which dubbed it 'The Toronto Blessing'. Responding to this, a report presented to the Methodist Church's Conference commented that it was perhaps unfortunate that the title had stuck, because of the undue focus on a particular place, and because it begs the question of whether or not it is indeed a 'Blessing'.[87] The report's misgivings about the strong focus on Toronto cannot erase the fact, however, that 'pilgrimage' to Toronto was an intrinsic part of the spread of the phenomena world-wide. Many thousands of Christians made the journey; the Methodist Report stated that by 1996 about 300,000 people had visited the Toronto Vineyard Fellowship. They went not just as tourists, to view what was going on, but to discover the spiritual refreshment of the 'Blessing' which could then be brought home with them. The vicar of one of my case study churches (St.E), upon his return from Toronto suggested in a sermon that this pilgrimage was a legitimate extension of the principle of the Naaman and Elisha story (2 Kgs. 5:1-14). In this story, Naaman, the Syrian general, had to travel to the waters of the Jordan to receive healing, despite his protest that the rivers in his homeland were superior. The vicar invited us to view Toronto, like the Jordan, as the place to which people travelled in order to receive healing and blessing.[88]

Opinion was divided over the issue of whether this new Pentecostal style phenomenon was a 'Blessing'. For many charismatics, it was 'the new thing that God was doing',[89] some initially heralding its arrival as a new 'revival'. However, the Dean of Worcester provoked debate in the correspondence section of the church press when he denied that the 'Toronto Blessing' was a sign of revival, preferring to describe it as 'an experience of mass hysteria for which there is ample historical prece-dence'.[90] Those who sought to give support to the 'Toronto Blessing' did so from a variety of approaches. Historically, apologists drew parallels with the ecstatic experiences of past revivals, such as Jonathan Edwards and the Great Awakening,[91] the Wesleys and the Evangelical Revival,[92] and even the 1859 Ulster revival.[93] Appeal was made to the bible on the basis that the Toronto ecstatic phenomena were 'uncannily like some of the experiences

---

[87] *The 'Toronto Blessing': Report to Conference 1996* by The Methodist Church Faith and Order Committee.

[88] St.E, sermon heard at 6.30pm service, visit 2.

[89] This was a typical informant description of the 'Toronto Blessing' from my case study churches most influenced by the 'Blessing'. Other descriptions included "a fresh outpouring of the Spirit" or a "new wave of the Spirit".

[90] *The Church of England Yearbook*, xxvi.

[91] G. Chevreau, *Catch The Fire: The Toronto Blessing*, Ch.4: 'A Well-Travelled Path'.

[92] N. Scotland, *Charismatics and the Next Millennium: Do they have a future?*, 215-17.

[93] D. Roberts, *The Toronto Blessing*.

of God which we find in the Bible'.[94] There were those who have pointed to the spiritual fruit of the 'Blessing' as validation of its authenticity as a work of God. 'Christians are really sorting out their lives', so Sue Hope, a vicar in Sheffield, was quoted as saying in the *Church of England Newspaper*: 'I think the fruit is good and Christ-like. It is about soaking ourselves in the love of God.'[95] Dr Patrick Dixon, a physician and leader in an independent church in West London, in his book *Signs of Revival*, examined the psychological benefits of the 'Toronto Blessing' at length.[96] He argued that the phenomena are best described psychologically as an alteration in conscious state, and rejected the view that the 'Blessing' was mass hysteria or corporate brainwashing. Dixon quoted Dr Simon Wesley, senior lecturer at King's College School of Medicine, who commented in *The Observer* on 4th September 1994:

> This religious experience appears to be cathartic. The people feel good about it and appear to go for the purpose of group ecstatic experience. It is not mass hysteria or any form of mental disorder – it may be rather un-English, but there is nothing sinister about it.[97]

Michael Mitton of A.R.M. reflected on his own experience of the 'Blessing' and affirmed it as a means through which God renews individuals in relation to their humanity, playfulness, spiritual darkness and love for God.[98]

It is important to recognize, along with the Church of England's Board of Mission report, that the phenomena associated with the 'Blessing' were neither new nor unusual within the overall context of world-wide charismatic movements.[99] Many of the ritual and ecstatic elements of Toronto had been witnessed previously at Vineyard conferences in the 1980s, when, as we have seen, prayers calling upon the Spirit were followed by behaviour such as falling down, bodily convulsions together with vocal expression such as laughter, screaming, crying. What appeared new was the scale and intensity of the behaviour, and certain ecstatic expressions such as the animal noises, and the enthusiasm with which the new 'Blessing' was received in Britain.

---

[94] M. Green, 'The Blessing? It's all in the Bible', *Church of England Newspaper*, (June 23, 1995).

[95] C. Hails, 'Toronto Blessing: what are the fruits?', *Church of England Newspaper* (May 19, 1995).

[96] P. Dixon, *Signs of Revival*, Ch.5, 'Medical Perspectives on Manifestations'.

[97] Dixon, *Signs*, 259.

[98] M. Mitton, *The Heart of Toronto: Exploring the Spirituality of the 'Toronto Blessing'*.

[99] *The Toronto Experience: An Exploration of the Issues*, Board of Mission Occasional Paper No.7.

The significance of the 'Toronto Blessing' is perhaps best regarded in historical terms as the latest in the succession of 'waves of experience' that have marked the development of the Charismatic Movement since its beginnings in the 1960s, each wave accompanied by associated charismatic phenomena.[100] Sociologically, these successive trends in religious collective behaviour could be characterized as 'crazes', a term originally applied to the Charismatic Movement by the sociologist John Moore in his description of the characteristics of the Roman Catholic charismatics.[101] By using the description 'craze', Moore is acknowledging the fact that certain aspects of religious public behaviour become normative for the way that a group establishes their relationship with the divine. For the early charismatics it was baptism in the Spirit accompanied by speaking in tongues, for the 1980s Wimber era it was 'words of knowledge' with 'prayer ministry', 'falling in the Spirit' and healings, and in the Toronto 'wave' a wide range of ecstatic behaviour, most notoriously animal noises and uncontrollable laughter.

Conclusion

The development of the Charismatic Movement has led to aspects of Pentecostal spirituality, albeit in adapted form, influencing many parts of the Church of England. Large, successful charismatic parishes have developed, bishops and others in leadership have been baptized in the Spirit, service agencies and conferences have grown, died and then re-emerged in new guises, and the term 'charismatic' has become another accepted churchmanship label. It seems that the desire of the original pioneers for the new movement of the Spirit to be spread throughout the church has, to a degree, been realized in the Church of England.

But what of the effect upon the public performance of worship in those parishes that have welcomed the charismatic experience, instances of which have been illustrated above? We move now to the next chapter, which begins to address this question by introducing the method of investigation used in studying the worship of my six case study parishes.

---

[100] Colin Buchanan uses this term in an editorial comment on the 'Toronto Blessing' in *News of Liturgy*, 237 (September 1994). This term is used in a more general sense than Peter Wagner's 'Wave' schematisation of Pentecostal history (see above).

[101] John Moore, 'The Catholic Pentecostal Movement' in Michael Hill (ed.) *Sociological Yearbook of Religion*, 6, 73-90.

CHAPTER 3

Methodology

Case Studies with a *Verstehen* Approach

In order to investigate the characteristics of charismatic worship in the Church of England I decided to use a case study approach, which Nisbet and Watt helpfully define as 'a systematic investigation into a specific instance'.[1] In my research I investigated the public worship of six churches, each a specific instance of a church that considered itself to have been influenced by Charismatic Renewal. I discovered that to conduct an investigation along these lines provided me with a unique perspective on the concrete realities of the practice of public worship, as succeeding chapters will demonstrate. Whilst large scale surveys have an important place in empirical research, to have used them in this context would have run the risk of creating an overview that blurs rather than clarifies the distinctive features of worship 'on the ground'.

However, whilst convinced of the advantages of the micro-level approach, I was also aware of my responsibilities to the macro-level: how can the conclusions drawn from a selection of case studies promote an understanding of charismatic worship in the Church of England at large? Understandably, critics of the case study approach point to its limitations when researchers wish to make generalizations. There is, however, another more promising and subtle way of defining the relationship between the specific instances of case studies and the wider set of instances of a phenomenon than that of generalizability. I would argue, following Michael Bassey, that the value of case study work to other social situations lies in its 'relatability' and it is this quality that is more important to a case study than its generalizability.[2] The relatability of my case study sample was a determining factor when it came to selecting churches. Three of the

---

[1] J. Nisbet and J. Watt, 'Case Study' in J. Bell, T. Bush, A. Fox, J. Goodey, and S. Goulding (eds.), *Conducting Small-Scale Investigations in Educational Management*, 74.

[2] M. Bassey, 'Pedagogic Research: on the relative merits of search for generalization and study of single events' in Bell et al., *Small-Scale*, 103-22.

churches were evangelical (St.B, St.C, and St.E), and were situated
respectively in a cosmopolitan city centre (St.B), an inner urban area (St.C)
and a middle class housing estate (St.E). One was anglo-catholic, situated in
a working class suburb (St.D). Another was modern catholic, situated in a
country village (St.A) and the final church (St.F) was situated in a deprived
outer urban estate and could be categorized by Josephine Bax's term
'radical' because of its engagement with local social issues.[3] This selection
of ecclesial traditions and sociological situations was a deliberate attempt to
relate the sample both to the variety and also overall constitution of
charismatic expression in the Church of England, features of which I have
already outlined in my historical overview. So, for example, the choice of
three evangelical churches in a sample of six represents the evangelical
dominance within Charismatic Renewal. Another feature that helped
establish the relatability of my sample was the coherent and strong identity
of the charismatic worship culture that these case study churches drew
upon. As my historical overview illustrated, the development of
Charismatic Renewal has, to a large extent, been determined by the rise and
fall of a succession of centralized networks, beginning with the Fountain
Trust and more recently with A.R.M. and the Vineyard church networks
associated with Wimber and the 'Toronto Blessing'. These networks have
successfully generated and sustained common cultures of charismatic
worship through conferences, teaching and training parishes, magazines and
song collections. This suggests that the liturgical practice in case study
worship is to a good degree relatable to the worship of other Church of
England charismatic parishes. Throughout both my sociological analysis
and theological appraisal, I will illustrate this kind of relatability by
including references to charismatic Anglican writing on worship which
draw attention to the way that worship in the case study churches relates to
the wider experience and interpretation of Anglican charismatic worship.

My analysis of the public worship in the case study churches was dependent upon ethnographic methods commonly used by social scientists in
the investigation of social groups. This approach can be summarized as a
Verstehen approach. *Verstehen* was a term coined by the sociologist Max
Weber to describe a research methodology that enabled the social
researcher to discover the social and cultural world of the group being
studied.[4] By using *Verstehen* the researcher is committed to two levels of

---

[3]   Two of the six churches were already known to me (St.B and St.E). Three were
chosen by recommendation: the radical parish (St.F) was suggested by the director of
A.R.M., the Revd Michael Mitton; the anglo-catholic parish (St.D) by a leading anglo-
catholic charismatic, the Revd Peter Peterken; the modern catholic country village
church (St.A) by a diocesan Renewal group chairman. The sixth (St.C) was discovered
after correspondence on an article in the A.R.M. journal, *Anglicans for Renewal*.

[4]   The literal translation of *Verstehen* is the noun 'understanding'.

enquiry. The first is to discover why social actors behave in the way that they do, or as Theodore Abel described it in an influential article, the work of 'bringing to the foreground the inner organic sequence intervening between a stimulus and response'.[5] This search for motivational sequences is what Weber called *erklärendes Verstehen*.[6] The second is the task of correctly identifying the meaning that social actors designate to their actions, which Weber called *aktuelles Verstehen*. The challenge for the researcher is to correctly identify the common-sense constructs pre-selected and pre-interpreted by those who participate in the social world under investigation. In the words of Schutz, 'the thought objects constructed by the social scientist, in order to grasp this social reality, have to be founded upon the thought objects constructed by the common-sense thinking of men living their daily life within their social world'.[7] The main strength for my purposes of a *Verstehen* approach, and its associated qualitative research methods of participant observation and interviews (see below), was its suitability for uncovering the relatively subtle and complex social processes of liturgical action. Because of its commitment to studying groups and individuals in their natural setting, where behaviour and 'common-sense' meanings are generated in social (and in this case, ritual) interaction, it has a distinct advantage over quantitative methods of enquiry. In considering the possibility of using questionnaires, for instance, I came to the conclusion that whilst undoubtedly of value in other fields of social enquiry this was a less than adequate means of capturing and understanding acts of public worship. As M. J. Wilson writes, 'Any social group is full of spontaneous activity which reflects a structure and set of beliefs which are difficult, if not impossible to capture by a formal [i.e. questionnaire] method of questioning.'[8] This, I suggest, is particularly true of a public ritual like worship, which is characterized by a whole series of ordered and spontaneous acts, the meanings of which would be inaccessible to questionnaires.

The *Verstehen* approach gave a distinctive shape to my research, evident in a number of disciplines that I followed. The first of these was a process of re-socialization whereby I familiarized myself with the social world of public worship that had been influenced by Charismatic Renewal. This was accomplished in two stages. The initial stage was a period of three and a half years of leading and participating in worship in the parish of St. John the Evangelist in Welling, Kent, where I served as curate from 1987 to

---

[5] T. Abel, 'The Operation Called *Verstehen*', *American Journal of Sociology* 54 (1948-9), 214.

[6] M. Weber, *Basic Concepts in Sociology*, 36.

[7] A. Schutz, 'Concepts, Constructs and Theory Formation', in M. Natanson (ed.), *Philosophy of the Social Sciences*.

[8] M.J. Wilson, 'Styles of Research', in J. Bell et al, *Small-Scale*, 30.

1991. Prior to 1987, the church had been introduced to the Vineyard charismatic culture, and for the duration of my curacy the public worship reflected aspects of that culture, most notably in the singing of modern worship songs and 'prayer ministry', an adaptation of the Wimber conference 'ministry time'. This experience gave me an in-depth example of my research topic, and prepared me for the subsequent main period of research, undertaken over a two year period between 1993–95, in which I made two weekend visits, a year apart, to each of the case study churches.[9] The advantage of the prior experience at St. John's in Welling was that I was able to enter this second period of research with focused notions of what needed to be observed and questions to be asked. In many ways I was simply re-entering the research field in which I had already, unintentionally, completed three and a half years of ethnography. The sequence of two visits to each church was also important. The second visits provided a comparison with the first visits, and they helped me identify the regular, occasional and developing features of each church's public worship. They also offered the opportunity to return to the research field with a more focused interview method (see below), and a developed sensitivity to the significant charismatic elements within worship, such as the role of music and song, 'prayer ministry', and the understanding of God's action in worship.[10]

Having chosen the case study approach because of its suitability to reveal the realities of worship 'on the ground' I wanted to allow the data gathered to control and generate subsequent interpretation. This led to a second research discipline in which, following in the steps of Glaser and Strauss and their grounded theory, I sought to avoid tailoring observations to fit predetermined theories and instead allowed the data collected to generate theory.[11] A classic ethnographic example of the converting nature of this process can be witnessed in Howard Becker's *Boys in White*. When Becker and his fellow researchers began research in a medical school, their

---

[9]   St.A: 4/5 Sept. 1993 and 3/4 Sept. 1994; St.B: 12/13 June 1993 and 5/6 Nov. 1994; St.C: 9/10 Oct. 1993 and 8/9 Oct. 1994; St.D: 22/23 Jan. 1994 and 14/15 Jan. 1995; St.E: 26/27 Feb. 1994 and 25/26 Feb.1995; St.F: 16/17 July 1994 and 17/18 June 1995.

[10]   The two-stage strategy I employed both within the main period of research and in the progression from St John's to the six case studies corresponds to the first two stages of case study research as prescribed by Nisbet and Watt. They suggest that a case study should start with an 'open phase', in which the emphasis is on a general review of the social situation without prejudgment, and then move to 'focus' on those aspects of the case study that are identified as of crucial importance. See 'Case Study' in J. Bell et al, *Small-Scale*, 78-80.

[11]   See B.G. Glaser and A.L. Strauss, *The Discovery of Grounded Theory: Strategies for Qualitative Research*. This theory is developed further in A.L. Strauss and J. Corbin, *Basics of Qualitative Research: Techniques and Procedures for Developing Grounded Theory*.

focus was upon the medical school as an organization in which a student acquired some basic perspectives for his or her career. However, in the final analysis of research data, a new research focus emerged, namely the problems experienced by the students in the level and direction of effort in their studies.[12] As I entered the main period of research with a fairly well defined focus due to my prior experience, I was also aware of the potential danger of previously held familiar assumptions distorting the way I handled and interpreted data. By inviting an Outside Observer to accompany me on my first visits, who then played the role of a 'stranger' to charismatic worship (see below), I introduced a significant check to such prejudice. The return visits were also important in this respect because they provided an opportunity to test developing hypotheses with further exposure to primary data.

The two research techniques that were crucial to the process of discovering the social and ritual processes of worship and the meaning attributed to them by participants were participation observation and informal interviews. Before I move on to explain how I adopted these methods I want to mention the third discipline of my research, which was to do with testing the adequacy of my descriptions of worship; how faithful to the social worlds of worship under study were my final descriptions? The discipline that I made use of was a practical procedure recommended by Alfred Schutz in which the researcher invites the social participants to judge the adequacy of the researcher's ethnographic description, and accompanying 'second order' interpretations.[13] Allowing informants the privilege of checking draft descriptions and interpretations is also strongly recommended by some research manuals.[14] In practice this meant that I submitted six ethnographic descriptions of worship observed, together with preliminary interpretation, to each of the respective case study churches, and invited comments from informants as to the fairness and accuracy of the material. After completing this consultation process I then proceeded to write-up the final form of description and interpretation.

---

[12] See H.S. Becker, *Boys in White: Student Culture in Medical School*.

[13] Which Schutz, following Weber, called the creation of Ideal Types. A. Schutz, 'The Problem of Rationality in the Social World', *Economica*, 19, 1943.

[14] For example, Nisbet and Watt recommend this process as the final stage of the case study research process; 'Case Study' in J. Bell et al, *Small-Scale*, 80-1.

Research Methods

Participation Observation

In understanding my role as a participant observer I found the definition in Cicourel's classic text on social research, *Method and Measurement in Sociology*, to be the most formative:

> For our purposes we define participant observation as a process in which the observer's presence in a social situation is maintained for the purpose of scientific investigation. The observer is in a face-to-face relationship with the observed, and, by participating with them in their natural life setting, he gathers data. Thus, the observer is part of the context being observed, and he both modifies and is influenced by this context.[15]

To supplement this definition, the role of participant observer can be categorized as follows:

> (a) The 'complete participant', whose sustained observer presence in the research field is concealed, for example in covert observation of groups;
> (b) The 'participant-as-observer', whose observer status is acknowledged and sustained over a lengthy period;
> (c) The 'observer-as-participant', whose contact with informants is brief, formal and openly classified as observation;
> (d) The 'complete observer', who is identified with an eavesdropping role and who may never really get to know the informants' views.[16]

As I participated in public worship, 'the natural life setting' of the six case study churches, my role was closest to the 'observer-as-participant'.[17] My visits were brief, and my hosts regarded me as someone who had come to 'look at' their worship. As a participant, I played the role of a member of the congregation in worship, following what was expected of congregational participation in its various forms: standing, sitting, kneeling, singing, greeting, and receiving the sacrament. As an observer, I was different to those around me in a number of respects. For example, whilst others were worshipping, and 'letting themselves go' in singing and acts of devotion, I was working, maintaining an analytical frame of mind that was anathema to the situational ethos. I also made use of a small, discrete cassette recorder in order to record my observations and the sequence of events in the services.

---

[15] A.V. Cicourel, *Method and Measurement in Sociology*, 41.

[16] This is the categorization outlined by R.G. Burgess, *In the Field: An Introduction to Field Research*, 79.

[17] Within this categorization my role in the initial period of three and a half years at St. John's, Welling could be described as 'complete participant'.

In working as an observer in what were relatively familiar surroundings I tried to take as much note of what appeared familiar and mundane, as I did those things that were unusual. Burgess suggests 'that researchers working within their own culture should adopt an artificial naiveté by recording as much detail as possible about the people present and topics of conversation regardless of their relevance'.[18] Partly in response to this need of maintaining an element of naiveté I invited a friend to accompany me on my first round of visits in the role of an Outside Observer. This person was a committed Anglican but prior to joining me had no first-hand experience of the Charismatic Movement. On each of the visits he took on the role of a participant observer in worship after which I interviewed him as an informant. The benefit of the Outside Observer was two-fold. First, as an outsider to the Charismatic Movement the Outside Observer had what has been called 'stranger value'. Burgess writes:

> The outsider ... has 'stranger value'. This idea of the researcher as a stranger rests on Simmel's notion of the individual who is free of commitments to those who are studied and therefore more likely to be objective ... This position is supported by Merton who maintains that 'it is the stranger ... who finds what is familiar to the group significantly unfamiliar and so is prompted to raise questions for inquiry less apt to be raised at all by insiders'.[19]

So, being an informant who was a 'stranger' to charismatic expression, the Outside Observer was in a unique position to observe with fresh eyes. His role had reached a natural conclusion by the completion of the first visits, as he was no longer a 'stranger', and so he did not accompany me on the second visits. Secondly, as a second observer, he performed the function of an informant, validating my observations and providing his own, often things that I missed. So, for example he would normally sit towards the back of the congregation, with a brief to take special note of congregational participation, whereas I would sit near the front where it was easier to observe the actions of those who led. This two-observer strategy has been used in other liturgical field studies, most notably in Mark Searle's study of Roman Catholic parish worship in the U.S.A.[20]

One of the strengths of participation observation as a research method is its naturalistic approach; it aims to help the researcher experience and observe people in their natural environment. Cicourel's definition, however, avoids the naïve assumption that participation observation can deliver a

---

[18] Burgess, *Field*, 24.

[19] Burgess, *Field*, 23.

[20] M. Searle 'The Notre Dame Study of Catholic Parish Life' in *Worship*, 60 (July 1986), 4:312-33.

pure naturalistic approach in which the social context remains unaffected by the researcher. An observer is inevitably part of the social context that is observed, and 'both modifies and is influenced by' this context. Although limited in my contact with each case study, I was nevertheless involved in social and ritual interaction with members of the churches. In general I attempted to lessen the impact of my presence, for example, by requesting that churches refrain from welcoming me publicly in services. However, the smaller the gathering for worship, the more difficult it became to remain anonymous, so that in the close community of the country parish church I visited (St.A), it was virtually impossible to maintain anonymity.[21]

Acknowledging, as Cicourel does, that the researcher is in genuine relationship with his context need not necessarily be a weakness for the research method. In fact it can be exploited to the researcher's advantage. For example, Hammersley and Atkinson argue that the interaction between researcher and participants is an inevitable part of the 'reflexivity' of ethnographic research, and the way that people respond to a researcher may be as informative as how they react to other situations.[22] The critical nature of an incident of public conflict in a service at St.A, for instance, was highlighted by the embarrassment expressed by informants that I should have been present as a witness.[23] Conversely, as Cicourel's definition notes, the way in which the Outside Observer and I were influenced by the social contexts of worship was just as significant a feature of this reflexivity. As will become clear in later analysis, taking stock of the existential experience of being at worship with each case study church was, for both of us, an important element in developing a clearer understanding of that worship, particularly in the rituals of the 'time of worship' (Chapter 5) and 'prayer ministry' (Chapter 6). This process of social knowledge gained through experience is illustrated by the work of Frederick Barth, an anthropologist who researched initiation rites among the Baktaman of Highland New Guinea.[24] Barth makes the point that if a researcher is to understand a ritual fully, they must participate in its performance, and so he went through a number of the initiation rites himself and attempted in his work to give expression to the experience. The most important aspect of the rites was the way they progressively altered his knowledge of the surrounding world; through the manipulation of symbolic equations, each rite presented a view

---

[21] Rather amusingly on my first visit to St.A my Outside Observer and I were prayed for by name in the main morning Eucharist in the intercessions by an enthusiastic member of the congregation who wanted to pray for God's blessing upon our research!

[22] M. Hammersley and P. Atkinson, *Ethnography: Principles in Practice*, 14-23.

[23] For further details, see description of St.A in Chapter 4.

[24] F. Barth, *Ritual and Knowledge among the Baktaman of New Guinea*. He is referred to by Martin Stringer in 'Liturgy and Anthropology: The History of a Relationship' in *Worship*, 63 (November 1989), 6:503-19.

and understanding of the world that was subtly different from the last.[25] Ely makes the same point in a more theoretical way in the book, *Doing Qualitative Research*. Ely argues that ethnographers need to take seriously the interplay between affect and cognition as they go about their research, concluding that 'qualitative research is forged in the transaction among what is done and learnt and felt by the researcher'.[26]

Interviews

The interview process complemented my participation observation in worship by providing a means of discovering how a selection of church members described and interpreted the acts of worship. This is implicit in Howard Becker's definition of the participant observer:

> The participant observer gathers data by participating in the daily life of the group or organisation he studies. He watches the people he is studying to see what situations they ordinarily meet and how they behave in them. He enters into conversation with some or all of the participants in these situations and discovers their interpretations of the events he has observed.[27]

The informants I selected on my first visit were three members of the congregation (chosen at random), a music leader[28] and the church minister. By including both leadership and congregational accounts of worship I was able to get a fuller picture of participant understandings, not least in the interesting comparison between what leaders hoped worship would achieve and what congregational members perceived to be important. The interview questions for the first visits can be found in Appendix A. Each of the five informants were sent a copy of the interview questions prior to my visit with the hope that foreknowledge would give them a sense of security, enabling a more relaxed interview. Each interview combined common core questions with questions specific to each category of informant. The core questions invited the informants to talk about the use of charismatic gifts in worship and to evaluate the worship in which they participated. Charismatic gifts appeared at the outset to be an important area of enquiry, although as the research progressed it became apparent that the use of charismatic gifts was only one amongst a number of symbolic actions that constituted the

---

[25] The total process involved seven initiations performed over the lifetime of an individual.

[26] M. Ely, *Doing Qualitative Research: Circles within Circles*, 1.

[27] Quoted in Burgess, *Field*, 79.

[28] A 'music leader' refers to a musician who was in charge of a music group that led worship.

charismatic worship culture. The category specific questions concerned the normal pattern of worship (congregational informants), the musical leadership and repertoire (music leader), and liturgical development and leadership (church minister). This information was an invaluable means of establishing the regular and occasional features of the worship I was observing as well as placing it within a situational and historical context.

The other interview that I conducted on the first round of visits was with the Outside Observer. After each service I invited him to reflect upon the worship that he had observed, and like the indigenous informants, the interview format developed from a more factual to evaluative analysis (see Appendix A4). As well as providing a check on my own observations, his role as 'stranger' enabled him to give important information about the realities of worship in each church.

On the second visit I made use of a different interview technique, the group interview. Having concentrated on the general experience of worship on my first visit, I wanted to interview informants with reference to the specific act of worship in which we had all participated. In this regard, these interviews were similar to those I conducted with the Outside Observer on my first visits. I selected two groups and interviewed them after the service, one with three members of the congregation, and the music leader and minister in the other. Re-selecting the three members of the congregation interviewed on the first visits proved practically impossible and so three more were again selected at random, with the proviso that they were comfortable with others in the group. The questions used are found in Appendix B. This interview was less structured and more spontaneous than the first visit interviews, since I fed the questions to the groups as the interviews progressed. The aim of the questions was to provide a framework within which the informants could discuss freely their experience of the service. The questions were predominantly evaluative, seeking to explore the meanings that the informants attached to worship. The fourth question, for example, explores the notion of God's presence that I discovered in the first visits to be a very important aspect of worship.

In general, informants found it very much more easy to talk descriptively about the events of a service than answer questions about the meaning of those events. For example, it was self evident to many of them that God was present, "at work", or "moving among" the worshipping congregation, but they found it very difficult to articulate what these common sense constructs actually meant. This illustrates the difficulty that participants have in articulating the full meaning of their acts, particularly when they are executed at a pre-reflective level, as is typically the case with religious ritual. Researchers in religious ritual witness to this fact. Barth, for instance, was surprised to discover in his research with the Baktaman that despite the very great importance of rites within their social and psychological world, the Baktaman very rarely discussed the meaning of these rites among themselves. Similarly, Martin Stringer, who researched the public worship of four churches in Manchester, discovered that many of those with whom he spoke in the congregations found it very hard to articulate what effect their liturgy had on them. They too affirmed that God was important to worship but often found it impossible to articulate this significance.[29] Whilst this does not invalidate interview work as a method, it does underscore the value of participant observation as a complementary means of discovery for the researcher who is seeking an interpretation of common-sense constructs.

In the presentation of interview data in the analysis of case study worship, I use the following codes to identify the sources of interview:

Visit 1	*Visit 2*
CI = congregational interview	CGI = congregational group interview
MLI = music leader's interview	LGI = service leader's group interview
LI = church leader's interview	
OI = outside observer's interview	

Research Strategy

Having introduced the ethnographic methods used in my research, I now turn to discuss the strategy that I employed. What was the procedural and theoretical framework that would give direction and focus to my participant observation and interviewing within the context of Christian worship? One of the challenges I faced in answering this question was the lack of comparative models upon which to draw. There are relatively few ethnographic studies of religious ritual in the First World and an almost complete absence on Christian ritual. The reasons for this are various.[30] In the past anthropologists have, on the whole, only been interested in the rituals of more 'exotic' societies in other parts of the world, and have not

---

[29] M.D. Stringer, *On the Perception of Worship: The Ethnography of Worship in Four Christian Congregations in Manchester.* See, for example, his discussion of the Baptist Chapel (Ch.4, esp. 90-7).

[30] In the following discussion I am indebted to Martin Stringer's analysis in his essay outlining the relationship between social science and the study of ritual. See Stringer, 'Liturgy and Anthropology'.

engaged in working with the more familiar Christian traditions.[31] Sociologists however have been more interested in Christianity, and the large
number of studies of churches in Europe and the United States have been
good at determining the social backgrounds of the people who attend the
churches and to a degree, why they might go. However, they tend to remain
silent on the activities of religious ritual within the churches. As Stringer
comments, 'it is almost as if the sociologist remains at the church door and
waits for the congregation to come out again'.[32] As with the anthropologists, there is no detailed work on the liturgy.

There are however a small number of studies on Christian ritual which
gave some preliminary details on methodological approaches. These
include two studies already referred to, Mark Searle's account of the Notre
Dame Study of Catholic parish life in America and Martin Stringer's study
of public worship in four Manchester churches. There are also a small
number of examples of work by social scientists specific to Christian ritual
in the Pentecostal tradition. Walter Pitts studied the Afro-Baptist ritual in
the African Diaspora,[33] and Terence Booth researched the life and worship
of the Church of Cherubim and Seraphim in Birmingham (a Pentecostal
African and Caribbean church).[34] Andrew Walker and James Atherton
wrote an ethnographic study of an Easter Pentecostal Convention.[35] Mary
Jo Neitz gave some ethnographic description in her study of a charismatic
Roman Catholic prayer group (the Precious Blood Prayer Group) but the
focus of her study is on the religious experience of charismatics rather than
the performance of ritual.[36] Though these studies were helpful for
comparative work, and gave some details on methodological approaches to
ritual, I had to look elsewhere for a more systematic basis for my research
strategy. Even Albrecht's *Rites in the Spirit*, the most recent and comprehensive study of Pentecostal ritual, gives little detailed information on
methodology.

In the end it was in the world of liturgical studies, rather than social
science, that I discovered a satisfactory and coherent methodological
framework that gave a sustainable focus to my fieldwork. The particular

---

[31] This may seem surprising, given that liturgists have made use of work done by
anthropologists, the most frequently quoted of these being Victor Turner's *The Ritual
Process*, Mary Douglas' *Natural Symbols*, and Clifford Geertz's *The Interpretation of
Cultures*. But as Stringer points out, none of these works is specifically about ritual.
Rather they address the place of religion and ritual within society as a whole.

[32] Stringer, 'Liturgy and Anthropology', 504.

[33] W. Pitts (Jr.), *Old Ship of Zion: The Afro-Baptist Ritual in the African Diaspora*.

[34] T.T. Booth, *We True Christians: The Church of the Cherubim and Seraphim*.

[35] A. Walker and J. Atherton, 'An Easter Pentecostal Convention: The Successful
Management of a "Time of Blessing" ' in *Sociological Review* (August 1971), 367-87.

[36] M.J. Neitz, *Charisma and Community: A Study of Religious Commitment within
Charismatic Renewal*.

strategy that I made use of is outlined by Margaret Kelleher, a Roman Catholic liturgist, in an essay 'Liturgical Theology: A Task and a Method'.[37] This strategy includes four main elements: acknowledging the public horizon of worship, observing it, interpreting it and assessing its theological adequacy.

The Public Horizon of Worship

As a focus for my research, I chose to concentrate on what Kelleher calls the 'public horizon' conveyed by the worship I observed. In her essay, she describes the public horizon as being constituted by a combination of the worshipping community's 'shared world of meaning and value, public spirituality, culture, common fund of knowledge, living tradition, corporate memory, and vision of reality'.[38] In its worship, a liturgical gathering or assembly conveys, or to use Kelleher's phrase, 'mediates' a public horizon. Rightly understood, this public world of meaning cannot be reduced to the meanings that are personally appropriated by members of the assembly. One of my case study churches, for instance, thought my presentation of their worship was limited because I had not give sufficient attention to how the worship had "changed the lives" of the worshippers.[39] This church clearly measured the authenticity of their worship according to the intensity of meanings appropriated by individual participants. The public horizon of worship however cannot be described solely in these terms. Individuals, after all, may not appropriate all that is publicly mediated, and their accounts of worship may be marginally related to it (although, as my interviewing sought to exploit, they may nevertheless give an invaluable insight into the public horizon). The public horizon is also to be distinguished from the meanings identified in official texts or commentaries on rite, since liturgical praxis may mediate meanings that are not included in the official rite. Lawrence Hoffman in his book *Beyond The Text* makes a similar point when he criticizes the tradition of liturgical scholarship as being too text-bound. He calls liturgical study to go beyond the text of prayer itself and recognize that liturgies are 'acted-out rituals involving prescribed texts, actions, timing, persons, and things, all coming together in a shared statement of community identity by those who live with, through, and by them'.[40] What Hoffman is in effect drawing attention to is the

---

[37] M.M. Kelleher, 'Liturgical Theology: A Task and a Method', *Worship*, 62 (January 1988), 1:2-25. I am indebted to Dr Carol Wilkinson for this reference.

[38] Kelleher, 'Liturgical Theology', 10.

[39] St.B.

[40] L.A. Hoffman, *Beyond the Text: A Holistic Approach to Liturgy*, 3.

inescapable social character of ritual.[41]

For Kelleher one of the chief tasks of liturgical theology is to scrutinize these horizons, questioning them, making them explicit and thematic. The task in which I engaged was similar, objectifying the horizons that were made public in the six cases of public worship selected for study.

Observing the Public Horizon

Having identified the public horizon as the field of study, it was important to ask what features of the ritual lay themselves open for empirical study. In this context, Kelleher draws upon social anthropology, and in particular Victor Turner's understanding of ritual action being a 'social symbolic process'. Liturgy is social because it has evolved within an ecclesial context, is performed by a community, and participates in the ongoing life of the church, which is a social reality. It is symbolic because its basic units are ritual symbols, ranging from objects, words and gestures to arrangements of space. It can be regarded as a process from a number of different perspectives. First, according to Turner, every ritual can be understood as a dynamic process, having an inner rhythm which may be described in terms of ultimate and intermediate goals which are either explicit or implicit.[42] Secondly, liturgy has an intimate relationship to the wider ecclesial process; liturgy has a history that is inextricably bound up with the history of the church. Finally, liturgy's own symbolic units are dynamic, gaining and losing meaning in the course of their lives. A good example of this in charismatic worship is the way that speaking in tongues, once a hallmark of charismatic gatherings, has become much less common in public worship, probably because other inspired or ecstatic phenomena now fulfil its symbolic function.

Corresponding to this understanding of ritual as a social symbolic process I worked with three observational categories: ritual subject, symbols, and ritual process.

RITUAL SUBJECT

The main objects of attention in observing the worshipping assembly as ritual subject were its composition, the distribution of roles and public reactions. My observation was guided by appropriately directed questions. For example: What are the numbers and age profile of the congregation?

---

[41] Ely lists nine major dimensions of social situations that the researcher needs to be aware of: space, actors, activity, objects, individual acts, events, time, goals and feelings; M. Ely, *Doing Qualitative Research: Circles within Circles*, 48. These all feature in my analysis of case study public worship.

[42] V. Turner, *The Forest of Symbols: Aspects of Ndembu Ritual*, 275; quoted in Kelleher, 'Liturgical Theology', 12.

Who takes a leadership role? How do they lead? What roles does the congregation play? How do people express their involvement in the service? The ritual subjects that featured most prominently in the public horizon conveyed by the worship observed were the congregation, worship leaders and music groups, 'prayer ministers', 'prayer ministry' leaders and God. One inherent problem for observation was how to pay proper attention to congregational demeanour and participation whilst taking note of what was happening at the front, by which I mean the area in the assembly where leadership was exercised and which was invariably the focus for congregational gaze (such as a sanctuary, leadership platform, chancel steps, pulpit or reading lectern). As mentioned above, my Outside Observer and I attempted to solve this by individually prioritizing observational gaze, he to the congregation and myself to the front.

SYMBOLS

As mentioned above, symbols can be objects, actions, relationships, words, gestures, or spatial arrangements. In exploring the symbolic life of the case study worship I was guided by what Victor Turner identified as the operational, positional and exegetical dimensions of meaning in ritual.[43] The operational dimension is what participants do with or in relation to ritual symbols. The positional is the relationships or associations established between or among symbols as the rite is performed. The exegetical covers what is said about symbols in ritual, the names given to symbols, and their appearance. Following Kelleher, I used a series of questions as a way of sensitizing myself to this three-dimensional symbolic 'map': Where does the ritual take place? How is the space organized? How is the place decorated? What symbolic objects appear? What symbolic actions take place? What relationships are established between and among persons, between persons and God, persons and objects, objects and actions? How are these relationships established? What dominant images are set out in the prayers, readings, sermon, and song?

Within the course of my participant observation, I became aware of the presence of a number of symbols. These included the human body in praise and prayer, charismatic gifts (typically prophecy, 'words of knowledge', and mental images offered by people), music, musical instrumentation, the use of technology, the spatial relationship of participants, the texts of songs, as well as the more familiar symbols of Christian worship such as bread and wine, altars, processions, and vestments. Even the use of liturgical texts was symbolic, so that, as will become apparent, in some churches their absence was linked to freedom of expression.

---

[43] V. Turner, 'Forms of Symbolic Action: Introduction', in *Forms of Symbolic Action: Proceedings of the 1969 Annual Meeting, American Ethnological Society*, 11-12, quoted by Kelleher, 'Liturgical Theology', 14.

RITUAL PROCESS

Kelleher suggests that questions asked about the ritual process by a participant observer may follow a number of lines of enquiry. One asks about the rhythm of the ritual itself: What is the order of events? Are there any variations? Are there distinct phases in the ritual? How are transitions made from one phase to another? One asks questions about the dynamics of the ritual symbols themselves, perhaps by focusing on one symbol for the duration of observation. One can also ask questions of the dynamics of the ritual in relationship to the dynamics of the worshipping assembly: Are there changes in the ritual process associated with changes in the assembly? If so, what are they?

In the course of my participant observation, the ritual process was important in a number of respects. I observed how charismatic elements were integrated into authorized liturgical provision, or alternatively how authorized liturgy was included in an unauthorized liturgical framework (see Chapter 4). Elements of process within specific units or frames of ritual were analysed, such as the period of congregational singing known as the 'time of worship' (Chapter 5), and the events of the public ministry of prayer known as 'prayer ministry' (Chapter 6). Relating the ritual process to the local ecclesial process was dependent on accounts given by participants of how worship had developed in each particular local setting. These accounts were an invaluable means of understanding the specific forms of ritual that had developed. Changes in the wider ecclesial process of Charismatic Renewal during my fieldwork also had an observable effect upon the worship in a number of my case study churches. The intervening period between the first and second visits coincided with the outbreak of the 'Toronto Blessing' which meant that on a number of second visits there had been significant changes in ritual process (most notably at St.B and St.E).

Interpreting the Public Horizon

It is one thing to describe what is seen in the observation of ritual. The process of understanding and expressing the public horizon conveyed by worship also engages an interpretative task that goes beyond participation observation. Kelleher suggests that for this stage a number of fresh sources have to be called upon in order to place the observations in a wider interpretative context, which include the people associated with the ritual, official interpretations of the rite in question, as well as historical and theological studies of the rite.

The interviews I conducted with participants gave me access to the history of liturgical development in each church, how people understood their roles, and the reasons for choices that had been made in relation to the content and structure of worship. With regard to Kelleher's reference to official texts and historical and theological studies, I was aware that the rituals I was studying were, in broad terms, examples of a convergence of two streams of liturgical tradition: Anglican, and Pentecostal.[44] As an ordained Anglican I familiarized myself with the characteristics of Pentecostal worship by attending Kensington Temple in London, a large Elim Pentecostal church, and by reading a number of studies already mentioned. I also researched the history of the development of charismatic worship in the Church of England, reading the literature of charismatics who write about worship, and drawing upon past experience, which included attendance at a number of Wimber Conferences in the mid-1980s and the three and a half year curacy at St. John the Evangelist, Welling.

In addition, I drew upon other historical instances of Christian worship and ritual when interpreting the two main foci of charismatic ritual practice, congregational singing and 'prayer ministry'. For example, there was significant resonance between the leadership style of sung worship and the leadership of Black gospel singing. The style of both the congregational singing and 'prayer ministry' mirrored elements of the large-scale meetings of the revivalist tradition. I also made use of a comparison with other forms of religious ritual, notably the traditional role of the shaman in shamanistic religion, when interpreting the role of the 'prayer ministry' leader. Strauss and Corbin recommend this kind of comparative analysis as a useful research technique for enhancing theoretical and interpretative sensitivity in qualitative research.[45] Its main value was the way it highlighted categories of behaviour that could have remained unnoticed because of familiarity. So, with the shaman comparison, three categories of the 'prayer ministry' were highlighted: the role of ecstatic behaviour, its control, and the amelioration of problems in the gathered community (see Chapter 6).

Whilst Kelleher is strong on drawing attention to ecclesial process as an essential element in the wider interpretative context for Christian worship, she makes no specific reference to wider cultural influences.[46] This is a curious omission given that worship is not a hermetically sealed environment, immune from cultural changes. As I will seek to demonstrate, wider cultural dynamics have had an important impact upon core characteristics of public charismatic expression. In the process of interpreting aspects of the charismatic worship observed, particularly the congregational singing, I found that the public horizon was rooted in wider cultural phenomena, such

---

[44] The word 'streams' embraces the reality of variety within each tradition. Within Anglican worship, for example, there are catholic, evangelical, and liberal variations in praxis. The Pentecostal influence is likewise multi-layered, and encompasses pre-Wimber, Wimber and Toronto variations in praxis.

[45] Strauss and Corbin, *Basics of Qualitative Research*.

[46] She does make mention of the larger society in which the church is situated but only in the context of liturgical praxis being a critique of such society ('Liturgical Theology', 19).

as the live performance culture of popular music and rituals associated with discotheques and nightclubs. For example, the three constitutive elements of live performance, presence, visibility and spontaneity, pervaded the ritual performance of congregational singing and 'prayer ministry'. The ritual of personal intimate encounter enacted in an evening at a discotheque appeared also to inform the ritual process of the 'time of worship'.

Judging the Public Horizon

The concluding main chapter of my study is devoted to a theological evaluation of the public horizons of worship I had observed. The necessity of this task, as Kelleher reminds us, arises from the theologian's and church's responsibility to God, to order worship so that it becomes a faithful representation of the life of the kingdom of God. Liturgical tradition can, of course, devalue, distort, dilute or corrupt this representation, and thereby become unauthentic. The theologian Bernard Lonergan, who is quoted liberally by Kelleher, defines an unauthentic tradition as one which 'may consist in a watering down of the original message, in recasting it into terms and meanings that fit into the assumptions and convictions of those that have dodged the issues of radical conversion.'[47] The questions suggested by Kelleher for evaluation include: Are there any elements of Christ's message that are consistently censored out of the public horizon? Are there any elements of the horizon which seem to contradict or distort that message? Are there signs of symbolic impoverishment or collective amnesia in the horizon? Does the vision of reality mediated address significant human questions in a way that is faithful to Christ's message? My own interrogation took on a less exclusive christological focus, being responsive to the implicit trinitarian patterns of language in case study worship. I decided to evaluate the authenticity of such trinitarian expression in relation to orthodox trinitarian doxology, the theology of which provided the means by which I could test the understandings of Christ and the Spirit mediated by the worship observed for evidence of the radical conversion that Lonergan highlights.

But before I get to this point I must turn first to the description and interpretation of the public horizons conveyed by the churches visited, beginning with the main liturgical characteristics of each case study church. For the remainder of the study, in order to preserve the anonymity of churches and people, names are fictionalized and the designation of churches follows the lettering scheme introduced at the beginning of this chapter.

---

[47] B. Lonergan, 'Merging Horizons: System, Common Sense, Scholarship,' *Cultural Hermeneutics* 1 (1973), quoted in Kelleher, 'Liturgical Theology', 14.

CHAPTER 4

Case Study Liturgies

Introduction

The analysis of the public horizons mediated by case study worship begins in this chapter with a consecutive examination of each church's liturgical celebration. The discussion of each case study is informed by three guiding questions: What is the liturgical structure of Sunday worship? How has this been influenced by Charismatic Renewal? What are the distinctive characteristics of the horizon of worship mediated by the charismatic elements present in the worship?

One of the potential difficulties in the following discussion is finding a satisfactory definition for a 'charismatic element'. On the one hand, a 'minimal' definition would encompass only the classical charismatic phenomena (such as speaking in tongues, words of prophecy, healing). Whilst this definition is laudable in what it affirms, its problem lies in what it neglects, such as the fact that these charismatic phenomena are part of a distinctive culture of worship in which, for example, individual contributions are nurtured and affirmed. To use a marine metaphor, charismatic phenomena are 'the tip of the iceberg', the body of the 'iceberg' being the worship culture. The 1981 General Synod Report recognized this and reported that along with the use of charismatic gifts such as speaking in tongues, prophecy and healing, worship in the Charismatic Movement promoted a particular 'style', the five features of which I outlined in Chapter 1. A 'maximal' definition states, on the other hand, that all aspects of the worship of a church that claims to be charismatic are to be regarded as elements of charismatic worship. However, this is an equally unsatisfactory definition because it lacks discriminatory power. In case study churches there were many aspects of public worship that had preceded the arrival of any influence from Charismatic Renewal, such as the authorized liturgy and historic local ways of celebrating the liturgy that were dependent upon churchmanship. Claiming the middle ground between minimal and maximal definitions, my own working definition states that a charismatic element is a recognizable feature of the public charismatic worship culture that has been fostered and mediated by large scale conferences (Fountain Trust in the 1970s, Wimber and the Vineyard in the 1980s and 1990s), travelling worship groups such as The Fisherfolk, and at a local level by small charismatic prayer meetings and influential charismatic parishes. The analysis of the next three chapters will identify the elements of this culture, and their adaptation, within case study worship: this chapter with its overview of case study worship, Chapter 5 on congregational sung worship and Chapter 6 on 'prayer ministry'.

As background to the discussion of this chapter, I will briefly outline informant descriptions of charismatic gifts that were present in public worship. 'Words of knowledge', which, as we have seen, have been a particular feature of the Vineyard 'ministry time', were described as messages received from God which related to conditions (often of need) of individuals present in the worshipping assembly. 'Prophecy' was invariably described as an inspired utterance that addressed the whole gathered assembly. Sometimes the designations 'word' or 'picture', describing the medium of communication, would be used as alternative nomenclature for either a 'word of knowledge' or prophecy. 'Singing in the Spirit' was observed as an act of praise in which members of the congregation improvised melodies around the closing chord of a song, some using the gift of tongues (hence the use of the phrase 'singing in tongues', which was used by one or two informants), others using ordinary words or simply vocalizing. The gift of 'speaking in tongues' was also mentioned, but informants regarded it as very seldom used in public worship. This confirms that what was originally a public mark of authenticity in the early Charismatic Movement had now been relegated to an aid to personal prayer.[1] Informants used 'healing' to refer to the presence of prayer for healing in their worship, which was most commonly called 'prayer ministry', modelled on methods from Vineyard church practice.

---

[1]   This was also the conclusion of the Church of England's Doctrine Commission who reported that interview work in an Anglican church revealed that speaking in tongues had ceased to be a feature of public worship, but informants spoke of using tongues as a regular discipline in private. *We Believe in the Holy Spirit: A Report by The Doctrine Commission of the General Synod of the Church of England*, Ch.2.

St.A: A Modern Catholic Approach

St.A was chosen as an example of a rural parish church. It served a small village community and the congregation consisted of Christians from a variety of traditions. There was a strong sense of community reflected in the way that people spoke of belonging both to the village and the church. The controlling vision of the parish priest was comprehensive, "drawing people from a variety of traditions within Anglicanism and beyond it to enrich one another"(LI).[2] The parish had developed a moderately catholic Parish Communion tradition. "Communion lies at the heart of worship", explained the priest, "and the expectation is that people build their pattern of worship around that."(LI) Since his arrival in 1984, as well as consolidating the modern catholic style of worship, the priest had also encouraged openness to Charismatic Renewal, which he regarded as an established tradition within Anglicanism. For example, on the weekend prior to my second visit, he celebrated the tenth anniversary of his ministry in the village by inviting a retired charismatic bishop to lead a parish weekend of renewal and healing. The priest identified a number of influences that had convinced him of the value of Charismatic Renewal: an experience of baptism in the Spirit, visits to Spring Harvest, a visit to Nigeria with a S.O.M.A. team and Anglican Renewal meetings.

I visited St.A on the first Sunday of the month for which the services were 8.00am Holy Communion, 9.30am Parish Eucharist, 11.15am Matins, and 7.30pm Evening Praise. The Parish Eucharist was the main act of worship, attracting 100–120 people representing a wide variety of ages who filled the small Norman church. The liturgy was Rite 'A' from the *Alternative Service Book* (*A.S.B.*), and it was celebrated with a due sense of catholic order and dignity. The priest was attempting to introduce musical and healing elements of charismatic worship within the Parish Eucharist sensitively. On the first visit, the psalm after the Old Testament reading was in the form of a song from *Songs of Fellowship* led by guitarists (the significance of this musical 'insertion' for musical leadership is explored in Chapter 5). The priest had introduced this with a public invitation to parishioners to compose other songs based on the psalms.[3] On the second visit I observed prayer for healing, with laying-on of hands, during and after the administration of Communion. The priest had introduced this for the first Sunday of the month, prayers always being administered by one of the clergy.[4]

---

[2] The interviewee codes are found in Chapter 3.

[3] Evidently a song based on Psalm 138 had already been composed for use in the following Sunday's Parish Eucharist.

[4] On my first visit, when the assistant non-stipendiary priest was away, there was no prayer offered because the parish priest was involved with administering the sacrament.

Evening Praise, according to the priest, "was designed to open up the possibilities of charismatic worship"(LI), and was described by one informant as "our charismatic rave-up!"(CI). With comparatively few attending (the congregation averaged twenty people), it had the feel of a small charismatic prayer meeting, and its relationship with the other acts of worship was not without tensions. The parish priest informed us that the Evening Praise style of worship was "resisted by a number of people in the mainstream of the congregation"(LI). For example, one member of the Parish Eucharist congregation objected to the introduction of the *Songs of Fellowship* guitar song mentioned above: "What's wrong with the traditional Anglican chants for the Psalms?" he said to me after the service. Some adherents of Evening Praise found the Parish Eucharist too staid. For example, the lay leader of Evening Praise never attended the Parish Eucharist when the assistant non-stipendiary priest presided because his style was "too formal, old fashioned and not relevant"(MLI). In order to illuminate the distinctive characteristics of Evening Praise, I will explore the juxtaposition of the other main acts of Sunday worship, and in particular the Parish Eucharist, with this informal charismatic service.

The service of Evening Praise was conducted without a written liturgy; the only printed text being the songbook, *Songs of Fellowship* (1991) and locally produced song supplements (an A5 sheet on the first visit and a blue booklet on the second). The leadership of the service had been delegated by the parish priest to a lay musician, who exercised his responsibility by determining the liturgical structure, choosing the theme of the service, its songs, and the person giving the talk (himself on both visits). The liturgical structure was the same on both visits and was observed to be as follows:

Notices (given by the priest)
Welcome by leader, and introductory prayer
Praise songs
Individual offerings of spoken praise and testimony [5]
Song
Reading and talk
Individuals share thoughts on the reading and talk
Worship songs
Individuals share 'words' from God
Praise songs
Closing prayer

---

[5] On the second visit this took the form of individual testimonies to healings and 'blessings' arising from the visit of the retired bishop the previous weekend.

'Face-to-Face' Worship

There were four main elements to the public horizon of worship mediated by Evening Praise that deserve comment. The first was a spatial arrangement that created a responsibility to relate to others in worship. The pews in the church had been re-arranged for Evening Praise so that the small congregation was seated, together with the leader and musicians, in an enclosed oblong. The congregation's gaze was thereby turned in upon itself, as the Outside Observer recognized:

> I was very aware of other people. If you look straight ahead you've got to look at somebody, and I didn't feel I really wanted to look up ... and you're forced to spend your time looking at the leader, and I can imagine if you looked at the leader too much at the wrong moment you might find yourself compelled to say something ... I did think that the square, or rectangle [his description of the seating arrangement] was claustrophobic.(OI)

In the words of the 1981 General Synod Report, Evening Praise was a prime example of the charismatic escape from the 'stately masked ball' of traditional Anglican worship,[6] epitomized by the 11.15am service of Matins that the Outside Observer attended in which he gained the impression that "one was expected to be completely oblivious of the people around you"(OI). At Evening Praise the masks were shed so that participants could discover each other within the liturgical action. One informant identified this as one of the great advantages of Evening Praise:

> Thinking of our local churches, you feel that people are putting up fronts and you're just longing for the masks to fall away and for them to really be open to the Spirit ... this frightfully formal traditional worship that they go to every Sunday morning ... they may feel that it is meeting their need, but having experienced something like Evening Praise and I suppose the whole charismatic thing, one just knows that there's so much more they can have. (CGI)

This however was not without its problems, as was illustrated in an incident which occurred on the second visit. The leader was in the middle of his talk when a member of the congregation interrupted him and challenged what he was saying. The leader was taken by surprise and silenced the person by saying firmly "Yes, I haven't finished yet; hang on there", and continued with his talk. Two or three minutes later, whilst the leader was still speaking, the person concerned stood up and walked out of church.

---

[6]   *The Charismatic Movement in the Church of England*, 42.

Although the leader managed to continue the service as if nothing major had happened, an informant reflected afterwards upon the trauma of the incident:

> Well, James, I actually felt at the end of Evening Praise tonight that I really wished it wasn't tonight that I was talking to you ... I found tonight incredibly difficult and I would rarely say that about Evening Praise ... I cannot remember the last time I felt so chewed up.(CGI)

This critical incident[7] revealed existing tensions between the leader and the person concerned; apparently that wasn't the first time that she had walked out in the middle of Evening Praise! The point to highlight, however, is that the close and personally demanding spatial environment created by the service exacerbated these tensions.

In the Parish Eucharist there was also an element of face-to-face encounter. The president, deacon and server, readily visible because of the small sized church, stood westwards facing the congregation from behind the altar for most of the service. But unlike Evening Praise, the focus of gaze for them and the congregation was not one another, but the ministry of the Word and Sacrament that took place at the lectern and altar in the small sanctuary area separating officiants and people. There was no symbolic equivalent in the space between participants at Evening Praise to direct our attention beyond ourselves, save an untidy pile of songbooks on a squat table in front of the musicians. The only way of escaping the gaze of others was either by looking at this table or by closing one's eyes! This inward looking gaze was also reflected in the fact that prayers offered at Evening Praise focused almost exclusively upon the spiritual needs of those present, whereas at Parish Eucharist intercessions were offered for the needs of the world and local community, alongside those of the congregation.

Inspired Individual Participation

The second element of worship to highlight at Evening Praise was the high public profile of individual contributions. The service afforded three structured opportunities for this to occur: the offering of words of praise, reflection on the reading and talk, and the sharing of 'words' from God. Almost everyone had made his or her own vocal contribution by the end of each service observed. The singing was also marked by a variety of individual bodily gestures and postures: some raised arms and hands, some clapped, and one or two knelt in the more devotional 'worship songs'. Informants spoke of this participative style as one of the most valuable

---

[7] In qualitative research, critical incidents are crisis moments which can be very useful for elucidating information about informants' basic beliefs and attitudes.

aspects of Evening Praise:

> I think that Evening Praise can be a wonderful opportunity for different members of the congregation to be making an active contribution to the worship. Praying, offering musical contributions, sharing what the Lord has done in their lives, and in many other ways too: praying in tongues, visions and prophecy.(CGI)

Charismatic gifts were observed in the opportunity given for 'words' from God. For example, on the first visit to Evening Praise, the service began with a time of quiet, followed by a good number of individual contributions. The leader had prepared us for this, encouraging us to be "open to the Lord as usual", and to speak out if we had received "a tongue or a picture or word". On this occasion, the period of individual participation began with three lengthy periods of congregational silence, broken by prayers on the theme of the talk, which was the armour of God in Ephesians 6. One lady, for example, prayed, "Lord, take us deeper into you that we may stand with courage, with your armour on our bodies and clothed with your love." A 'picture' was then offered:

> The Lord showed me a depot and it was absolutely stacked from here to there with white robes ['robes of righteousness' had been mentioned earlier in the service] neatly folded ready to put on; and then packs of armour, all neatly in order which you put on ... and there are masses there. Plenty for everybody. And we don't have to buy it.

Someone added: "God has provided for us, all we've got to do is pick it up ... sometimes we don't." Someone else drew our attention to the mention of a shield in Psalm 33. Another said that she had been reminded of Luther's hymn 'A safe stronghold our God is still', which we proceeded to sing unaccompanied after much laughter (partly because the leader could not play it on his guitar). The parish priest followed this by offering a 'prophecy' which took us away from the armour of God theme:

> I sensed that the Lord was saying to us afresh, "I long for your worship, the worship of your hearts; that you will give all to me and hold nothing back. I know the cost of worship; I know there are times when it's difficult to offer that worship. But the decision, the will to offer it is precious in my sight".

Another 'picture' was then offered: "I saw Jesus walking into the room, walking around everybody, and he said, 'You are my children, I love you very dearly. Feast your eyes upon me and I will light your path'." We returned obliquely to the armour of God theme with a testimony that explained how a difficult situation had been overcome by "putting on the Lord Jesus Christ".[8] The service leader then drew the sharing to a close.

The ritual process of this period of individual participation seemed, in the main, to function rather like word, or image association, many of the contributions being improvisations on the content of the talk. The language used could also convey different degrees of inspiration, or authenticity. The picture of the depot, the Lord speaking to us about worship, and Jesus being seen walking in the room presented themselves as the three most inspired contributions on account of their ability to communicate a fresh and dynamic revelation from God. It is interesting to note that despite the encouragement of the leader's invitation, no one spoke in tongues.

Compared with Parish Eucharist, the style of participation in Evening Praise was much more dependant upon individual performance for its authenticity. This can be illustrated with regard to the liturgical posture of kneeling. In Evening Praise, kneeling appeared to be an individual expression of worship, which was a measure of personal engagement and even spiritual progress. This is evident in the leader's description of his wife's kneeling during the 'worship' song section:

> Seeing people freely express themselves in worship was another sign that to me they had gone past the group around them and they were actually focusing on God ... the fact that Maggie [wife] knelt down and worshipped the Lord in front of the group was a big thing for her to do. She felt it was like a culmination of four years of what God had been doing in her. (LGI)

In the Parish Eucharist, kneeling was a sign, not of 'going beyond' others in the congregation, but of incorporation with others in the common act of worship. One knelt, with everyone else, during the intercessions, and even when kneeling was more individualized, such as at the altar rail, and for devotional prayer after receiving the sacrament, it was nevertheless something that everyone did, and not a self-conscious display of individual worship. This contrast between the spontaneous individual expression of Evening Praise and the corporate action of Parish Eucharist reveals a different set of authenticities and priorities in worship.

However, participation at Evening Praise was not merely a matter of self expression, for there were indications that these individual contributions were offered within a communitarian environment shaped by the Pauline metaphor of the 'body of Christ', where 'to each one the manifestation of the Spirit is given for the common good' (1 Cor. 12:7). For example, in his opening prayer on the first visit, the leader prayed: "We've gathered here as one body to worship you and we come with many gifts." At the end of that

---

[8]   A reference to Romans 13:8.

service, as we were standing in a circle with inter-linked arms, he prayed: "Thank you for the encouragement that you give through each other, and that you've given us to one another as one body to stand together."

Journey to Intimacy

The third distinctive element of the public horizon of worship in Evening Praise was the ritual process conveyed by the sung worship. This was a journey from praise to intimacy with God, which, as we shall see in Chapter 5, was typical of the corporate sung worship in other case study churches. The leader of Evening Praise described the difference between the 'praise' songs (sung at the beginning of the service) and the 'worship' songs (what he called the 'time of worship') as follows:

> The praise is the lifting up of Jesus, putting him in his rightful place. It's like a spiritual battle if you like; we're claiming Jesus, we're staking our ground and we're getting people to realize that we are in the kingdom. But when we get to the time of worship it's meant to be an intimate time. Although done as a group, it is more down inside, something between you and God, you enter into a deeper time.(LI)

The sense of intimacy was mediated by the slow, ballad-style music, the demeanour of intense devotion on people's faces, epitomized by the closing of eyes, and the language used by the leader to introduce the worship songs: "Let's be open to the Lord and really close to him now ... 'Holy Spirit, we pray that you would come and melt our hearts'." This context of intimacy became the appropriate place for the congregation to receive communication from God, and so the sharing of 'words' from God followed the 'worship songs'.

The Parish Eucharist also mediated a ritual process which was similar in respect of being a journey where one drew near with faith[9] into the sanctuary to receive the sacrament. However, the climax of the journey was not an intuitive 'tuning-in' to communication from God but the altar around which we gathered to receive bread and wine, symbols of God's salvation through Jesus Christ.

Liturgical Time

The fourth characteristic of Evening Praise, highlighted again by the contrast with Parish Eucharist, was the experience of liturgical time. The Outside Observer described Parish Eucharist as an 'act' of worship in

---

[9] In the *A.S.B.* Rite A, the President begins his invitation to receive the sacrament with the words "Draw near with faith".

which "we did certain things together and we did them under God in the best way we could and once they were done we left them behind and went on to the next thing"(OI). He contrasted this with the word 'time' used frequently by the leader in referring to activities in Evening Praise ("time of worship", "time of prayer"): "Somehow the word 'time' indicates something that was quite shapeless whereas the word 'act' conveys a very definite shape"(OI). This contrast between 'act' and 'time' reveals a fundamental difference between worship understood as a highly structured corporate event, and worship understood as a flexible event with encouragement given for individual expression and improvisations on a shared theme. In the former, time is experienced as a linear progression, whereas in the latter, time is experienced as 'openness' to the promptings of the divine Spirit, which for the Outside Observer was a 'shapeless' experience. In some ways this is akin to the contrast between performances of classical music and those of modern jazz, in that the former emphasizes the linear progression through a received musical score, whereas the latter emphasizes the improvisational skills of the performers. We have seen an example of the jazz approach to liturgical time illustrated above, in the improvisations on 'words' from God, and further examples will be encountered in Chapters 5 and 6 when the spontaneity of both human and divine 'performers' will be highlighted in the 'time of worship' and what was sometimes called the 'time of ministry' (or more commonly, 'prayer ministry'). The more classical, linear, approach to liturgical celebration tended to be viewed critically by case study informants at St.A and elsewhere, for whom it was too traditional, predictable, and not flexible enough to respond to the Spirit's promptings. The two churches that epitomized this view were St.B and St.E.

St.B and St.E: 'Free' Evangelical Approaches

The congregation of St.B was established in 1988 as a church 'plant' from a large parent charismatic church. They had moved into a large unused and empty Victorian church, which they had furnished for their worshipping needs: a raised leadership platform, situated in the original chancel and sanctuary, extended towards the congregation, and portable modern seating had replaced wooden pews. The congregation was large and eclectic, attracting a high proportion of young professional people. The numbers at each service were between 200–300, many of whom were under forty-five years of age. A large lay leadership team supported the ordained minister, including a lay curate, children's and young people's leaders and administrative staff. There were two services on a Sunday, 10.30am and 6.30pm, with Communion once a month in both services.

The modern building in which the congregation at St.E worshipped was situated in a 1970s middle class estate, and was originally built as a community centre for the estate and church hall for the main parish church. Worship took place in a multi-purpose hall, and so congregational chairs and the various pieces of liturgical furniture had to be assembled each Sunday. The worshipping congregation had developed, in effect, as a church 'plant' from the main parish church, its growth in numbers due partly to outreach work on the estate and partly to its reputation as a charismatic church, attracting a variety of charismatics from the local area (the pastoral groups advertised covered an area of about five miles in radius). The regular pattern of Sunday services was a 9.30am Family Service (Communion once a month), an 11.00am service (Communion twice a month) and 6.30pm service (Communion once a month). There were, on average, about hundred at each service.

Free and Flexible Worship

St.B and St.E are considered together on account of two similar features. First, both represented an evangelical charismatic tradition that had a cavalier attitude to authorized liturgical provision, and a general ambivalence to the institutional life of the Church of England (hence my designation, 'free' evangelical, above). St.B self-consciously promoted itself as a lively alternative to "dead" and "out of date" traditional forms of worship.[10] For instance, in a sermon on evangelism,[11] the preacher suggested that members of the congregation could promote St.B on the basis that its worship was led by a rock band, the leaders weren't robed, and there were no pews! In the four services attended, all non-eucharistic, the only recognizable authorized liturgy that was used was for an infant baptism in the morning service on the second visit, the traditional version of the Lord's Prayer to conclude intercessions, and the formal Blessing at the end of services.[12] There was no form of creed or confession, and only one scripture reading. Freedoms from a set liturgy and flexibility to change the service structure and "go with what we discern to be the direction of God's Spirit"(LGI) were regarded by the minister as the most valuable assets of worship at St.B.

Although St.E was advertised on the church notice board as the Anglican church for the estate, the Outside Observer suggested that in ethos it was attempting to be as "un-Anglican as it could get away with"(OI), reflected in the rather apologetic introductory announcement by a service leader at

[10] These were phrases regularly used by congregational informants when describing their previous experience of worship in the Church of England or other established denominations.

[11] Visit 1, 10.30am service.

[12] The vicar said that an authorized Eucharistic Prayer was used at Holy Communion.

one service: "You might recognize this as an Anglican service!"[13] St.E used more authorized liturgy than St.B, but sparingly and flexibly. In the non-eucharistic services, the authorized liturgy was regarded by the Outside Observer as a "walk-on part"(OI) – the congregation followed the *A.S.B.* Morning or Evening Prayer booklets for the Introduction and Confession, but then closed them and left them on their seats for the remainder of the service. The flexible use of liturgy was epitomized in the 11.00am Communion on the second visit, when the service leader announced at the beginning that we would have Communion first, followed by the ministry of the Word, concluding with a 'time of ministry'. This complete reorganization of the *A.S.B.* Communion liturgy led to the bizarre situation of praying the post-Communion prayer, with its petition 'send us out in the power of your Spirit, to live and work to your praise and glory', after only a third of the service had been completed! However, this kind of flexibility was viewed by one informant as a great strength of St.E: "I think one of the strengths of St.E is that the services tend not to be the same, so you never go to sleep because you don't know what comes next, which I imagine takes a lot of work. It keeps 'the punters' awake!"(CI) Since his arrival in 1993, the new vicar had tried to regularize aspects of worship, which included ensuring that there was a licensed person involved in the leadership at each service,[14] and introducing an authorized form of confession and creed to the 9.30am Family Service.

Vineyard Ritual

The second feature that St.B and St.E shared was a liturgical pattern and style that had been heavily influenced by the Vineyard worship culture. This culture, mediated by the Wimber conferences, is characterized, as we have seen, by a three-fold liturgical structure: an extended period of sung worship, a talk, and a 'ministry time', or more simply, 'Worship-Word-Ministry'. St.B and St.E were also the two case study churches most influenced by the outbreak of ecstatic behaviour associated with the Toronto Vineyard church, the 'Toronto Blessing', the arrival of which in Britain coincided with the interim period between my first and second visits. I made the second visit to St.B just over five months after the 'Blessing' had been introduced to the church. My second visit to St.E coincided with the return of the vicar from a one-week visit to the Toronto Vineyard Fellowship. The main element that was different on the post-Toronto visits at St.B and St.E was the higher public profile of 'prayer ministry' and a greater frequency and intensity of ecstatic behaviour within

---

[13] St.E, 6.30pm service, visit 2.

[14] St.E had developed its own leadership, or 'eldership' team, who though unlicensed, led non-eucharistic worship.

the 'prayer ministry'. This included somatic expression, such as falling down, bodily convulsions, and bouncing up and down, together with vocal noises, such as hysterical laughter, animal noises, screaming and deep breathing.

The liturgical structure of St.B was very obviously based on a Worship-Word-Ministry pattern, and the vicar happily acknowledged that the Vineyard model had played an important part in the ongoing development of services at St.B. All four services attended had the following structure:

Welcome
Time of worship
Prayers
Notices
Break
Reading and sermon
Prayer ministry

The dependence upon the Vineyard culture was evident in the large proportion of time spent on the three main liturgical items. The 'time of worship' was anything from twenty to forty minutes of continuous singing in the Wimber pattern of seamless music, finishing with devotional songs (a high proportion of the songs were Vineyard songs). The prayers, which were led by members of the congregation, lasted only five to ten minutes, and the notices and break (in which we were invited to informally greet our neighbours) were effectively an interlude before we returned to the serious business of the Word.[15] The sermon was a minimum of half an hour,[16] and the 'prayer ministry', which went on beyond the time when the minister announced an ending to the service, was of indeterminate length, and in character typically Vineyard in style with a public calling upon the Spirit, a 'prayer ministry' team moving among the respondents, and, most noticeably after Toronto, ecstatic behaviour among the congregation.

St.E was more varied in its liturgical structure. On the first visit, the two main services had the following liturgical structure (the elements of the service that used authorized liturgy from the *Alternative Service Book* are

---

[15] One of the striking features of the notices was the high level of humour, which the Outside Observer judged had the effect of providing a 'breather' after the spiritual intensity of the singing and prayers. The 'seriousness' of the Word was evident in the length of time that participants were required to concentrate.

[16] The exception being a Family Service attended in which the sermon was much shorter on account of children being present (10.30am service, visit 2).

indicated as '*A.S.B.*'):[17]

> 11.00am Morning Worship
> Preliminary songs
> Welcome and notices
> Introduction and Confession (*A.S.B.*)
> Time of worship
> Intercessions
> Reading and sermon
> Concluding song
>
> 6.30pm Holy Communion (Rite 'A')
> Preliminary songs
> Welcome and notices
> Greeting and Confession (*A.S.B.*)
> Time of worship
> Reading and sermon
> Prayer ministry
> Intercession
> Prayer of Humble Access (*A.S.B.*)
> Peace (*A.S.B.*)
> Communion (*A.S.B.*)
> Closing song

The most obvious feature of the Vineyard worship culture on this first visit was the 'time of worship', which consisted of five or six songs, again mainly Vineyard, sung consecutively. There was also a form of 'prayer ministry', though without a 'ministry team', after the sermon in the evening service, for which the congregation sat prayerfully whilst the preacher called upon the Spirit and applied the points of his sermon, which had been on the theme of repentance. The applications functioned rather like a rite of reconciliation. So, for example:

> I think that there are some people struggling here to forgive themselves for sexual sins. Let the Spirit show you your heart. Are you repentant? Ashamed? See yourself as Jesus sees you. [Pause] Jesus sees us, once we have confessed, as his bride, without spot, without blemish. We're forgiven. Be free! See yourself as Jesus sees you.

On the second, post-Toronto visit, the equivalent services embodied a

---

[17] The 9.30am Family Service could be described in terms of the elements present (songs, confession, prayers, talk/presentation), but there wasn't a recognizable structure to the service.

more obvious Vineyard Worship-Word-Ministry structure. This pattern can be recognized after the Communion at the 11.00am service, and after the Introduction and Confession at the 6.30pm service, which was called a 'Come Holy Spirit' Service:

11.00am Holy Communion
Preliminary songs
Greeting and welcome
Collect for Purity and Confession (*A.S.B.*)
Peace (*A.S.B.*)
Communion (*A.S.B.*)
Time of worship
Intercessions
Reading and sermon
Prayer ministry

6.30pm 'Come Holy Spirit' Service
Preliminary songs
Welcome and notices
Introduction and Confession (*A.S.B.*)
Time of worship
Reading and sermon
Break
Prayer ministry

As mentioned above, in the 11.00am service the *A.S.B.* Rite 'A' structure had been rearranged so that it began with Communion and ended with 'prayer ministry'. The service leader justified this pragmatically on the basis that the sermon could then be followed by the 'prayer ministry'. This irregularity[18] not only reveals the Vineyard praxis of 'works' always following 'words', but also, by inference, the preference for 'prayer ministry' to conclude a service. It is worth noting that the Rite 'A' structure could have been maintained, with the 'prayer ministry' following the ministry of the Word before the Communion, as was the practice at St.D (see below). I suggest that by using it as a conclusion to the service the strategy at St.E allowed 'prayer ministry' to transcend time constraints and maintain its essential character as an open-ended spontaneous liturgical item.[19] The 6.30pm 'Come Holy Spirit' Service coincided with the return of the vicar from his visit to the Toronto Vineyard church, and the pattern of 'prayer ministry' reflected the Toronto Vineyard in format: chairs were

---

[18] This was the first time in over twenty years of regular participation in Christian worship that I had witnessed a service beginning with Communion.

[19] See further, Chapter 6.

removed from the congregational seating area during a break,[20] the Spirit was called upon, and ecstatic behaviour of great variety was observed.

'Words of the Lord'

With regard to the use of charismatic gifts, informants at St.B spoke of "prophecy", "pictures", "words of knowledge", "healing" and very occasionally "singing in tongues" as a feature of public worship at St.B. They informed me that it was commonly understood that if an individual received a 'word of knowledge' or prophecy during the service, they were to write this down and pass it to the service leader, who would then read it out before the 'prayer ministry'. This allowed the service leader to test the authenticity and appropriateness of contributions. I witnessed one occasion, however, when there was a more public opportunity for charismatic contributions. This was during the 'time of worship' at the 6.30pm service on the first visit, when the service leader interrupted the more devotional songs by moving from his place in the front row of the congregation onto the leadership platform.[21] After announcing that the Spirit was present, he asked the congregation to remain standing in silence, "opening ourselves to God", and he then led us in a brief prayer asking God to "cleanse us". He remained on the platform whilst we sang two final songs, and then invited members of the congregation to offer prophecies. There was a long pause, after which four members of the congregation (C1, C2 etc.) moved to the platform and offered their prophecies. Note how these inspired utterances were presented in a 'picture' format, each with an introductory image that is linked to an assuring word about, or from, God for the congregation:

C1:   I saw a picture of a worm in a can, and the can was capped. I believe the worm to represent the worries we have, and God is able to 'cap' them, and keep them under control.

C2:   On the way to church I looked at all the people who passed me in the street, and became aware of my own impotence to reach them for the Gospel. I felt God saying that I shouldn't worry, because he will give the power we need.

---

[20] It was normal practice at the Vineyard Toronto for a space to be cleared of obstructions and then used for the 'ministry time'.

[21] He had previously signalled to the music group leader who was leading the worship on the leadership platform that he wanted to intervene. This intervention was unusual, as was confirmed by my neighbour who whispered that I had chosen an exciting service to observe "because this is quite different from our normal pattern".

C3: I had a vision of a tree with lovely fruit, and Christ standing with his arms around the tree. The tree represents our life, which Christ will surround and protect.

C4: I had a vision of passing through fire; I'm not sure whether it was the fire of testing or purification, but we are not to worry because Jesus is with us.

At St.E informants identified "words from the Lord", which included "prophecies" and "pictures", and occasionally "singing in tongues" as occurring in their public worship, and even more occasionally someone would speak publicly in tongues. The regular place for the 'words' was during the 'time of worship', which I witnessed at the 11.00am service on my first visit. At the end of the fifth and final song, a slow devotional song, the service leader moved to the leader's podium, a discrete, portable raised step, next to the music group in front of the congregation on the hall floor. With the congregation still standing, he told us that he believed the Lord may be wanting to say something to us and that if anyone believed they had a 'word', that they were to shout it out. There was a long pause for about a minute, the silence of which was interrupted by the sound of a distressed baby from the crèche. Two inspired utterances were then offered by members of the congregation (C1, C2):

C1: My children, I receive your love. My children, I hear your praises. And as I receive your love and hear your praises, so I shower each one of you with my blessings. I tell you now my children, do not be afraid of what lies ahead, for I go before you. I have made plans for this place, and I will carry out those plans. So my children, I want you to rest in my love. For as you worship me so I pour out my love upon you. Do not be afraid. I want you to walk tall in my presence. I want you to listen to my voice. O my children, my love for you knows no bounds. My children, will you hold my hand? Will you walk with me? Will you listen to my voice? For I have great things in store for you. Do not be afraid.

C2: As you have heard the child crying and the child has needs, so I know that you have needs my children. I see your needs and I want to fulfil your needs. I want to be the source for you; I want to be your source.

These inspired utterances differ from those observed at St.B in their style of communication, presenting themselves as a direct address from God to the congregation who are his "children". This familial language is typical of the prophecies Mary Jo Neitz encountered in her regular observations at a charismatic Roman Catholic prayer meeting in the late 1970s. In those prophecies, God addressed the participants as his 'children', using the syntax and vocabulary that a parent might use with a five-year-old, presenting himself as a loving and affirming Father who reassures them of his constant care and providence.[22] The Father-child relationship was also promoted during instances of case study 'prayer ministry', which will be discussed further in Chapter 6.

The other aspect of the inspired utterances witnessed at St.B and St.E was their rather ordinary and unsurprising content. They were, at best, words of encouragement for the anxious, and they had no observable impact upon the course of the public worship, none of them being referred to subsequently by service leaders, intercessors, or preachers. Terance Booth, in his research into the Church of Cherubim and Seraphim in Birmingham, makes a similar observation with regard to the visions that were presented in worship.[23] Booth comments that the content of these inspired utterances was not the revelation of something new or exciting, but a reiteration of what was well known to the congregation, which leads him to conclude that 'the content of the messages is far less radical than the means used to convey them'.[24] Walker and Atherton made a similar observation with regard to the public interpretation of tongues in their study of a Pentecostal convention, insisting that what matters was *that* God spoke rather than the content of what he said.[25] The superficiality of the interpretations of glossolalic utterances in American white Pentecostal churches led Samarin to make the suggestion that 'it might be more important *that* a message be interpreted than *what* it has to communicate' (italics original).[26] Samarin goes on to suggest that speaking in tongues functions as a linguistic symbol of the sacred: 'Glossolalia says "God is here" (Just as a Gothic cathedral says, "Behold, God is majestic")'.[27] In a similar way, I would suggest that the primary ritual function of the inspired utterances at St.B and St.E was connected to their ritual performance as symbols of the dynamic presence of God among the congregation, rather than their content. This is confirmed by the fact that in both cases they were invited and offered at the climactic devotional stage of a 'time of worship', which, as will be discussed at greater length in Chapter 5, is a stage associated with intimate communion with God (note the significance of the service leader's

[22] M.J. Neitz, *Charisma and Community: A Study of Religious Commitment within Charismatic Renewal*, 132.
[23] T.T. Booth, *We True Christians: The Church of the Cherubim and Seraphim*, 84.
[24] Booth, *Christians*, 243.
[25] A. Walker and J. Atherton, 'An Easter Pentecostal Convention: The Successful Management of a "Time of Blessing"', in *Sociological Review* (August 1971), 387 n.19.
[26] W.J. Samarin, *Tongues of Men and of Angels: The Religious Language of Pentecostalism*, 166.
[27] Samarin, *Tongues*, 223.

announcement of God's presence prior to inviting the inspired contributions in the description at St.B above).

St.C: An Anglican Evangelical Approach

St.C was situated in a large city, with sections of the parish regarded by informants as characteristically inner city. The church was built in the 1930s, and the hundred or so worshippers at the main Sunday morning service, who between them covered a wide a variety of ages, were comfortably accommodated in its spacious interior. The interior design and architecture was cruciform in shape, with a longitudinal nave, chancel and sanctuary axis. Although evangelical in tradition, St.C differed from St.B and St.E by being self consciously Anglican in ethos, something which informants saw as giving it a certain distinctiveness among evangelical charismatic Anglicans:

> I'd say we are very Anglican. We have wafers, we have robes, we have candles and the appropriate colours on the altar frontal ... we do really follow the rules, far more so than some of the really charismatic evangelical Anglican churches.(MLI)

St.C kept almost entirely within the authorized *A.S.B.* liturgies in the services I attended. The one relatively minor departure from the Holy Communion liturgy was the 'block worship' (St.C's version of the 'time of worship'), but significantly the musical director argued that it was much to St.C's credit that it was able to include this extended period of singing "without destroying the shape of the liturgy"(LGI).

The church had been influenced by the Charismatic Renewal in the mid-1980s through its previous vicar.[28] After attending one of the early Wimber conferences, in which his ministry, according to one informant, "was to a considerable degree turned around"(CI), the previous vicar introduced a weekly Sunday evening Vineyard style service at 8.00pm after Evensong. Eventually elements of the Vineyard liturgical praxis were introduced into the main Sunday services. An extended period of congregational singing was established at the beginning of the main morning Communion service and called 'block worship'. When the Sunday 8.00pm services became monthly, a 'prayer ministry', or as St.C called it, the 'Come Holy Spirit' time was introduced at the end of Evensong. A 'prayer ministry' team also offered prayer during the administration of Communion in the main morning service.

---

[28] My first visit to St.C was during the interregnum; by the time of my second visit, a new vicar had been inducted.

The Choir and Liturgy

The pattern of Sunday services was a 9.00am Holy Communion, a main Holy Communion at 10.30am (Family Service on the first Sunday of the month), and Evening Prayer at 6.00pm (Communion on the first Sunday of the month). The 8.00pm service described above occurs on the last Sunday of the month and attracts people from a number of local churches. My two visits were on the second Sunday of the month. The liturgical structure for the 10.30am Holy Communion I attended was as follows:

Entrance procession (choir, service leaders, server)
Notices
Greeting and Collect for Purity
Block worship
Confession and Collect
Old/New Testament reading
Gospel
Sermon
Creed
Intercessions
Peace
Offertory hymn
Eucharistic Prayer
Administration of Communion (with 'prayer ministry' in side chapel and songs led by choir)
Hymn
Blessing and Dismissal
Exit procession (choir, service leaders and server)

The only significant departure from the *A.S.B.* Rite 'A' in this liturgy was the inclusion of the 'block worship' between the Collect for Purity and the Confession. The musical director regarded the 'block worship' as the liturgical substitute for the Gloria,[29] and so when, on my second visit, the vicar included the Gloria (spoken) in its orthodox position after the Confession, the musical director criticized this as being unnecessary because "we had done that bit" in the 'block worship'(GLI). This was indicative of the musical director's commitment to the liturgy, which he saw as providing a "balanced environment for the Spirit to work" (MLI). As well as composing songs, he had also written musical settings for the Communion liturgy.[30] He had also choreographed the choir's participation

---

[29] If this was the case then strictly speaking the 'block worship' should have followed the Confession, not preceded it.

[30] This included the Offertory Acclamation, the Sanctus and Acclamations in the Eucharistic Prayer, the Lord's Prayer and Agnus Dei.

in a way that embodied, in microcosm, the liturgical process of the Communion service. This was in exact accord with the prevailing ideology of charismatic music groups, which, as we shall see from the description of 'block worship' in Chapter 5, demanded that they model the process of worship. As leaders of worship, the choir participated in the preparatory prayer meeting in the vestry along with service officiants and the 'prayer ministry' team. Their entry and exit processions marked the beginning and end of the service. Moving from their choir stalls to the chancel steps, they gave a visible lead in the 'block worship',[31] after which they sat in the front rows of the nave, and joined and identified with the congregation in the Confession, the ministry of the Word, the Creed, and Intercessions. The Peace was characterized by people moving significant distances to greet others in the church, including choir members who, by virtue of their distinctive robes, could be seen greeting people as far back as the rear of the nave. In returning to their stalls in the chancel during the Offertory hymn, the choir established a focus on the altar and the forthcoming Communion. During the administration of Communion, they gathered round the piano, positioned unobtrusively to the right of the chancel steps, and led the singing of devotional songs. This was a background role and so unlike the 'block worship', it was not necessary for them to be a visible focus. Returning to their stalls at the end of the administration, they drew attention once again to the altar and the eucharistic president for the post-Communion prayers, final hymn and Blessing.

'Words of Knowledge'

The 6.00pm Evening Prayer followed the authorized *A.S.B.* order and concluded with a 'Come Holy Spirit' time.[32] This was the context in which the 'words of knowledge' were observed, the one charismatic gift that informants spoke of as featuring regularly in worship at St.C. The use of this gift will be given a more detailed analysis in Chapter 6, but it is sufficient to note here that the 'words of knowledge' arose from a preparatory prayer meeting in the vestry, and also, in the case of the first visit, from the assembled congregation during the 'Come Holy Spirit' time. I did not observe 'words of knowledge' in the 10.30am Communion Service, but informants said when they did occur, then usually they would have been received in the preparatory prayer meeting, and passed on to the service leader. The leader would announce them in the service, as a way of

---

[31] See Chapter 5 for an extended description and analysis of their leadership in this liturgical item.

[32] On the first visit this followed directly after the service, and on the second visit it was included within the service as the conclusion. This was the equivalent to the 'prayer ministry' at St.B, St.D and St.E.

encouraging individuals to receive prayer from the 'prayer ministry' team during the administration of the sacrament. The team operated in a side chapel that was screened from congregational view by a curtain, and accessible to individuals as they returned from receiving the sacrament. The element of privacy this granted was seen by informants as making it easier for members of the congregation to receive prayer. It also meant that prayer could continue beyond the end of the service without the congregation or the praying disturbing each other. I was familiar with a similar arrangement for managing 'words of knowledge' at St. John's, Welling in the late 1980s. The 'prayer ministry' team would meet for prayer beforehand, and 'words of knowledge' received were written on paper and handed to the service leader. These were read out at the end of the service, and respondents made their way to the chancel area where the 'prayer ministers' prayed for them in relative privacy.

St.D: An Anglo-Catholic Approach

St.D was situated in an outer suburban working class estate. The church building had been built in the 1960s, and unlike the more traditional cruciform shaped building of St.C, its design was modern, with a spacious square arena set aside for worship.[33] The centrepiece was the altar, standing on a modest, raised sanctuary area, which was one step above ground level. St.D was chosen because of its anglo-catholic tradition, and the parish priest commented that he knew of no other church in the Church of England that was as explicitly anglo-catholic and charismatic. The priest had been baptized in the Spirit whilst serving a curacy, and since his arrival at St.D in 1987 had initiated and encouraged a charismatic dimension to the church's worship. This had developed from the experience of charismatic worship in small groups, such as the mid-week homegroups and daily Masses. Visiting teams from St. Andrew's, Chorleywood had helped St.D develop 'prayer ministry'. The 'Toronto Blessing' had influenced St.D briefly in the intervening time between the two visits, but by the time of the second visit its influence had subsided. The priest told me informally that the 'Blessing' "blew into St.D and then out again within the space of a month", though this did not disappoint him since he considered that St.D had been experiencing aspects of the 'Toronto Blessing' for a long time, "though in a quieter, gentler way".

The main Sunday service was the 10.00am Parish Mass which was attended by just over a hundred people of a wide variety of ages, ranging from the elderly ladies welcoming and distributing service books to the

---

[33] This was rather like an ecclesiastical version of a large sports hall!

seven or eight year olds in the serving team.[34] Although the parish was anglo-catholic, there were a variety of traditions represented in the congregation; two of the informants, for example, had evangelical backgrounds. The liturgy for the 10.00am Mass was based on the *A.S.B.* Rite 'A' and was printed in a green booklet entitled: 'The Eucharist – often called the Mass':

Preparatory songs
Processional hymn/song
Greeting
Song (visit 1) / Act of Penance (visit 2)
Gloria[35] (visit 2)
Collect
Song (children leave for Sunday School)
O.T. and Epistle
Gradual song/hymn
Gospel
Sermon
Act of Penance (visit 1)
Prayer ministry with songs and intercessions
Peace (visit 1)
Offertory hymn
Eucharistic Prayer
Lord's Prayer, Peace (visit 2), Breaking of Bread, Agnus Dei
Administration of Communion (with songs)
Prayer
Notices
Blessing and Dismissal
Recessional hymn

Catholic, Evangelical and Charismatic

The manner in which the Eucharist was celebrated was described by the priest as being "anglo-catholic in ritual, charismatic in its openness to the Spirit and in its 'prayer ministry', and evangelical in its style of preaching"(LI). Traditional catholic ritual permeated the whole service. The procession of the priest (dressed in traditional eucharistic vestments) and the sanctuary party marked the beginning and end of worship. The

---

[34] There were also two very small said celebrations (4–6 people) of Mass at 8.00am and 6.00pm on Sundays.

[35] The priest informed us that on the one Sunday a month when the 'prayer ministry' occurred within the liturgy (the Sunday of my visits), the Gloria and the Creed were normally omitted to save the Mass becoming too long.

congregation crossed themselves at appropriate points, for example, corporately upon the priest's greeting in the name of the Trinity, the Absolution, the raising of the consecrated elements, and the final Blessing, and individually whilst receiving the sacraments. The gospel book was processed, censed, read, and then raised and kissed at the conclusion to the reading. The altar was kissed at the arrival of the priest, and censed in preparation for the Eucharistic Prayer. The eucharistic elements were raised during the institution narrative and a bell rung to indicate their consecration. Elements of the Roman rite were also used, such as prayers in the Offertory, and a Roman Eucharistic Prayer (on my second visit), and the Roman lectionary for readings.[36]

The evangelical commitment was reflected in the ministry of the Word. There were copies of the *Good News Bible* in the pews so that the congregation could follow the readings, and the preaching was based on the scriptures and challenged the congregation with the message of the gospel. The Roman lectionary was preferred on the basis that it had a much more systematic approach to the biblical text than the thematic approach of the *A.S.B.* lectionary. The parish priest admitted to hating preaching in his early years of priesthood, but since being baptized in the Spirit he had got "really excited by the scriptures"(LI).

The charismatic dimension to the Mass was evident in the Vineyard style 'prayer ministry', with its opportunity for inspired utterances (informants identified these as "words of knowledge" and "prophecy"), extempore prayers offered by the priest calling upon the Spirit at various points in the Mass, the large number of contemporary songs led by the music group, and the enthusiastic and spontaneous participation of the congregation, evident in the raising of hands and clapping during singing, and on the first visit, corporate singing in tongues.

Charismatic Liturgy

The most distinctive and striking characteristic of St.D was the way in which these elements of charismatic worship had been thoroughly integrated within the celebration of the Mass. The priest's extempore prayers for the Spirit, for instance, were all offered at moments with liturgical significance: at the beginning in the preparatory gathering rites, in the preparation for the ministry of the Word, and at the beginning of the 'prayer ministry'. This integration of the charismatic with the liturgical can be further illustrated by discussing the liturgical use of songs, the integration of the 'prayer ministry' with the intercessions, and the priest's style of

---

[36] It was on account of the use of the Roman liturgy that a prospective curate from an evangelical training college, whilst attracted in many ways to St D's, eventually turned down the parish on the basis that it used unauthorized liturgy!

presidency.

On both visits, the songs had been carefully chosen by the priest to complement the liturgy, St.D being the only case study church whose priest or vicar had kept the responsibility for choosing songs. Virtually all were songs associated with the Charismatic Movement (the exception being one or two traditional hymns). Although there were two regular points in the Mass when songs were played and sung in succession (as a background to the 'prayer ministry' and as a devotional accompaniment to the administration of Communion), the majority were chosen as single items with the intention of enhancing the flow and meaning of the liturgy. This liturgical use of songs can be illustrated from the first Mass attended. The entrance song for the priest and sanctuary procession matched the liturgical movement:

> I will enter His gates with thanksgiving in my heart,
> I will enter His courts with praise;
> I will say that this is the day that the Lord has made,
> I will rejoice for He has made me glad.[37]

Extract taken from the song 'He has made me glad' by Leona van Brethorst

After the Greeting, we sang a song set to words from Psalm 84 as a prayer of preparation. Having entered the 'house of the Lord', we now turned our attention to seeking him:

> One thing I ask, one thing I seek,
> that I may dwell in Your house, O Lord,
> all the days, all of my life –
> that I may see You, Lord.
> One thing I ask,
> one thing I desire
> is to see You,
> is to see You.[38]

Extract taken from the song 'One thing I ask' by Andy Park

In place of a said prayer of Confession, and before the Absolution we sang:

---

[37] *Mission Praise* [*MP*] (1990), No.307. Copyright © 1976 Maranatha! Music/CopyCare music@copycare.com* (* denotes address in song index).
[38] *New Mission Praise* [*NMP*], No.115. Copyright © 1989 Mercy/Vineyard Publishing/ CopyCare music@copycare.com*.

Purify my heart,
cleanse me from within
and make me holy;
purify my heart,
cleanse me from my sin,
deep within.

Refiner's fire,
my heart's one desire
is to be holy,
set apart for You, Lord;
I choose to be holy,
set apart for You, my Master,
ready to do Your will.[39]

Extract taken from the song 'Refiner's fire' by Brian Doerksen

During the Peace, as people greeted one another, we sang the following:

Let there be love shared among us,
let there be love in our eyes;
may now Your love sweep this nation,
cause us, O Lord, to arise:
give us a fresh understanding
of brotherly love that is real;
let there be love shared among us, let there be love.[40]

Extract taken from the song 'Let there be love shared among us' by Dave Bilbrough

At the conclusion of the administration of Communion, we sang a version of Isaiah 6, originally popularized by the Fisherfolk, as a fulfilment of the desire expressed in the preparatory song (see above) and a climactic expression of union with God around the altar:

We see the Lord,
we see the Lord,
and He is high and lifted up,
and His train fills the temple.[41]

---

[39] *NMP*, No.123, verse 2 and refrain. Copyright © 1990 Mercy/Vineyard Publishing/CopyCare music@copycare.com*.
[40] *MP* (1990), No.411. Copyright © 1979 Thankyou Music*.
[41] From *MP* (1990), No.736. Copyright control.

To conclude the service, as the priest and sanctuary party processed out, we sang a song which like the entrance song, matched the liturgical movement:

You shall go out with joy
and be led forth with peace,
and the mountains and the hills
shall break forth before you.[42]

Extract taken from the song 'The trees of the field' by Stuart Dauermann/Steffi Geiser Rubin

Secondly, I observed the practice of public 'prayer ministry' at St.D combined with the intercessions, a practice that was unique amongst the case study churches. This pattern was followed on one Sunday of the month (on other Sundays the 'prayer ministry' took place after the conclusion of the service), and was considered by the priest to be an important monthly reminder that the 'prayer ministry' belonged to the whole congregation. An example of this kind 'prayer ministry' will be described and discussed at length in Chapter 6. Here it is sufficient to note that the role of the priest in leading the intercessions, whilst the 'prayer ministry' team prayed for respondents at the front, gave those who hadn't gone forward for prayer the opportunity to be incorporated within intercession for the wider church, world, and local community during the 'prayer ministry'.

Thirdly, as the choice of songs and leading of the 'prayer ministry' illustrate, the key factor in the integration of the charismatic with the liturgical was the presidency of the parish priest. This was further demonstrated in the style of his liturgical presidency. With apparent ease, he would blend extempore prayer with liturgical prayer. For example, the confession he led on the second visit used a traditional *Kyrie* with extempore prayer based on the Gospel for the day, Jesus at the wedding in Cana (congregational response is in bold type):

Lord change the water of our doubt into the wine of faith.
Lord have mercy.
Lord have mercy.

Lord Jesus, change the water of despair into the wine of hope.
Christ have mercy.
Christ have mercy.

---

[42] From *MP* (1990) No.796. Copyright © 1975 Lillenas Publishing Co/CopyCare music@copycare.com*.

Lord Jesus, change the water of selfishness into the wine of love.
Lord have mercy.
Lord have mercy.

May Almighty God have mercy upon us, forgive us our sins, and bring us
to everlasting life, through Jesus Christ our Lord.
Amen.

The manner of his praying was also significant, as the Outside Observer
observed:

> All the prayers were said in the same way. They were all meaningful, they
> were all impassioned, whether they were written down or whether they
> came extemporarily ... you haven't got this vast yawning gap between one
> kind of prayer [liturgical] and another kind of prayer [extempore].(OI)

The parish priest summarized the integrative ethos of St.D: "Renewed
catholic liturgy is wonderful. The liturgy has got all the ingredients and the
Holy Spirit actually puts life into those ingredients."(LI)

This integrative approach of the charismatic with the liturgical is not
without historical precedent, for charismatic expression was formalized in
the liturgy of the nineteenth-century Catholic Apostolic Church.[43] The
catalyst to the Catholic Apostolic Church's formation was the series of
'Irvingite' Albury conferences in the late 1820s, where speaking in tongues
and prophecy had become an important feature. These charismatic elements
were retained by the Catholic Apostolic Church by being given a formal
place within their liturgy; in their Eucharistic Liturgy, the 'Exercise of
Prophecy and Tongues' occurs directly after the Communion.[44] Within
Anglican Charismatic Renewal it has been the anglo-catholics who have
maintained the view that charismatic expression and liturgy enrich each
other. John Gunstone, for example, has repeatedly affirmed, that the
liturgical revision process leading to the authorization of the *Alternative
Service Book* was very much in Anglican charismatics' favour. In a number
of articles he has argued that the *A.S.B.* rites, particularly the Eucharistic
rites, embody a charismatic ethos, drawing attention to their participative
style, their recognition of the worshipping assembly's character as the
'body of Christ', their flexibility, and the more prominent place they give to

---

[43] In view of the present discussion of an anglo-catholic church, it is interesting to
note that the Catholic Apostolic Church was formed in the very same decade (1830) that
saw the birth of Tractarianism in the Church of England.

[44] C. Flegg, *Gathered Under Apostles: A Study of the Catholic Apostolic Church*,
235.

the Holy Spirit in the liturgical text.[45] This leads Gunstone to give thanks to God 'that there were people like Ronald Jasper and Geoffrey Cuming preparing the way for the Spirit-filled worship of the Lord'.[46] Gunstone even goes so far as to suggest that 'the Charismatic Movement is an important means of popularizing ... the objectives of liturgical revision'.[47] Not all Anglican charismatics would agree with Gunstone, particularly those representative of churches like St.B and St.E, but what Gunstone represents, like St.D, is the charismatic anglo-catholic concern for charismatic life and the church's liturgy to inform and enrich one another.[48]

St.F: A 'Radical' Approach

St.F served an outer urban council estate with a high level of social deprivation, including high levels of unemployment (especially among youth), crime, long term illness and over-crowding. Informants explained that St.F formed the heart of the estate's community life, the parish priest being regarded by some as the estate's natural leader. Realities of the estate made themselves present in worship in a number of ways. Violence at home was reflected in the children who thumped each other when sitting in their seats at church. On my first visit there was no amplification system because it had been stolen and before the second visit, after being replaced, it had been stolen again. On account of illiteracy, the congregation used the colourfully illustrated Holy Communion booklets, *The Lord is Here!*, which provided an easy way to follow the *A.S.B.* Rite 'A'.[49] The priest explained that in order to avoid an over-load of words in worship he omitted the Creed, and used only one of the three possible lectionary readings (on both Sundays I was present, only the Gospel was read). He also saw an important role for colour in the context of what he described as "a monochrome estate", vestments having an important role to play in this respect.

---

[45] J. Gunstone, 'The Spirit's Freedom in the Spirit's Framework' in K. Stevenson (ed.), *Liturgy Reshaped*, 4-16; 'Preparing for Renewed Worship: 10 Years of *A.S.B.*', *Anglicans for Renewal* 41 (Summer 1990), 30.

[46] Gunstone, 'Preparing for Renewed Worship', 30. Jasper and Cuming were two leading members of the Church of England's Liturgical Commission that steered the liturgical revisions through church government in the 1970s.

[47] Gunstone, 'The Spirit's Freedom', 16. For an assessment of the relationship between the worship of Charismatic Renewal and the Liturgical Movement, see J.R.K. Fenwick & B.D. Spinks, *Worship in Transition: The Twentieth Century Liturgical Movement*, 111-3.

[48] See further: P. Peterken, ' "All Things Should be Done Decently and in Order" ', *ARMLink* 34 (Autumn 1988), 9-11; N de Keyser, 'Catholic Worship: A "Charismatic" Appreciation', *ARMLink* 38 (Autumn 1989), 13-6.

[49] Arranged by Paul Jenkins and Leslie Francis, published by Collins.

St.F was chosen as an example of a parish that combines charismatic spirituality with a commitment to social concern, a 'radical' charismatic parish in Josephine Bax's terminology. At the time of visiting there were plans being made to re-order the church building so as to enhance community education and care projects, as well as worship. I was given to understand by informants that if there was to be regeneration in the estate's community life then the church would be the chief means by which it would come about.

The main morning service at St.F was Holy Communion, which followed the *A.S.B.* Rite 'A'.[50] There were between forty and fifty adults present, with about the same number of young children (St.F boasted the largest Junior Church in the diocese). The order observed was as follows:

Visit 1	Visit 2
Preparatory songs	Preparatory songs
Greeting	Notices
Song	Song
Notices	Greeting
	Induction of head server*
(Junior Church leaves)	(Junior Church leaves)
Confession	Collect for Purity and Confession
Gloria	Gloria
Collect	Collect
Bible reading	Bible reading
	Sermon
Song	Song
Sermon	Intercessions
Commissioning of ministry team*	
Peace	Peace
Song	Song
Eucharistic Prayer	Eucharistic Prayer
(Junior Church returns)	(Junior Church returns)
Lord's Prayer / Breaking of Bread	Lord's Prayer / Breaking of Bread
Communion (with songs)	Communion (with songs)
Blessing	Blessing
Song	Song
Dismissal	Dismissal

(* denotes special item)

---

[50] Apart form the first Sunday of the month when a 9.00am Holy Communion was followed by a 10.30am Family Service. There was also a small gathering for Evening Worship at 6.00pm on Sundays, which I did not attend.

Earthed Charismatic Worship

St.F differed from the other charismatic parishes visited in that some of the typical charismatic elements were absent from the public horizon of worship. There was no liturgical provision for a public 'prayer ministry', nor developed 'time of worship' in which songs were sung in succession. The charismatic gifts that had been a feature of other churches, such as the inspired utterances of 'words of knowledge' and prophecies, were absent, and, significantly, when I interviewed members of the congregation, none of them understood what I meant by 'charismatic gifts' (St.F was unique in this respect).

However, through the influence of the priest and his wife, both of whom had been involved in the Charismatic Renewal since the 1970s, there was a charismatic dimension to the worship of the parish. There were frequent extempore prayers to the Spirit made by the priest in his leading of the liturgy, and a general congregational awareness of the reality of the Spirit; one little boy sitting next to me said proudly that "he knew all about the Holy Spirit"![51] The priest had formed a music group and a 'prayer ministry' team, both of which were evident in the worship I observed, though the latter functioned discretely in a side chapel. The small music group was led by a gifted church musician who had the responsibility for choosing the songs for each service. The repertoire of songs drew upon a broad range of folk and charismatic sources, including Fisherfolk songs alongside the most recent Vineyard songs, and like other case study churches, the selection was almost exclusively post-1970s. Again, like other case study churches, a series of songs were sung during the administration of Communion, which was the nearest St.F got to a 'time of worship'.

The 'prayer ministry' team had its annual commissioning ceremony on my first visit. Although a group from St. Andrew's, Chorleywood had helped in the initial training for this ministry, the way it had developed differed from standard Vineyard practice. The side chapel situated to the left of the sanctuary had been designated as the 'prayer ministry' area, which made the ministry unobtrusive to the gaze of those sitting in the congregation. It was not linked to any public liturgical action (such as calling upon the Spirit and the offering of 'words of knowledge') but was available at any point in the service; it was understood that anyone who moved to the side chapel would be joined by a member of the 'prayer ministry' team. However, despite these differences in liturgical style, the 'prayer ministry' was firmly located within the action of the Spirit, as the priest made clear when he introduced the prayer team's commissioning as "an important moment when the Holy Spirit comes in power on the church for this ministry of prayer". Informants clearly appreciated the significance

---

[51] Visit 2.

of this ministry of healing: "there is a lot of healing there"(CGI), said one
lady with regard to worship at St.F; "I should by rights be in a wheelchair,
but you serve the Lord here and I'm walking!", said a lady churchwarden in
casual conversation.

With regard to charismatic gifts, the priest had a policy of what he
described as "making the supernatural natural by earthing it"(LI). As an
example, he related the occasion when he encouraged the congregation to
respond to his sermon by asking them "what would Jesus say to us here?",
and then explained to them "that if anything comes across your mind just
shout it out as best you can"(LI). This is an 'earthed' version of what other
case study churches might have introduced in terms of 'a time for words,
pictures, or prophecies'. The priest explained: "There is no holy feel about
it, it is just plain earthiness."(LI) With regard to speaking in tongues, he
said:

> If anyone used the gift of tongues, I would say "Right, thank you very
> much Margaret. Margaret has spoken a language that nobody understands
> at all so what we are going to do about it is ask God what it is all about,
> so let's just wait on God." ... One Pentecost Sunday I started off my
> sermon by speaking for about 2 minutes in tongues, and I said "Now what
> do you think about that?", and the people just gave a reflection back: "It
> sounds a bit like this or that." We just throw the gifts around without
> anyone getting tense or hyped-up about it.(LI)

The same applied to the instructions the priest gave the 'prayer ministers':

> When they ask me what the 'laying-on of hands' means, I say, "Lay your
> hands on them and just touch them. Don't start doing this hovering
> business over the top or whatever."[52] The key thing is not to be
> emotionally unreal; so often people can start speaking in strange voices or
> do odd things. I will have none of it. I'll say, "Stop that! Just realize that
> this is a gift from God, it is not you. You are just there and if you are
> really still, just lay a hand on them and you will probably get more insight
> than if you are fidgeting around." That has worked really well and we
> have been able to cut away the froth that often the Charismatic Movement
> has brought and get down to help people. Also, they will then realize that
> God is quite normal and not this strange sort of being.(LI)

The creation of this 'natural' environment for the charismatic life of St.F
was identified by my Outside Observer, who said that the worship was "not

---

[52] The priest is referring to the Vineyard practice of 'prayer ministers' holding their
hands above people during prayer. See Chapter 6.

overtly charismatic ... there were no 'words of knowledge' or anything like that, and somehow I felt that would have been inappropriate; one of the things that fascinated me was that they were not out to be religious."(OI)

Synagogue and Temple Worship

Alongside a 'down to earth' approach to charismatic gifts and expression, the other distinctive feature of the worship at St.F was its ritual process. There were two distinct phases to the celebration of Rite 'A' Communion. The first phase, up to and including the Peace, was dominated by what the priest called "Synagogue Worship" This phase had many of the characteristics of a folk celebration: the emphasis was upon people gathering to meet one another, sharing together in an informal manner. This was demonstrated in the high intensity of communication, evident in the sharing of news in the notices, the sharing of prayer requests in small groups for intercession,[53] the priest's dialogue sermons,[54] and the Peace, during which people greeted one another and shared in conversation for about five minutes. This folk environment reflected the kind of community informants experienced at St.F. "We're like a large family", said one; "It's like a community centre – everybody welcomes you"(CGI), said another.

The 'Synagogue' phase created a community in which the experience of being present *to* each other (as distinct from merely being in each others' company) was heightened, and the sharing of gifts encouraged. This was reminiscent of the community experienced at St.A's Evening Praise, though more hospitable to the presence of the local and wider community (evident in the dialogue sermons, notices, intercessions, and even in song[55]), and less self consciously charismatic (see above). This heightened sense of presence was expressed in the directions of the music leader:

> Right now, everybody in church, we're part of one family, so we're going to sing this song to one another. This is a way of encouraging one another to praise God, and there are also some actions. So I want you to find one partner; look around, introduce yourself to one another.[56]

For two members of the congregation, this kind of community created the responsibility and opportunity to resolve a dispute, which they did by going

---

[53] Visit 2.

[54] These sermons took the form of a conversation between the priest and the congregation about the content of the reading.

[55] St.F was unique among case study churches in singing a song that mentioned the local community by name. The song concerned was an improvised version of 'This little light of mine' (*Junior Praise*, No.258.), sung on visit 1.

[56] Visit 1.

to the side chapel during the intercessions.[57] The priest played a crucial role in the creation of this community. He had a strong leadership presence. "He doesn't miss a thing"(CGI), said one lady; "He caught my eye this morning. He could see that I had got problems and he does not have to say anything. You just see him look or glance and you know that he is reading you"(CGI), said another. He was also very aware of the congregation's presence, which was apparent in the way he described his role as president:

> You have got to be really aware in your guts of what is going on, and I personally feel the whole business of transference and transfer onto others very, very deeply. I work on intuition and perception and that sort of stuff. People talk about 'working an audience' or whatever, but I feel everything that comes out of that and know exactly where they are.(LI)

He encouraged and facilitated the use of gifts within the liturgy. "Mark brings out the skills in all of us"(CGI), said one member of the congregation. This was illustrated in the way he welcomed individual contributions in the dialogue sermon, including one lady who shared her gardening knowledge and skills with the congregation, which was useful both to aspiring gardeners, and to all present by illuminating the Gospel message of Jesus as the Vine.[58] Both visits were marked by the commissioning of special ministries present in the congregation, the 'prayer ministry' team on the first visit and the induction of the chief server on the second.

The Offertory song after the Peace marked the transition to the second phase of worship, which the priest called "Temple Worship". We observed the priest remove himself from the congregation to put on a chasuble, and then he moved behind the altar to face westward, towards the congregation. The people's offerings and the eucharistic elements were brought up in an orderly procession, and received by servers. The movements of those at the focus of congregational gaze (priest, servers and acolytes) had been carefully choreographed to communicate dignity, formality and orderliness. It was also evident that the priest had taken great care in thinking through and rehearsing his manual actions (what he called 'priest-craft') for the Eucharistic Prayer.

The priest described 'Temple Worship' as emphasizing the transcendence and holiness of God, which is typically formal, highly structured and mediated by the 'professional' priest. The presence of God in this phase was focused by the altar. He explained:

> I always tell the people the holy space, or the place where God is, is the space above the altar. The words are said through it, we sing towards it,

---

[57] I discovered this during an interview after the service (CGI, visit 2).

[58] John 15:5-11 was the set reading.

the elements are brought into it and given back out. It is all happening within that space and that for me is invisible too. It is not the altar; the altar gives the framework or frame around it.(LI)

The children had evidently received this message. "The only time the children are really quiet is when they go up to the Communion rail"(CGI), said one member of the congregation. One little boy said to me at the beginning of the service, pointing to the sanctuary area, "No one is allowed to go there, but I've been there!"[59] The reverence created by the act of receiving Communion was evident in the priest's personal reflections: "When folk come to the altar and they kneel down and all the kids are there, the holiness and the reverence that actually comes there just completely overwhelms me."(LI) The sense of the numinous in the sanctuary was heightened for one lady by a vision she had in worship, which she related to me in the course of conversation in church after the service:[60]

I can remember saying to Mark [the priest], "Did you see what I saw? Was it my imagination?" He said, "No. What was it?" I replied, "There were old men all at the back, all the way round there [she pointed to the wall behind the altar], and they were holding their hands out. They'd all got beards, and they were all in white." And I said to Mark, pointing to the back wall, "It was there, all at the back." And he said "Like at Communion?" I said, "Yes, just as if they were putting their hands out." And I told my husband and I said, "It was really beautiful Mike." He said, "It's like the communion of saints." You know, they were all at the back, where Mark was. They were with him and they'd got their hands out.

The significance of drawing attention to the ritual process at St.F is that it provides an interesting example of how divine presence is mediated. In contrast to the more overt charismatic worship culture in other case study churches, which apprehends the numinous, or the Holy, in such things as 'words' and prophecies, St.F appears to have minimized the numinal symbolic value of classical charismatic expression, interpreting it within a folk environment of community sharing. However a high numinal value was ascribed to the eucharistic celebration around the altar, which is where worshippers at St.F encountered the Holy.

Conclusion

The discussion of each case study's worship has revealed a number of significant features. We have seen a variety of strategies by which

---

[59] Visit 2.

[60] Visit 1.

charismatic elements have been regularized in Sunday public worship: a charismatic service separate to the main service (St.A), the main service ordered with a charismatic liturgical structure (St.B and St.E), the main service in which the charismatic is integrated into authorized liturgy (St.D and to a lesser extent St.C), and the main service in which charismatic culture is an undercurrent that informs the performance of the liturgy (St.F). We have noticed that the development of these patterns of public worship has been strongly influenced by the priest or vicar (most obviously at St.A, St.C, St.D and St.F), and by the tradition of churchmanship represented by each case study. It is also possible to discern two main styles of worship representing two sources of charismatic worship culture: the Vineyard style dominating at St.B, St.C, St.D and St.E, and the more communal Fisherfolk culture in the ascendancy at St.A and St.F. Finally, some of the distinctive characteristics of the public horizon of worship mediated by charismatic expression have been explored, further details of which will be revealed as I turn to a more detailed analysis of the two main charismatic elements within case study worship, congregational singing and 'prayer ministry'.

CHAPTER 5

Singing God's Praise

Introduction

As I have already indicated, congregational singing has been one of the chief mediums for the expression and conveyance of charismatic worship culture. From large conference venues to the smaller prayer group meeting, participants in charismatic worship have experienced sustained periods of congregational singing, which have typically been led by a group of musicians playing a succession of modern worship songs. In case study worship this style of singing was expressed liturgically in a variety of ways: preparing and gathering people for worship before the service (St.D and St.F), aiding devotion during the administration of Communion (St.C, St.D, St.E. and St.F), enhancing the spiritual atmosphere during public prayer ministry (St.B, St.D, St.E),[1] and standing as a distinct liturgical item, variously referred to as the 'time of worship', 'worship time' or 'block worship' (St.A, St.B, St.C, and St.E). There were also instances when, in a more traditional manner, songs and hymns were sung as single items. At St.D, for example, I have already illustrated how individual songs were used to serve the whole liturgical action.

The aim of this chapter is to explore in depth the horizon of worship mediated by instances of songs sung in succession, focusing upon the 'time of worship' as the primary field of study, from which the other forms of successive singing summarized above appeared to be variations. Unlike the account given in Chapter 4, which offered a description and analysis of case study churches in their individual particularity, the approach of this and the following chapter will be to demonstrate the common characteristics of sung worship and 'prayer ministry' across the case study churches. This is not an artificial attempt to harmonize accounts, but an exercise in discerning shared ritual elements that were present, in varying degrees, in every church. As with the following chapter, the discussion begins with an

---

[1]   The phenomenon of songs in 'prayer ministry' is treated in greater depth in Chapter 6.

account of a specific instance of the liturgical practice under investigation. A 'time of worship' observed at St.C has been selected because it includes many of the ritual elements common to other 'times of worship' and because it lends itself to a compact description. This account forms the basis for the analysis of the chief ritual components present in the 'time of worship', which are successively identified as the music group[2] (understood as leaders of ritual), the songs (understood as liturgical text), and the ritual process (understood as transformation).

The 'Time of Worship' at St.C: 'Block Worship'

The occasion of my first visit to St.C coincided with an interregnum. The 10.30am service of Holy Communion was led by a retired priest who was well known to the congregation. Having welcomed people to the service, and read the introductory parish notices, the retired priest looked momentarily bewildered as he tried to find the number for the announcement of the first hymn. One or two agitated members of the robed choir marched briskly forward from the choir stalls, calling out " 'block worship', 'block worship' " (so called because of the 'block' of songs sung one after the other). Realizing that there was no first hymn, the priest gave way to the choir, and seated himself in his leading stall at the end of the choir stalls.

The choir, eight in all, assembled themselves on the chancel steps, facing the congregation. One choir member, the leader of the 'block worship' (I shall refer to her as the 'worship leader'[3]), asked the congregation to take the *Praise God!* songbooks and turn to the inside cover.[4] "The Lord is here", announced the worship leader. "His Spirit is with us", responded the congregation, who then joined the worship leader in the Collect for Purity. The worship leader then added an extempore prayer, and announced the first song: "Lord Jesus, fill us with a spirit of worship, a spirit of praise this morning; we claim this ground for you. We sing number 26 in *Praise God!*" The congregation stood as the keyboard player, who together with a clarinettist accompanied the songs, began to play. Like the choir, the instrumentalists were robed, and were situated to the right of the choir in

---

[2]   I use the term 'music group' to encompass the various groups of musicians and singers observed, though they were given a variety of designations by case study churches, ranging from 'worship group' to 'musicians'.

[3]   This was the most common designation in case study worship given to those individuals within a music group who provided leadership when songs were sung in succession. For an analysis of their role, see further below.

[4]   St.C had published *Praise God!* and it contained 54 songs with some eucharistic liturgy, including this standard liturgical introduction to the *A.S.B.* Rite 'A' Holy Communion Service.

front of the chancel steps.[5] The positioning made it easy for the worship leader and keyboard player to maintain eye contact, and throughout the 'block worship' they cued each other, ensuring that the choir and instrumentalists were co-ordinated in the various repetitions of songs. The song was sung with energy, with the choir clapping to a strong up-tempo rhythm. This soon had a number in the congregation clapping, as we 'claimed the ground' from evil influence:

> In the name of Jesus, in the name of Jesus,
> we have the victory.
> In the name of Jesus, in the name of Jesus,
> demons will have to flee.
> Who can tell what God can do?
> Who can tell of His love for you?
> In the name of Jesus, Jesus,
> we have the victory.[6]

Author unknown

When the song was repeated for the third time, the tune was transposed up a tone and a number of people raised their hands in the air, including the server standing in the choir stalls. Without delay, the next song began with the worship leader announcing the number from *Praise God!* as the keyboard player played the tune. This was a three-verse song with repeated refrain:

> I will never stop praising the Lord,
> I will always give Him thanks!
> I will praise Him for all that He's done,
> the oppressed may now be glad!
>
> (*Refrain*)
> Proclaim with me
> that the Lord is great!
> And so let us
> together praise His name![7]

Extract taken from the song 'I will never stop praising the Lord' by Roger Jones

---

[5] On my second visit the instrumental accompaniment included percussion, flute, clarinet, trombone, trumpet, guitar and keyboard, all robed.

[6] *Mission Praise* [MP] (1990), No.339. Copyright control.

[7] *Ways to Praise* (successor to *Praise God!*) No.6, v1 and Refrain. Copyright © 1993 Christian Music Ministries* (* denotes address in song index).

By being present on the chancel steps, the choir engaged the congregation's gaze and encouraged us to "proclaim" with them "that the Lord is great!" One large choir member, positioned at one of the two choir microphone stands, was particularly enthusiastic in her expression of worship, raising her hands and on occasions closing her eyes in intense engagement. A few members of the congregation swayed to the rhythm, and some followed the choir's lead in raising hands for the refrain.

Again, without a break, the third song was introduced. "Great and wonderful are Your deeds, Lord God the Almighty. Number 30 in *Praise God!*", announced the worship leader as the keyboard began playing the tune of the third song. This was a modern musical version of the *A.S.B.* Morning Prayer canticle 'Great and Wonderful',[8] composed by the musical director at St.C, and sung at a similar tempo to the preceding songs. The concluding doxology celebrated a common theme in songs used by the case study churches:

> To Him who sits on the throne and to the Lamb
> be praise and honour, glory and power.[9]

Extract taken from the song 'Great and wonderful are your deeds' by Roger Jones

The advent of the fourth song brought with it a marked change in mood as the musical tempo slowed considerably. The worship leader introduced it with another 'voice-over',[10] this time at length by reading out the verse, and then announced the number from another songbook, *Songs of Fellowship*. After swapping songbooks, we were singing with the choir again:

> For Thou, O Lord, art high above all the earth;
> Thou art exalted far above all gods.
> For Thou, O Lord, art high above all the earth;
> Thou art exalted far above all gods.

---

[8]   Based on the song of the martyrs in Revelation 15:3b-4, with a doxology from Revelation 5:13.

[9]   *Ways to Praise*, No.1. Copyright © 1993 Christian Music Ministries*.

[10]   John Leach recommends the 'voice-over' as a useful skill for a worship leader to develop. He suggests that whilst the musicians are playing, the leader can encourage the congregation to worship or alternatively offer prayers on behalf of the congregation. See J. Leach, *Liturgy and Liberty*, 163.

(Refrain)
I exalt Thee, I exalt Thee,
I exalt Thee, O Lord.
I exalt Thee, I exalt Thee,
I exalt Thee, O Lord.[11]

Extract taken from the song 'For Thou O Lord art high' by Pete Sanchez Jnr.

The atmosphere was now more devotional and most choir members were singing with their eyes closed and arms raised in front of their chests with the palms of their hands facing upwards. The one or two whose eyes remained open, and hands by their sides, looked singularly unmoved and out of place, compared with their neighbours. The worship leader announced the next song in a quieter voice, reinforcing the devotional atmosphere. For the two elderly nuns standing in the row behind me, regular visitors from a local convent, it was clearly too quiet. One of them made a point of walking to the end of their empty row in order to see the song numbers on the hymn board. With minimum keyboard accompaniment, we then sang repeatedly and very slowly a Vineyard song:

Jesus, Jesus,
holy and anointed One, Jesus.
Jesus, Jesus,
risen and exalted One, Jesus.

Your name is like honey on my lips,
Your Spirit like water to my soul,
Your word is a lamp unto my feet,
Jesus I love You, I love You.[12]

Extract taken from the song 'Holy and anointed One' by John Barnett

During this song one or two in the congregation sat down, which was a pattern of behaviour that I noticed elsewhere on my fieldwork visits when a good number of songs were sung in succession. There seemed to be two reasons for the change of posture. Sitting was both a more appropriate posture for the less energetic and more contemplative spirituality encouraged by the devotional worship, and also a rest from long periods of standing. The vicar at St.E, for example, informed me that he would quite

---

[11] *Songs of Fellowship [SF]* (1991) No.115. Based on Psalm 97:9, one of a number of psalms celebrating God's kingship. Copyright © 1977 Pete Sanchez Jnr*.
[12] *SF* (1991), No.293. Copyright © 1980 Mercy/Vineyard Publishing/CopyCare music@copycare.com*.

regularly sit during the 'time of worship' on account of varicose veins!

The song ended and after a short pause the worship leader spoke again: "Jesus, you are worthy of our praise. Rejoice in the Lord you who are righteous; praise his holy name. Number 481 in *Songs of Fellowship*." The keyboard broke the devotional mood with a rousing introduction to the last song, and we returned to a racing tempo:

(*Repeated refrain*)
Rejoice, rejoice, rejoice!
Rejoice, rejoice, rejoice!
My soul rejoices in the Lord.

My soul magnifies the Lord,
and my spirit rejoices in God my Saviour;
my soul magnifies the Lord,
and my spirit rejoices in my God.[13]

Extract taken from the song 'Rejoice, rejoice, rejoice' by Chris Bowater

We sang this two and a half times, the choir and congregation clapping during the refrain. This was an energetic climax to the 'block worship', and the choir and congregation applauded at the end of the song.[14] The choir and instrumentalists now moved to the front nave seats as the congregation sat down. As I turned to sit down, one of the nuns behind me caught my eye and gave me an exasperated look. "Sometimes they go on and on with those choruses," they said to me after the service, "sometimes three or more times over they sing them!"

The Music Group and Sung Worship

The constitution of the music group at St.C, a robed choir supported by robed instrumentalists, would probably be regarded by many charismatics as rather atypical. The influence of Charismatic Renewal in public worship has often been associated with a shift from a traditional robed choir to a more informal and modern music group or band. At St.D, for instance, the priest, soon after his arrival in the parish, dismissed the organist, disbanded the choir and formed a music group (keyboard, percussion, bass guitar, and

---

[13] *SF* (1991), No.481. Copyright © 1986 Sovereign Lifestyle Music*.

[14] Applause at the end of a song or series of songs is a phenomenon that has spread from large conference venues, such as Spring Harvest, and is viewed as an extension of the congregation's act of worship. The object of the applause is not the musicians or singers (for they too were clapping), but God.

lead guitar) with singers.[15] Moreover, the leadership model of a choral group with instrumental accompaniment belongs more to the Fisherfolk era of the 1970s, as is illustrated in Andrew Maries' account of St. Michael-le-Belfry's music group, which was essentially a singing group with instrumental support.[16] Since the 1980s, music groups have been modelled more on the professional 'band', with a worship leader (the equivalent to the lead vocalist) supported by instrumentalists and vocalists.[17] This was the case with the music groups at St.B (lead, rhythm and bass guitars, percussion, keyboards, and vocalists) and St.E (guitar, bass guitar, keyboard, vocalist, and electronic drum machine). However, the groups at St.A's Evening Praise (guitars and a clarinet) and St.F (piano, guitars, violin, and vocalist) tended to be less professional and more folk oriented.

Despite the relative unorthodoxy of its appearance and constitution, the music group at St.C shared similar functions with the other music groups. In common with other churches, St.C used their music group to accompany all the sung items in a service, which, like St.D and St.F, included musical settings of the authorized eucharistic liturgy. The worship leader at St.C was typical of other music group leaders in having the responsibility for overseeing music group rehearsals, selecting songs,[18] and in the 'time of worship' taking on the responsibility of leading the act of worship. The performative role of the choir at St.C in the 'time of worship' was also similar to other music groups. It is to this role and its implications for the leadership of worship that I now turn.

The Music Group as 'Live' Performers

One way of analysing the role of the music group in 'time of worship' at fieldwork churches is to consider it within the milieu of live performance. In charting the recent history of popular music, Sarah Thornton, in her book *Club Cultures*, identifies three elements that are distinctive of the live performance, or 'gig': visibility, presence, and spontaneity.[19] Visibility at a live concert is enhanced by large-screen high definition video, enlarging the spectacle of the performance and offering 'live' close-ups of the performers. Concert technology also intensifies the presence of the performer. On

---

[15] St. John's, Welling also reflected this change. The choir had disbanded in 1983, and whilst I was there, the choir stalls remained empty for worship whilst the vicar encouraged a music group to work alongside the organist.

[16] A. Maries, *One Heart, One Voice: The Rich and Varied Resource of Music in Worship*, esp. Ch.5. For the Fisherfolk model, see B. Pulkingham's *Sing a Simple Song*.

[17] This approach is reflected in Leach, *Liturgy and Liberty*, Ch.10: 'The Worship Group'.

[18] St.D was an exception to this; see below.

[19] S. Thornton, *Club Cultures: Music, Media and Subcultural Capital*, 76-85.

his famous Dangerous tour, for example, Michael Jackson opened the show by emerging 'mysteriously' from clouds of smoke and ended the spectacle without an encore by seeming to ascend to heaven in an astronaut suit. The third principle of 'live' music, spontaneity, is mediated through musical and behavioural improvisation. This could be a well rehearsed deviation from the record track in the form of the guitar or drum solo, the introduction of a special guest musician star on stage, drug induced dramatic and involuntary behaviour[20] or the smashing of one's instruments on stage.[21] These spontaneous elements help to make the 'gig' a unique event, and all three core elements, so Thornton argues, are indispensable constituents of the 'liveness', or authenticity of a popular music concert (Thornton explains that 'authenticity is arguably the most important value ascribed to popular music'; music is perceived as authentic 'when it rings true, or feels real, when it has credibility and comes across as genuine').[22]

In case study worship, visibility was established by positioning the music groups in front of the congregation. As indicated above, the choir at St.C moved from their conventional place in the choir stalls and positioned themselves nearer the congregation on the chancel steps (which also meant that they were raised above floor level). This transformation of space was made all the more obvious by the unintentional blunder of the presiding priest and the momentary conflict that subsequently arose. At St.B, St.E and St.F, the music groups were positioned at the front, with visibility at St.B enhanced by the raised platform, and at St.A's Evening Praise, the musicians sat in the enclosed gathering. The only exception to this was St.D, where the musicians, though positioned at the front, were placed to the left of the sanctuary, leaving the presiding priest at the altar as the visible focus for congregational gaze. The reasons for this will be explored below.

As well as making the choir at St.C more visible, their movement to the chancel steps also transformed their presence. They were able to engage the congregation's gaze and thereby involve us in the act of worship by their distinctive dress, and personal face-to-face interaction (which would have been almost impossible from their 'side-on' positioning in their collegiate choir stalls in the chancel). The presence of other music groups was enhanced by the amount of physical space that they and their accompanying technology occupied, which in the case of St.B and St.E was virtually the

---

[20]   Thornton comments that people like Jimi Hendrix and Jim Morrison have legendary status as live performers, not only because they were innovative musicians but because their abuse of drugs and alcohol made them appear out of control on stage.

[21]   Common to live performances of The Who, and subsequent punk groups.

[22]   Thornton, *Club*, 26.

whole of the front platform or leadership area.[23] Presence was also enhanced aurally through sound reinforcement. The loudspeaker systems at St.B, St.D, and St.E were particularly effective, and at times sung worship was reminiscent of the high volume, continuous music of discotheques or live popular music concerts.[24] The small size of the gathering at St.A's Evening Praise meant that the musicians needed no sound reinforcement for their presence to be obvious. This was a contrast to the morning Parish Eucharist where the singing was accompanied by an organist whose organ console was positioned to the rear of the church, rendering him invisible to the congregation.

The spontaneity of performance, rather like the secular context of the 'gig', was mediated through musical, vocal and behavioural improvisation. The music group at St.C illustrated many of the techniques employed by the other music groups observed that enhanced an impression of spontaneity:[25] the number of times a song, or its refrain, might be repeated, the transposition of musical key within a song, and the apparently 'ad lib' verbal comments of the worship leader between songs. With other music groups, a sense of spontaneity within the sequence of songs was conveyed with the help of an overhead projector. For instance, in contrast to St.C, where we could check the progress of songs against the numbers on the hymn board, during the 'time of worship' at St.B and St.E the sequence progressed as each song was projected onto the overhead projector screen, giving the impression of a spontaneous unfolding of events of which the congregation had no prior knowledge. One of the worship leaders at St.B reinforced this impression of spontaneity by the way he deliberately paused between each song. In these pauses he closed his eyes whilst he continued gently to pluck his guitar strings, keeping us in suspense and giving the impression that he was making a prayerful decision about which song to sing next.[26] This impression is backed-up by the practice of the worship leader interviewed at St.B who said that she would sometimes make choices about song selection during a 'time of worship'.

---

[23] This had the effect of visually overwhelming other items of furniture. For example, at St.B a large wooden cross placed to the rear of the platform was half-hidden by microphones, and the small portable holy table at St.E was dwarfed by the neighbouring overhead projector.

[24] In the case of St.D and St.E, neighbours to the churches had complained of the loud music, even to the extent of calling the police (St.D)! I noticed that the music group at St.E used a different and far more effective loudspeaker system than that used by leaders and preachers at the leading lectern.

[25] The word 'impression' is used deliberately, since in conversation with the worship leader afterwards I discovered that many spontaneous elements had, in fact, been rehearsed.

[26] St.B, visit 1, 6.30pm service.

The Music Group as the Leaders of Worship

As well as enabling a style of performance, the transformation of space that occurred with the movement of the choir at the beginning of the 'block worship' at St.C established a new set of relationships. The accidental and momentary conflict between the retired priest and choir emphasized the change of leadership from the priest, who gave way and sat himself in his stall, to the choir, musicians and worship leader, who became the visible focus for congregational gaze on the chancel steps. This delegation of leadership to the music group in sung worship was a common pattern in case study worship. For example, at St.B and St.E this was emphasized by the vicar or service leader vacating the leadership platform[27] and joining the congregation for the 'time of worship'. Indeed, on one occasion at St.B, after vacating the platform, the vicar proceeded to wander around and greet people during the 'time of worship'![28] At St.A the music group leader led the whole of Evening Praise, whilst the vicar sat as one of the participants. At St.F, I observed one or two occasions when the presiding priest joined the music group with his guitar, temporarily relinquishing service leadership to the worship leader, another member of the group. The exception to this was St.D where the parish priest presided over the sung worship, introducing each item himself. As mentioned above, this was symbolized in a spatial arrangement where the music group, situated in the area to the left of the altar, was in a subsidiary position to the priest who faced westward from behind the altar, the eucharistic president's position of authority and focus for congregational gaze.

As well as the priest relinquishing his leadership, equally important for the leadership role of the choir at St.C was their ability to be present to the congregation, which, as discussed above, was established by their movement to the chancel steps. In common with other music groups, their visibility and presence were essential to a leadership style that relied upon a high level of engagement with the congregation. This is quite different from a more traditional musical accompaniment in Anglican worship based upon the organ and choir, where musicians are much less obtrusive. A memorable illustration of this occurred at St.A when the priest invited two guitarists to lead a song in place of the Gradual hymn in the main Parish Eucharist.[29] Up until that point in the service, an organist situated unobtrusively at the rear of church had accompanied the singing, but in the two guitarists, large men positioned in the small chancel and sanctuary area,[30] the congregation

---

[27]   Although St.E did not have a raised platform, I use the word 'platform' to refer to the area at the front of the church that was used by service leaders and music group.

[28]   St.B, 6.30pm service, visit 2.

[29]   St.A, visit 1. This incident is also referred to in Chapter 4.

[30]   The presence of the guitarists was further exaggerated by the small size of St.A, which was described by one participant as "architecturally intimate".

was now suddenly faced with musicians who were visible and present. Significantly, we were no longer simply being accompanied, but visually engaged by musicians and encouraged to join in through the presence of their guitars, musical symbols of the folk spirit of participation.[31]

In being visible and present to the congregation, the music groups exercised leadership in a variety of ways. The role of worship leader was clearly a crucial one. In the 'block worship' at St.C the worship leader could be seen to facilitate the progression of the singing by offering prayer, announcing the numbers of songs, drawing attention to some of the song lyrics, as well as co-ordinating the musicians with the choir by eye contact. Other worship leaders made more use of facial communication, and some were clearly gifted at animating congregational singing. At St.F, I witnessed the priest's wife, acting as worship leader, rescue a rather half-hearted attempt at singing during the administration of Communion simply by engaging the congregation with encouraging facial language.[32] Equally impressive was a worship leader observed at St.B.[33] Occupying the front of the raised platform area, with the instrumentalists and vocalists behind her, she was in an excellent position to facilitate an expressive dialogue between her and the congregation. During the up-tempo songs she would smile at the congregation, conveying a sense of corporate enjoyment, and in the slower more devotional songs she closed her eyes, conveying a sense of communion with God. Although she said less than the worship leader at St.C (she had no need to announce songs since they were all provided on the overhead projector screen) her vocal communication was subtler and just as important to the congregation's participation. As lead singer, she would give us cues for improvisations during the singing of songs, which could be a repetition of a verse or refrain. The cues were sometimes sung, as in two responsive songs in which we repeated her vocal lead. Twice at the end of songs, whilst the instrumentalists improvised on the melody, she encouraged us to speak out our own praises to God, and then quietly offered her own spoken praise which had the effect of prompting a hubbub of praise from the congregation.

The parish priest at St.D, who, as we have seen, retained the responsibility for leading the sung worship, exercised a similar pattern of leadership. Facing the congregation from behind the altar with his vestments and radio-microphone, he was visible and present to us in a way that the leader of the music group, standing with his back to us as he co-ordinated the musicians, could never be. The priest combined the variety of leadership techniques

---

[31] For an extended discussion of the power and meaning attributed to musical instruments in ritual contexts see Sue Carole DeVale's 'Power and Meaning in Musical Instruments' in *Concilium 202: Music and the Experience of God*, 94-110.

[32] St.F, visit 1.

[33] St.B, 6.30pm service, visit 2.

already identified. I observed him give vocal cues to the repetitions of refrains, prompt some singing in tongues, and offer prayers and praise as a 'voice-over' in the pause between songs or even between verses of a song. If he clapped, the congregation would soon follow, and an intense demeanour on his face would encourage a more devotional approach to our singing. He was all that a live performer at worship should be, visible and present to the congregation and effectively conveying a natural spontaneity in his leadership.

Alongside the worship leaders, the other members of music groups also had an important leadership function. In common with other music group vocalists, members of the choir at St.C exercised leadership not only in their singing but also by their bodily gesture and facial expression. As we have seen, they could either initiate or reinforce behaviour, such as clapping and the raising of hands. Like the worship leaders described above, their facial expressions were a subtler, though no less suggestive, medium of leadership, conveying the appropriate level of engagement with the ritual process.

The Songs as Liturgical Text

The textual medium at the disposal of music groups was provided by the songs. It was a medium that they made full use of, for with the congregations in the twenty-two services attended I had sung 195 separate items.[34] One striking feature of the overall constitution of these songs was the relative paucity of traditional hymns. We sang only 17 songs that would be regarded as traditional congregational hymns (structured as a succession of metrical verses) and if the two Parish Eucharists at St.A are discounted, that number drops to nine. There were three other sung items that could fall into the category of hymns, which linked a series of verses with a repeated refrain.[35] However, the vast majority of songs, which for convenience I call 'charismatic songs', were structured either as a single verse, or as one of two verses accompanied by a repeated refrain. This lack of traditional hymnody is reflected in the participants' own estimation of their song repertoire. For example, the vicar at St.B estimated that the congregation might only sing 15 traditional hymns in the course of a year.

It is possible to discern a number of reasons for this move away from traditional hymnody. One is connected to the different musical genres of the traditional hymn and the charismatic song. The guitar and keyboard musical instrumentation of the music groups is better suited to the medium of the charismatic song, with its emphasis upon rhythm and ease of improvisation,

---

[34] This is a separation in sequence, not in kind. After taking into account repetitions, the total number of songs was smaller, about 150.

[35] For example, 'The Servant King', by Graham Kendrick, *MP* (1990), No.162.

than the more classical medium of the hymn, which is better served by the organ.[36] This was strikingly illustrated at St.A's Evening Praise when a member of the congregation chose Luther's hymn 'A safe stronghold our God is still', which we had to sing unaccompanied because the guitarists were not able to play it.[37] Another reason is that hymns do not fit the symbolic world of the sung worship of Charismatic Renewal, epitomized by the 'time of worship'. For example, whereas the shorter charismatic songs can be used to create a sense of spontaneity by various forms of improvised repetition, traditional hymns, with uniform rhythm, and a linear sequence of verses are much more predictable. Hence, apart from an occasion at St.B, when two hymns had been musically arranged for use in the 'time of worship',[38] and the Parish Eucharists at St.A,[39] hymns in case study worship were used only at the beginning of a service (St.C), at the Offertory (St.C, St.D, St.F) or at a service's conclusion (St.C and St.F).

As part of their leadership of sung worship, the music groups were given the responsibility for selecting songs in services (the exception being at St.D where the priest chose). Each church used a variety of song resources. As we have seen, St.C used a conventional songbook, *Songs of Fellowship* alongside its own songbook, *Praise God!*, which included songs written since the publication of their conventional songbook and some which had been locally composed by their musical director. St.D and St.A's Evening Praise used a similar strategy, combining their own printed supplementary songbook or sheet, which contained the most recent songs (St.D) and locally composed songs (St.A), with a conventional songbook (*Mission Praise* at St.D and *Songs of Fellowship* at St.A). Another means by which churches kept abreast of new songs, which are generated continually at big conference venues such as Spring Harvest and New Wine, was by using overhead projector slides. Alongside *Mission Praise*, St.F used an overhead projector for a good number of its songs, particularly during the singing at the administration of Communion. There was no songbook at either St.B or St.E, and instead the texts of all songs were projected onto an overhead projector screen. The only church to use a traditional hymnbook was St.A where *Ancient & Modern New Standard* was used at the main Parish

---

[36] For a helpful discussion on the differences between the music of charismatic songs and traditional hymns, see J. Leach, *Hymns and Spiritual Songs: The Use of Traditional and Modern in Worship*, 6-10.

[37] St.A, visit 1, as mentioned in Chapter 4.

[38] St.B, 6.30pm service, visit 1: 'Immortal, invisible, God only wise' and 'Abide with me'. These hymns were sung devotionally, and some of the words had been changed to make them more individual.

[39] Hymns were used throughout the Parish Eucharist in the standard positions: Introduction, Gradual, Offertory, Communion, and Dismissal.

Eucharist.[40]

The songs within a 'time of worship' provided a shared liturgical text, the characteristics of which can be illustrated with reference to the example of 'block worship' at St.C, and to the 'time of worship' at St.E and St.B. The musical director at St.C instructed his worship leaders[41] to choose songs according to a structure of 'Invitation – Proclamation – Adoration', a pattern that the 'time of worship' at St.B and St.E appeared also to follow.[42] For example, a worship leader at St.E described their song progression as beginning with the proclamation of who God is, moving to praising him for what he has done, and then climaxing in a personal response of love and devotion. My observation was that by keeping to this liturgical scheme, the songs chosen did not engage with seasonal or biblical themes present in other parts of the service (this contrasts with song selection in services at St.A, St.D and St.F, where thematic or seasonal considerations were evident). Thus, the 'time of worship' presented itself as a relatively self-contained liturgical act.

The 'block worship' at St.C began with a claim upon the space in which the worship was about to take place. After stating in prayer that we were claiming "this ground" for God, the worship leader led us into a song that celebrated the victory of Jesus over evil, or "demons". As a participant, I was struck by the incongruity of this exorcism. It was, after all, a consecrated church building in which worship had taken place for many years, and everything within it spoke of its use as a place of worship. Although incongruous, it is important to recognize that claiming space for worship through song is something that occurs within the charismatic tradition. As I have mentioned, the idea of 'claiming the ground' is present in Restorationist songs, of which this song is an example.[43] There were echoes of a similar consecratory formula in other songs sung in case study worship, most typically songs which contained requests for God to become present within the worshipping assembly. For example, the Vineyard song 'We are all together', sung at St.B and St.E as a preparation for worship,[44] contains the repeated refrain:

---

[40] A good number of traditional hymns are also to be found in the 1991 edition of *Songs of Fellowship* and all *Mission Praise* editions.

[41] There were a number of adults in the choir who had been trained to lead the 'block worship'.

[42] This pattern also appeared to determine the overall liturgical shape of Evening Praise at St.A.

[43] This first 'block worship' song, 'In the name of Jesus' was originally published in *Songs of Fellowship Book 3*, No.398.

[44] St.B, 6.30pm service, visit 2 and St.E, 11.00am and 6.30pm services, visit 1.

Lord, we welcome You,
we welcome You,
we welcome You,
come fill this place.[45]

Extract taken from the song 'We welcome you' by Danny Daniels

The second song, the invitatory 'I will never stop praising the Lord', mediates a vision of worship that is involving ('I will always give Him thanks!') and, in asserting our responsibility to sing together, demanding of participation ('let us together praise His name'). This theme is reflected in other songs used as invitations to worship on fieldwork visits:

And we will worship, worship,
we will worship Jesus the Lord.
we will worship, worship,
we will worship Jesus the Lord.[46]

Extract taken from the song 'Shout for joy and sing' by Dave Bilbrough

We are all together
to call upon Your name;
there is nothing we like better,
than to sing and give You praise.[47]

Extract taken from the song 'We welcome you' by Danny Daniels

I will enter His gates with thanksgiving in my heart,
I will enter His courts with praise.[48]

Extract taken from the song 'He has made me glad' by Leona van Brethorst

---

[45] *SF* (1991), No.564 (italics added). Copyright © 1987 Mercy/Vineyard Publishing/CopyCare music@copycare.com*.

[46] *SF* (1991), No.495 (refrain). Copyright © 1983 Thankyou Music*. Evening Praise, St.A, visit 1.

[47] *SF* (1991), No.564 (v.1). Copyright © 1987 Mercy/Vineyard Publishing/ CopyCare music@copycare.com*. St.B, 6.30pm service, visit 2 and St.E, 11.00am and 6.30pm services, visit 1.

[48] From *MP* (1990), No.307. Copyright © 1976 Maranatha! Music/ CopyCare music@copycare.com*. St D, visits 1 and 2.

Jubilate, everybody,
serve the Lord in all your ways, and
come before His presence singing:
enter now His courts with praise.[49]

Extract taken from the song 'Jubilate everybody' by Fred Dunn (1907 – 1979)

The music accompanying these songs mediated the themes of the text: the melodic range was narrow and the tunes repetitive, making it easy for congregations to participate, whilst the rhythm and melody communicated the joy of celebration. The high level of involvement anticipated by these song lyrics was reflected in the time demand made upon congregations. The 'block worship' at St.C described above was nearly 15 minutes long, which was shorter than the average 'time of worship' observed at St.E and St.B, where one 'time of worship' lasted 45 minutes![50] It was not surprising that I regularly observed some members of the congregations at St.C, St.B and St.E taking the opportunity to sit down before a 'time of worship' had finished. Though other case study churches did not have a developed 'time of worship', their sung worship was similarly demanding of time. At St.D participants identified the amount of time spent singing as a major contributory factor to the Masses running for over two hours in length.[51] On my first visit to St.D, for example, we sang 17 songs at the Mass together with a sung setting of the liturgy. At St.E this commitment to song was also symbolized architecturally by the large overhead projector screen that had been permanently fixed to the section of wall at the centre of congregational gaze, a position where one would normally expect a cross to be hung.[52]

The third song in the 'block worship' at St.C, 'Great and wonderful are Your deeds', takes us into the proclamation stage of the 'block worship' with a doxology that celebrates the kingdom of God and the exalted Lamb. This theme of divine kingship was the dominant theological vision of the songs sung on case study visits. Some songs presented the theme through passages of scripture, which tended to be either from the Book of Revelation, such as the doxology at St.C, or from the Psalms, such as Graham Kendrick's 'My heart is full of admiration',[53] which celebrates Jesus' kingship using Psalm 45, a Davidic kingship psalm. Other songs placed kingship within a narrative celebration of the crucifixion, resurrection and

---

[49] From *MP* (1990), No.394. Copyright © 1977 Thankyou Music*. St.G, visit 1.

[50] St.B, 6.30pm service, visit 1.

[51] The most common complaint of participants at St.D, particularly those with young children, was of the excessive length of services.

[52] The cross at St.E hung on a section of wall to the left of the O.H.P. screen.

[53] *New Mission Praise* [*NMP*], No. 95; St.E, 11.00am service, visit 2.

ascension, such as 'You laid aside Your majesty'.[54] Restorationist songs developed kingship in a militant fashion, as in 'Through our God we shall do valiantly' which proclaims that God will tread down enemies as the congregation sings and shouts that Christ is King.[55] In the Vineyard song 'He is the Lord, and He reigns on high', the authority of Christ is an encouragement for the congregation to invoke God's power in a refrain which includes the petition 'Show Your power, O Lord our God'.[56] Other songs celebrated the reality of the kingdom in the act of worship:

May Your kingdom be established in our praises
as Your people declare Your mighty works.[57]

Extract taken from the song 'Father in heaven' by Bob Fitts

Typically, in celebrating God's kingship, songs encouraged participants to 'lift up', 'magnify', and 'glorify' the name of Jesus, such as the popular charismatic song 'Majesty'.[58]

The fourth and fifth songs in the 'block worship' at St.C further illustrate the pervasiveness of the kingdom theme. The 'Lord', or 'Jesus' is still the 'exalted One', but this theme now informs a devotional rather than a proclamatory milieu. The devotional is communicated primarily by the slower rhythm and lower volume of the music, the intensity of facial expression of choir members, and in part by the lyrical content ('Jesus I love you, I love you'). Whereas the worshipping response of the proclamation songs is typically to 'exalt' or 'lift high' the name of Jesus, in these devotional songs one also 'bows' before the King in surrender and offers one's heart or life to him. For example, in a devotional song sung during Communion at St.C we sang:

---

[54] *MP* (1990), No.795; St.D, visit 2.

[55] *SF* (1991), No.558; St.E, 6.30pm service, visit 1.

[56] *NMP*,No.45; 'Show your power' by Kevin Prosch. St.B, 10.30am service, visit 1.

[57] *MP* (1990), No.135. Copyright © 1985 Scripture in Song (A Div. of Integrity! Music, Inc)/Sovereign Music UK*. St.E, 11.00am service, visit 2.

[58] *MP* (1990) No.454; St.C, 10.30am Holy Communion, visit 2. This was one of the most widely known charismatic songs in the 1980s, and used often when I was at St. John's, Welling.

Lord Jesus, here I stand before You,
to worship You, glorify Your name,
I humbly bow the knee before Your majesty,
give You the glory, give You the praise.
I love You, lay my life before You,
I trust You for my every need;
I lift my hands to You, surrender everything,
You are my Saviour, my Lord and King.[59]

Extract taken from the song 'Lord Jesus here I stand' by Rae Ranford

I shall have more to say about the characteristics of this devotional climax
as I now turn to an extended analysis and interpretation of the ritual process
of the 'time of worship', which will demonstrate the inter-relations of the
music group leadership, the liturgical text of songs, and, what has yet to be
discussed in any depth, congregational participation.

Ritual Process as Transformation

In providing an interpretation of the ritual process associated with the 'time
of worship' I draw upon research work done by Mellonee Burnim on the
Black gospel music tradition.[60] As I shall demonstrate, this tradition
provides us with a sacred form of live performance that shares many
characteristics of the 'time of worship'. The most fundamental of these is
the concept of performance as 'transformation', the process of becoming
something different from what was before. In the following discussion, the
'time of worship' will be analysed and interpreted with reference to the two
key processes of change highlighted by Burnim in the Black gospel
performance: the transformation of place and the transformation of
personae.

Transformation of Place

Mellonee Burnim writes that the transformation of space is characteristic of
performances of Black gospel music, an ability that has been transferred
from the worship of the African slaves in the New World who had to meet
for worship in secluded places away from their slave masters, such as
woods, gullies, ravines and thickets. Burnim demonstrates that because
Black gospel music is viewed by its performers as worship ("We didn't

---

[59] *SF* (1991), No.358. Copyright © 1990 Thankyou Music*. St.C, 10.30am
Communion service, visit 1.

[60] M. Burnim, 'Black Gospel Music as Transformation' in M. Collins, D. Power,
and M. Burnim (eds.), *Concilium 202: Music and the Experience of God*, 52-61.

come to put on a show; we came to have church!" is a typical admonition that indicates this attitude[61]) and because it is so frequently performed outside the confines of the church building, black people consciously engage in ritual acts that transform secular contexts into sacred ones. These would include prayer meetings before a performance, draping furniture in white (symbolizing a cleansing of the venue), and the designation of performances as 'services'. Like Black gospel performances, many of the large gatherings characteristic of the Charismatic Movement have also been held in secular places, such as Butlins Holiday Camps for Spring Harvest, conference arenas for Wimber Conferences, local schools for independent Restorationist fellowships or city streets for Praise Marches. The process of adapting worship to these secular places may explain the origin of charismatic songs that emphasize the transformation of space, such as those already mentioned above. Although performed within the sacred environment of a church, these songs invited participants to view their ritual space in a new way, as a space in which evil is banished and God becomes present. Rather like incense in anglo-catholic ritual, these songs function symbolically as a means of creating holy space. For example, in a song that alludes to the reference in Psalm 22 of God being enthroned on the praises of Israel, the worshipping assembly enthrones Jesus and transforms itself into the throne room of the King:

Jesus, we enthrone You,
we proclaim You our King.
Standing here in the midst of us
we raise You up with our praise,
and as we worship build a throne,
and as we worship build a throne,
and as we worship build a throne,
come Lord Jesus, and take Your place.[62]

Extract taken from the song 'Jesus we enthrone You' by Paul Kyle

This transformation of space was also reinforced by the physical position of the music group. For example, the movement of the choir at St.C from their stalls to the chancel steps, from where they led 'block worship', had the effect of defining the space within which the divine was experienced, as the Outside Observer observed:

---

[61] Burnim, 'Black Gospel', 58.
[62] *MP* (1990), No.388. Copyright © 1980 Thankyou Music*. St.A (Evening Praise), visit 2.

The choir's position [on the chancel steps facing the congregation] says something about where they think God is in all of this, that he's not somewhere remote but he's there in the midst of the congregation as they worship him ... had the choir been standing side-on in their choir stalls, worship would have been directed to God who is 'out there', beyond the altar.(OI)

Transformation of Personae

The 'personae' that Burnim refers to are the performers and audience, both of whom are included within the transformative process of a Black gospel performance. Burnim identifies the Black gospel performer's 'style of delivery' as a critical element in the process of transformation. It is a style that depends upon various aspects of performance: dress, facial expression, gestures, religious dance and performer-audience interplay. Dress, for example, functions both as a way of distinguishing performer from audience, and also as a symbol of the cultural value of dressing well; both performer and audience put on their 'Sunday-go-to-meetin' best' for a gospel concert. Gospel performers also use their bodies to communicate with God and the audience, some in a style that is overtly demonstrative, and others who sing 'flat footed', often with their eyes closed. Burnim comments, 'The closing of the eyes is not intended to shut off the communication with the congregation, but is directed toward opening up communion with God'.[63] An important ingredient to the seasoned black listener is the performer's communication of sincerity, so that the presentation is 'convincing'. Again, Burnim writes, 'Members of the congregation look for evidence that the performer is 'gettin' into the song, a syntactic phrase which implies *a process of becoming*, or the transformation of the individual or group from one state of being to another.'[64] One way in which this individual transformation is often described is in terms of 'anointing'. As Burnim mentions, in the film about gospel music, *Say Amen, Somebody*, one of the main characters, Mother Smith, contends that the ultimate goal of the gospel performer is 'anointed singing'. The process of transformation is complete when the congregation responds with verbal and physical affirmation during the performance, such as shouting "Praise the Lord!" or waving a hand. The congregation have not merely been engaged, but inspired, and they too have become participants in the transformational process.

I observed the musical leadership and congregation engaging in a similar transformative process in the 'times of worship'. I consider first the 'performers', the music group.

---

[63]   Burnim, 'Black Gospel', 55.

[64]   Burnim, 'Black Gospel', 56 (italics original).

THE MUSIC GROUP

Like the gospel music performers, the members of the music groups have a 'style of delivery' through which they communicate with the congregation and with God. Of the elements of performance that Burnim identifies, the most significant, as we have seen, were the bodily movements, such as facial expression and gestures (raising hands), and the interplay between the music group and congregation. The heightened sense of visibility and presence of the music groups enhanced the degree to which they were able to encourage the congregation to participate in the transformative process (Burnim comments that worship in the context of a typical Black church structure minimizes the distance between performer and congregation enhancing visibility and presence of the performer and facilitating the dialogue between audience and performer).

Informants in all the churches, particularly the church ministers and music group leaders, confirmed the necessity for music group members to take a lead in the process of transformation. They all stressed the need for their musicians and worship leaders to be worshippers first and foremost, an emphasis that is reflected in the designation 'worship group', used to refer to the music groups at St.B, St.D, and St.E. This reflects the advice of charismatics who write about worship, such as John Leach, who writes, 'The most important quality in musicians ... is that they should be worshippers themselves.'[65] The musicians' preparation for the Sunday service was part of the transformative process: all the musicians inter-viewed spoke of their music group rehearsals as opportunities for worship, and some worship leaders (at St.B and St.A) spoke of choosing songs whilst worshipping individually at home. Before most services observed, musicians gathered for prayer, which was an anticipation of their transfor-mative role within the service. Worship leader informants eschewed the notion that they were 'performers', preferring to see their role primarily in terms of their responsibility to worship God that would, in turn, encourage the congregation in their worship. As the main worship leader at St.D, for example, the priest spoke of how his experience of Charismatic Renewal had changed him from a religious performer to a worshipper:

> Before Renewal, it was all a matter of going through the motions, of saying the right words at the right time and putting the right actions to go with the words and then I had done my bit for God and the people should be grateful I've done it. Now in my leadership of worship it's worship for me too. I want to worship God and experience him through the worship, as well as wanting the people to really have an encounter with God.(LI)

---

[65] Leach, *Liturgy*, 191.

The worship leader had the primary responsibility for ensuring that the 'time of worship' was a transformative process. This responsibility began with preparing songs, and when asked how they choose songs, worship leaders emphasized their dependence upon the Spirit's inspiration.[66] A worship leader at St.B spoke of using songs that had a special "anointing", indicating their enhanced spiritual potency for facilitating transformation among the congregation. Like the gospel performer, the worship leaders saw their responsibility within a 'time of worship' as being to God and the congregation. For example, this was how the worship leader involved in the 'block worship' at St.C described her leadership:

> I try to be led by the way I feel things are going, which I believe to be the way the Spirit leads me, and how people are responding. I don't know why, but it does tend to differ from week to week; sometimes people seem ready to praise and worship and there are other weeks when you almost feel whatever you did it would be difficult to get people moving.(CI)

The weight of responsibility towards the congregation was illustrated in one post-service interview at St.B where the worship leader expressed to the vicar his deep disappointment and feeling of discouragement after failing to engage the congregation in worship:

> The whole reason for leading worship is to lead people into a place of heart-felt worship, and when you fail that you haven't done what you're there to do, and that gets me annoyed.(LGI)

Later in the same interview he explained what he was looking for in congregational engagement and transformation:

> You look up and you see that most of the congregation has got their eyes closed and are not looking at you any longer ... but they are actually worshipping, with their spiritual eyes fixed on God, and you think, 'Ah, alleluia! This is why we have a 'time of worship''.(LGI)

An important contribution of the worship leader to a successful 'time of worship' was their ability, like the gospel performer, to communicate sincerity and to embody the transformative process themselves. This will, in part, depend upon the sense of spontaneity the worship leader is able to convey through such things as vocal interjections and prayerful hesitations. As I will explore further in a moment, changes in facial expression and the volume and intensity of vocal cues, were also signs to the congregation that

---

[66] This was particularly the case at St.A (Evening Praise), St.B, and St.E.

the worship leader was 'gettin' into' the worship. Unfortunately this did not always work, as I discovered from the congregational interview on my second visit to St C:

> Kate's leadership this morning ... I don't know how I would describe it, but it was certainly not helpful. She did not seem herself today; Kate has done it better than that before now. She just stood there and she just said the numbers, and if all the person leading is going to do is say the numbers then that is a waste of time. It becomes a distraction because the numbers are on the hymn board; we did not need just to be told the numbers.(CGI)

The responsibility to communicate sincerity in worship was shared by members of the music group, particularly vocalists who, unencumbered by musical instruments, were best able to engage in an expressive dialogue with the congregation. Here too there were occasions when the role was not fulfilled. For example, in the 'block worship' at St.C described above, the one or two younger choir members who kept their eyes open and hands to the side looked lifeless and curiously unmoved compared to the energetic and intense engagement in worship exhibited by the other choir members who were 'gettin' into' the songs.

THE CONGREGATION

The nature of the congregational involvement in the transformative process was neatly illustrated in the introduction to a 'time of worship' at St.E as the service leader (L) handed over leadership to the worship leader (WL), who then prayed for the congregation:

> L: [Addressing the congregation] We're going to have a 'time of worship' now. Please stand as we begin the worship. If you feel the Lord wants you to sit then sit, if you want to dance, then dance! [This was followed by excited chuckles in the congregation].

> WL: We invite you [God] to come into this place and ask that you would release us, Lord, with your spirit of worship. Father, help us to worship before you, that we may stand before you also, that we may dance before you Lord also, that we may be free to express the love that you have put in our hearts.[67]

This introduction reveals that the reality of a truly inspired and transformative participation in a 'time of worship' is conveyed by the individual expressions of worship offered by members of the congregation. The most

---

[67] 6.30pm service, visit 2.

common bodily gesture observed in sung worship was the raising of arms
and hands, most often in an extended position above the head, and
occasionally in the more devotional songs, forearms were extended in front
of the chest with palms of the hands facing upwards. The raising of hands
in worship has been a distinctive visual symbol associated with charismatic
worship; indeed it has been described by one commentator as the 'party
badge of those affected by renewal'.[68] It was most prominent among the
congregations at St.B and St.E, and one reason for this may have been the
fact that neither St.B nor St.E used songbooks, leaving the hands of the
worshippers free (this was one of the advantages identified by informants at
St.B and St.E for the use of overhead projectors in congregational singing).
However the raising of hands occurred in varying degrees in each of the
churches, and cues for such activity were various: the lyric of a song (such
as 'I lift my hands',[69] or a phrase like 'so exalt, lift up on high the name of
Jesus'[70]), the actions of the vocalists or worship leader, one's neighbour, or
even the personal and corporate memory that suggested that 'we always
tend to put our hands up in this song.' The refrains of songs were also
regular occasions for the raising of hands, particularly when refrains were
repeated to mark the climax and conclusion of a song. At these moments it
was most obvious that raised hands were a visible sign that members of the
congregation were really 'gettin' into' the worship. It is important to note
here the significant role of song repetition in encouraging the congregation
to 'get into' the worship. The nuns' comment, reported at the end of the
description of 'block worship' at St.C, that the congregation could "go on
and on with those choruses" singing them "three or more times over" draws
attention to this familiar feature of charismatic worship. For some, like the
nuns, repetition is a frustrating experience, but for congregations wanting to
enter into the affective style and transformative flow of charismatic sung
worship, repetition builds a cumulative intensity of personal engagement.[71]

Congregations also used hands to clap to the rhythms of the faster songs
of praise, proclamation and celebration, and that was nearly always cued by
worship leaders or vocalists. I observed little that passed for dancing (even
on the occasion above at St.E when this was specifically encouraged),
although bodies did sway and feet tapped to rock rhythms.[72] During the

---

[68] D. Bebbington, *Evangelicalism in Modern Britain: A History from the 1730s to the 1980s*, 241.

[69] 'I lift my hands, I raise my voice', *MP* (1990), No. 280; St.E, 11.00am Service, visit 2.

[70] 'Majesty', *MP* (1990), No. 454; St.C, 10.30am Communion, visit 2.

[71] Repetition also enhances a non-rational approach to worship, a key quality of the intimate climax of the 'time of worship'. See my comments below on the mystical approach to worship under 'Intimacy, Prayer and God'.

[72] There were individual jigs during a closing song after Mass at St.D. See below.

more devotional phase of a 'time of worship', I observed instances when some would sit and very occasionally kneel, especially when the song text suggested that we 'bow' before the Lord. Individual members of the congregation could also offer vocal contributions within sung worship, such as the inspired utterances I discussed in Chapter 4 at St.B and St.E.

The controlling ethos or milieu within which all these expressions of worship took place was the freedom of expression for individuals, a feature that I have already noted with regard to Evening Praise at St.A, and which was reflected in the introduction to the 'time of worship' quoted above. This permissive environment encouraged diversity of expression, neatly portrayed in a couple I observed in the 'time of worship' at St.E: at one point the woman sunk to her knees with her eyes closed and hands raised whilst her male partner stood motionless looking completely unmoved by the worship.[73] As participants within this environment, the Outside Observer and I felt no embarrassment at maintaining a relative detachment from the acts of sung worship we observed; it was a case of us doing 'our thing' (observation), whilst everyone else did 'their thing'. Bebbington reflects our observations in his comment, 'For charismatics, worship was expressive, not functional ... it was a Christian version of "doing your own thing", a principle near the heart of the expressive revolution.[74] An informant at St.D, captures the essence of this freedom:

It's wonderful. You can do what you like, worship however you like. No one stares at you or anything. It's just natural. If you want to dance around, you can do it. Nobody takes a blind bit of notice. Wonderful; I wouldn't have it any other way![75]

These expressions of worship however were viewed not merely as human action, but as visible signs that the congregation was being transformed and caught up in God's inspiration, or as one informant put it, "really knowing God":

I found it was a great privilege just to be there because I thought, 'Isn't this wonderful, all this wonderful worship and people raising their hands, and really knowing God?' How different from a cold traditional service. It's magnetic somehow. I found it a wonderful privilege to be with so many people who know the Lord.[76] (CGI)

Similarly, in Chapter 4 we have also seen how a participant kneeling in

---

[73] St.E, 11.00am service, visit 1.
[74] Bebbington, *Evangelicalism*, 241.
[75] Informal conversation after Mass.
[76] St.E, visit 2 (in relation to the 6.30pm service).

sung worship at St.A's Evening Praise was interpreted as a visible sign of divine transformation of the individual concerned, and how inspired utterances during sung worship at St.B and St.E were also public signs of divine presence and transformation.

The desire for divine inspiration was given public form in the prayers of invocation that usually initiated a 'time of worship', which were offered either by the service leader or the worship leader. The worship leader's opening prayer in the 'block worship' described above, "Lord Jesus fill us with a spirit of worship", was mirrored by the opening prayer quoted from St.E, which asked God to "release" the congregation with a spirit of worship. These prayers reflected the invocatory emphasis of some of the introductory songs (see above), and rather like the liturgical request 'O Lord upon our lips',[77] both they and the songs acknowledged the priority of God's inspiration for the worship that was about to take place. In being inspired, like Burnim's gospel performers, the congregation thus became 'anointed' for worship, as we sang at St.E:

You have anointed us with sacred oil,
And the songs of Zion burn within.[78]

Extract taken from the song 'Blessed are they' by Kevin Prosch

The implications of the term 'release' for worship are expounded in the Anglican Renewal Ministries' teaching programme on worship, *Saints in Worship!*. 'Release' is understood to be a grace of the Holy Spirit which enables the participants to offer their 'whole being' in worship, understood biblically as including singing, speaking, shouting, waiting on God in silence, kneeling and bowing, lifting hands, clapping and dancing.[79] This was reflected in a song that was sung at the end of Mass at St.D. As the Jewish folk melody speeded up as the song progressed, members of the congregation participated in physical movements (clapping, little individual jigs for 'dance', and hands raised for 'praise'), and in so doing evoked the memory of King David's worship and celebrated the inspiration of the Spirit within them:[80]

---

[77] Morning and Evening Prayer, *A.S.B.*

[78] *NewWine '93Songbook*, No.3. Copyright© Mercy/Vineyard Publishing/CopyCare music@copycare.com*. St.E, 6.30pm service, visit 2.

[79] D. Howell, *Saints in Worship!*, Session 5: 'Release in Worship'.

[80] It is interesting to note that the music group leader at St.E spoke of David's worship before the Ark of the Covenant (1 Chron. 15:29) as a biblical precedent for the freedom of individual expression in worship (MLI). See also J.H.S. Steven, *Worship in the Restoration Movement*, 14, for a discussion of David as a model worshipper for Restorationist worship.

When the Spirit of the Lord is within my heart
I will sing as David sang.
When the Spirit of the Lord is within my heart
I will sing as David sang.
I will sing, I will sing,
I will sing as David sang.
I will sing, I will sing,
I will sing as David sang.

When the Spirit of the Lord is within my heart,
I will clap ... dance ... praise ... [81]

Author unknown

Transformation as 'Flow'

The word used most often by music group informants to describe the nature of this transformative ritual process was 'flow'. Charismatic literature also regularly uses this term. The *Saints in Worship!* training manual, for example, gives specific advice on how to create worship flow in a 'time of worship', offering practical guidance on musical links, vocal interpolations, and planning the overall structure, or 'worship shape'.[82] John Leach's *Liturgy and Liberty* also includes a chapter with similar advice for music groups planning the flow in a 'time of worship'.[83]

The experience of flow has been documented by social scientists, most notably Mihaly Csikszentmihalyi. In interviewing rock climbers, dancers, chess masters, surgeons and others who engage in activities requiring much concentration, Csikszentmihalyi discovered that when their skill and the requirements of the task match, they can attain an identifiable state of consciousness in which they become one with their activity, and thus the 'flow' experience emerges. Csikszentmihalyi defines flow as

The holistic sensation when we act with total involvement. We experience it as a unified flowing from one moment to the next, in which we feel in control of our actions, and in which there is little distinction between self and environment; between stimulus and response; or between past, present and future.[84]

---

[81]   *SF* (1991) No.598. Copyright control. St.D, visit 2.
[82]   Howell, *Saints*, Leader's Manual, 108-13.
[83]   Leach, *Liturgy*, Ch.9: 'Handling the Planning'.
[84]   Quoted by J.V. Spickard, 'For a Sociology of Religious Experience' in W.H. Swatos (ed.), *A Future for Religion? New paradigms for social analysis*, 113.

Victor Turner has applied this concept of flow more specifically to ritual, and suggests that it is clearly what is going on in successful ritual action.[85] Mary Jo Neitz and James Spickard have likewise applied Csikszentmihalyi's insights to their research with religious informants, and discovered that with significant religious experiences 'all sense of individual self vanishes. The person feels in a time out of time, connected to "the way things really are"'.[86] Individual participants spoke of the success of the flow in the 'time of worship' in terms of whether it brought them "close to God", helped them be "open" or "tuned-in" to God, and whether it allowed God to "get through" to them.

The Goal of Ritual Process: 'Intimacy' in Worship

The successful flow in a 'time of worship' led to communion with God, or 'intimacy' as informants preferred to call it. This is evident in the way a worship leader at St.B described her leadership in the 'time of worship':

> I find the congregation is not ready to go into an intimate time of worship when they come into church. It's really good practically to get the voices working, get them moving, getting them to feel comfortable. So I tend to start with praise songs, maybe an odd action song if children are present, just to get the people going. Gradually then I move from songs which I call 'starters' to songs which link the 'starters' to the more intimate worship. That's the way I go to get the flow.(MLI)

Looking more closely at the ritual process of the 'time of worship' we discover how the various ritual subjects function to create a sense of intimacy with God. As we have seen, song lyrics developed from a communal proclamation and celebration of God's praise to a more individual expression of devotion. The music developed from up-tempo songs conveying the sense of a high-energy celebration to appreciably slower songs with ballad melodies. The music group communicated this transformation through facial communication and bodily gesture. As I have indicated, relaxed smiles of enjoyment changed into an intense demeanour with closed eyes, which, like Burnim's gospel performer, expressed communion, or intimacy, with God. Bodily posture and gesture also conveyed the ritual process, moving from the more overtly demonstrative actions, such as clapping and swaying to the rhythm, to an attentive stillness. Arms and hands were raised in various ways throughout the 'times of worship', though it was difficult to be certain about how this gesture reflected the ritual process. If there was a general progression to be

---

[85] V. Turner, 'Ritual, Tribal, and Catholic', in *Worship* 50 (November 1976) 6.
[86] Spickard, 'Sociology', 114.

discerned it was from the more triumphant posture of arms raised above the head in the songs of praise and proclamation, to arms raised in front of chests with palms of the hands facing upwards in a more receptive and passive posture (as we witnessed at St.C in the description above). This same behavioural change was also observed among individuals within a congregation, and could include the additional element of individuals sitting for the more devotional songs. The manner of vocal communication by the worship leader was also significant. In the 'block worship' at St.C, the progression into intimacy was reflected in the appreciably softer voice used by the worship leader, which, despite the aid of a microphone, made it difficult for the hard-of-hearing to hear what she was saying. At St.B and St.E the journey into intimacy was marked by the increasing absence of any vocal interjection by the worship leaders, which accords with the advice of the musical director at St.C, who saw the journey into intimacy as needing a diminution of the spoken word: "I always encourage the worship leaders to realize that the further we move from the invitation stage and the nearer to adoration the less they need to say."(MLI)

Having summarized how the various ritual subjects functioned symbolically to create a journey into intimacy, the characteristics of the intimacy that is conveyed in the public horizon of worship need to be analysed. In doing so, I turn to a comparison suggested by the Outside Observer. He suggested a connection between the behaviour and atmosphere he experienced in the 'time of worship' and his experience of the ritual of a night at a discotheque. Commenting on the 'time of worship' at St.E, he said: "There was a definite progression from the fast to the slow, à la disco mode; the sort of jolly tune to start with and then slowing right down to the more affective type of thing."(OI) He also experienced this with the progression of music in St.A's Evening Praise: "I had to liken it to a dance or a disco. You know, they moved from the 'boppier' numbers to the 'slows'. I can't but help draw that comparison ... and we were invited to draw really close to the Lord."(OI)

The ritual similarity that the Outside Observer recognized between the 'time of worship' and the disco was the goal of an intimate encounter. Typical of a school or party disco, in which most young people from the late 1950s onwards will have participated, is the progression from the high energy dance songs to the end of night 'slow dances', when the music slows, the lights may be dimmed, and dancers pair off in an intimate exchange.[87] The refrain of 'Save the Last Dance for Me' by The Drifters, a popular romantic dance-song from the 1950s, expressed this ethos:

---

[87] Within mainstream club culture however, this ritual process is rare. Thornton states that 'although end-of-night "slow dances" linger at school discos, and are occasionally subject to ironic revival, they have been marginal to club culture for almost 30 years'. Thornton, *Club*, 93.

'Cos don't forget who's taking you home
within whose arms you're going to be.
So darling, save the last dance for me.[88]

Central to both the intimate exchange at the disco and the intimacy
conveyed by the ritual of the 'time of worship' is the notion of romance.
This can be demonstrated in the similarities between the lyrics of popular
'slow dance' love songs and some of the songs used in more intimate stages
of case study worship. From observation, this included not only the climax
of a 'time of worship' but also the devotional singing at St.A's Evening
Praise and the singing during the administration of Communion at St.C,
St.D, St.E and St.F (the musical director at St.C identified the administration of Communion as the most appropriate place in a liturgy for "singing
love songs to Jesus"[MLI]).

In the songs of intimacy the public worshipping assembly became the
solitary 'I' who encountered the divine 'You'. In true romantic fashion,
intimate worship celebrated 'Just the Two of Us'.[89] In worship we sang
songs of love that we hoped would delight the Beloved:

I love You, Lord,
and I lift my voice
to worship You,
O my soul rejoice.
Take joy, my King,
in what You hear,
may it be a sweet,
sweet sound in Your ear.[90]

Extract taken from the song 'I love you Lord' by Laurie Klein

We sought the object of our desire:

---

[88] 'Save the Last Dance for Me' by Doc Pomus and Mort Shuman © 1960
(Renewed) Unichappell Music Inc – Lyric reproduced by kind permission of Carlin
Music Corp.*.
[89] Name of a love song CD (1990 CBS United Kingdom Ltd.).
[90] *MP* (1990) No.287. Copyright © 1978 House of Mercy Music/Maranatha!
Music/CopyCare music@copycare.com*. St.A (Evening Praise), visit 1; St.E, 6.30pm
service, visit 1.

O Lord, You're beautiful,
Your face is all I seek.[91]

Extract taken from the song 'O Lord, You're beautiful' by Keith Green

Love and desire were expressed in romantic language of the heart:

You alone are my heart's desire
and I long to worship You.[92]

Extract taken from the song 'As the deer pants' by Martin Nystrom

Jesus, Jesus, Jesus,
Your love has melted my heart.[93]

Extract taken from the song 'Jesus, Jesus, Jesus' by Chris Bowater

I've got a love song in my heart,
it is for You, Lord my God.
I've got a passion in my heart;
it is for You, Lord my God.[94]

Extract taken from the song 'I've got a love song' by Matt Redman

There was a cherishing of every moment spent together:

To be in Your presence,
to sit at Your feet,
where Your love surrounds me,
and makes me complete:

---

[91] From *SF* (1991), No.432. Copyright © 1980 BMG Songs Inc/Birdwing Music/EMI Christian Music Publishing/CopyCare music@copycare.com*. St.B, 6.30pm service, visit 1.

[92] From *MP* (1990) No.37. Copyright © 1983 Restoration Music Ltd/Sovereign Music UK*. St.A (Evening Praise), visit 2.

[93] *MP* (1990) No.370. Copyright © 1979 Sovereign Lifestyle Music*. St.A, visit 1 and St.D visit 1.

[94] Copyright © 1993 Thankyou Music*. St.B, 6.30pm service, visit 2.

(*Refrain*)
This is my desire, O Lord,
this is my desire.
This is my desire, O Lord,
this is my desire.

To rest in Your presence,
not rushing away,
to cherish each moment –
here would I stay.[95]

Extract taken from the song 'To be in Your presence' by Noel Richards

This closeness was typically expressed in terms of a physical embrace or touch:

By Your side I would stay,
in Your arms I would lay.
Jesus, lover of my soul,
nothing from You I withhold.[96]

Extract taken from the song 'By Your side' by Noel and Tricia Richards

Secular romantic love songs celebrate many of these themes. The heart symbolizes the centre of affection, and the place where romantic secrets are laid bare. Romance is the cherishing of the beloved's presence:

But after all's said and done,
there's nothing sweeter:
so close to you, where I want to be,
you and me, and it feels so good.
So close to you, feels so good.[97]

Extract taken from the song 'So close' by Dina Carroll

Communication is through physical embrace:

---

[95] *NMP* No.153. Copyright © 1991 Thankyou Music*. St.F, visit 1 and St.E, 6.30pm service, visit 1.
[96] From *NMP* No.12. Copyright © 1989 Thankyou Music*.; St.D, visit 1.
[97] Words and Music by Dina Carroll and Nigel Lowis. Copyright © 1992 Polygram Music Publishing Limited*, (50%)/MCA Music Limited*, (50%). Used by permission of Music Sales Ltd. All rights reserved. International Copyright Secured.

I want you to be mine,
now you're by my side, and I feel so good.
I know I want you baby, so hold me so tight.
Put your arms around me; you make me feel so safe.
Can you whisper in my ear, that you're here to stay?[98]

Extract taken from the song 'Dreams' by Gabrielle

Three further characteristics of the romantic intimacy mediated by case study worship were its non-rationality, its eroticism and intensity of emotion. The non-rationality is reflected in the Outside Observer's comments on his experience of the ritual 'flow' into intimate songs:

As we went more towards the end of the service, the words of the choruses became less and less important, they were more and more repetitive, and there was less and less content.(OI)[99]

My major criticism of the service would be that [in the 'block worship'] there was nothing to interrupt the songs and so they just went on getting more and more bland... we sang one, and perhaps you paid quite careful attention to it, but by the second or third one, the words became increasingly meaningless and by the time you had the musical link between the songs, the sort of 'wallpaper' type music, the atmosphere becomes all important and the actual substance gets lost.
[I then asked him what he meant by 'bland']
By the time you have sung something two or three times, you know, unless it is very powerful poetry, very striking, and unless you have a bit of silence in between what you have sung previously you can't really get hold of it. You can't really think about what you are doing, and so your mind just switches off.(OI)[100]

This non-rational basis of the intimacy epitomized in the climax of a 'time of worship' is a further reason why the shorter and simpler songs were used in preference to congregational hymns, as the vicar at St.E explained:

My own feeling is that the whole purpose of a 'time of worship' is to be worshipping in spirit. It's a kind of moving more into the holy of holies,

---

[99] Evening Praise, St.A.
[100] St.C

you know, approaching through the outer courts and so on.[101] So you may begin with a hymn (although we don't get many at St.E) with theological meat, leading more towards the end to the 'I love you, Lord' or 'Jesus, Jesus, Jesus,' songs. That is when you are worshipping in spirit; you are no longer having to be thinking in your mind, 'Is this theologically sound?'(LI)

The fact that hymns fail to embody the symbolic values of intimate worship is confirmed by charismatic literature on worship. The *Saints in Worship!* training manual, for example, states that

Many of out traditional hymns allow us to glorify God, as we sing of his greatness. They can however keep us at a dignified distance. Some of the modern songs are short, simple, yet allow us to draw near to God our loving Father and he to us.[102]

Andrew Maries also writes

It is the difference between singing *to* God and singing *about him*. You don't present the person you love with a doctrinal thesis on their nature and place in the universe; you just say 'I love you'. In informal worship, when the people offer their prayers or songs spontaneously to express the love and adoration they feel towards God at that moment, they need simple, versatile forms. Prayers read out of books or complicated six-verse hymns would be quite inappropriate.[103]

This non-rationality is also typical of the more erotic elements present in secular love songs, such as Lisa Stansfield's 'Time to make you mine':

I've waited for this moment,
the moment when we share ourselves.
This moment can't be thought about;
it has to be felt.[104]

Extract taken from the song 'Time to make you mine' by Lisa Stansfield

In charismatic literature, this eroticism is a feature of the way in which the

---

[101] A reference to an Old Testament cultic model for the 'time of worship'; see below.
[102] Howell, *Saints*, 45.
[103] Maries, *One Heart*, 84.
[104] 'Time to make you mine', written by Stansfield/Devaney/Morris published by Big Life Music Ltd*.

more intimate worship is described. Wimber, for example, has drawn upon the Song of Songs and described the intimate stage in a 'time of worship' as a climax 'not unlike physical lovemaking'.[105] Others have romanticized one of the New Testament words for worship, *proskuneo*, by playing on its more literal meaning of 'come towards to kiss' (*kuneo* means 'to kiss').[106] Andrew Maries, for example, writes that in intimate worship we are filled with the Spirit and so allow ourselves 'to be "kissed" and embraced by God'.[107] In case study worship, this eroticism was suggested at a subliminal level by the combination of ballad style music, the facial demeanour of music group and worship leaders and by some song lyrics (see above).[108] It is perhaps not surprising therefore that my Outside Observer often referred to this kind of worship as 'claustrophobic'!

The Outside Observer also identified the high level of emotion, or feeling, mediated by the intimate songs:

> I want to make a comment about the word 'feel' used ten or fifteen times by the worship leader. It was used particularly at the point of the slower songs, when we were expected to feel a certain emotion, and this was backed up by the singing of the emotional choruses.(OI)[109]

> In the silences between the songs I felt that people were waiting for an emotional moment, an emotional highpoint.(OI)[110]

> I found the songs kept on driving me back into an emotional expression of worship; a good old-fashioned hymn would have cleared the air!(OI)[111]

Participants also spoke of the emotional content of worship, such as the informant at St.A who spoke honestly about the demands of Evening Praise: "I don't always find Evening Praise an easy form of worship. I find it is sometimes far too emotional for me and I find it very difficult to show my emotions and so I find it extremely painful sometimes, although I enjoy going to it."(CGI) This is not unlike what Sandra Sizer refers to as 'the

---

[105] J. Wimber 'Intimacy with God', *Worship*, 8 (Winter 1988).

[106] In New Testament usage *proskuneo* meant 'to make obeisance, or do reverence to' God, Jesus, or a human superior. G. Abbott-Smith, *Manual Greek Lexicon of the New Testament*.

[107] Maries, *One Heart*, 50. David Watson, Maries' vicar, often spoke of the ministry of God's Spirit in terms of a 'kiss'.

[108] This eroticism has been explored systematically by Martyn Percy in 'Sweet Rapture: Subliminal Eroticism in Contemporary Charismatic Worship', *Theology and Sexuality* 6 (1997), 71-105.

[109] Evening Praise, St.A.

[110] St.B.

[111] St.E.

community of feeling' created by gospel hymns of the American revivals in the nineteenth century. These hymns typically portrayed Jesus as a friend, charming, beautiful, strong, and as the Saviour who enfolds the sinner in his arms, and in whose presence is heavenly bliss, which encouraged communities of intense emotion and feeling.[112] The intimate songs of case study worship appear to follow in this tradition, drawing upon a hinterland of popular secular romanticism to evoke communities whose language is primarily one of emotion and feeling.

Intimacy, Prayer and God

This intimate, non-rational worship not only has its secular parallels, as has been illustrated above, but also, in the mystical tradition, a religious one too. Lawrence Hoffman's description of the Jewish mystics *yordei merkavah* illustrates this well.[113] These mystics embodied a Jewish gnosticism that can be traced to the third or fourth centuries (A.D.). The name *yordei merkavah* means 'those who go down into the chariot', a reference to the way their pattern of prayer took them on a ritual journey to the seventh heaven where God dwelt in a chariot of glory.[114] These mystics have been of particular interest to liturgists on account of the way that their liturgy incorporates the Kedushah, the sanctification of the name of God in the recitation of Isaiah 6:3, 'Holy Holy Holy is the Lord of Hosts'. Hoffman describes their use of the Kedushah:

> Rhythm, repetition, sound, elaborate praise of God, without, however, burdening the mind with conceptualizations of the deity being praised: these were some of the formal characteristics that enabled the mystic to escape the fetters of the mundane reality and to enter the realm of the numinous. The last mentioned characteristic is especially significant. Words in prayer were not always intended to convey information about reality. The very reverse was often the goal. The mind was to be freed from the normal strictures of thought, so that, in the extreme instance, a trance might set in. We deal with a form of mantra. True, these mantras are not strings of totally meaningless syllables, but they are mantras nevertheless, in that otherwise meaningful words are used in meaningless ways: that is, the sentences they constitute do follow the normal rules of syntax and are thus translatable into conceptually valid statements, but

---

[112] S. Sizer, *Gospel Hymns and Social Religion: The Rhetoric of Nineteenth-Century Revivalism*, 36-9.

[113] L. Hoffman, *Beyond the Text: A Holistic Approach to Liturgy*, 154-8.

[114] In order to gain an experience of self-transcendence, it was common practice for them to recite their prayers after several days of fasting and in a posture whereby the head was placed between the knees, thus allowing the blood to rush quickly to the brain!

their function is irrelevant to their message, and their cognitive content is not allowed to intrude upon their rhythmic affective function. Indeed the theologically disparate concept-signifying words, *kadosh* and *barukh*, often appear interchangeably in *merkavah* liturgy, since their normal 'meanings' – we would say 'holy' and 'blessed' – were irrelevant to a liturgical experience that presented words for the purposes of their rhythm, their sound, their affect, not their sense values, their dictionary-defined equivalents.[115]

In this description there are significant parallels with the 'time of worship'. The increasing lack of doctrinal content and repetition of songs freed the mind (or as the Outside Observer put it, "your mind just switches off"). The cognitive element was progressively reduced so as not to intrude unnecessarily upon the songs' affective function (for example, explanation was eschewed in intervals between songs) and the experience of participation suggested that the songs' liturgical function was defined primarily by their rhythm, sound and affect rather than their cognitive value (Outside Observer: "the atmosphere becomes all important and the actual substance gets lost").[116] The result for the participants was not a trance in the strict sense of the word, but as mentioned above, getting 'in touch' with God.

As is the tendency with prayer in the mystical tradition, the amount of time spent in the 'time of worship' was also seen as important. A number of informants told me that the great advantage of the succession of songs in the 'time of worship' was that it enabled them to "focus upon God" in a way that was impossible with the more traditional pattern of singing single item hymns sandwiched within the liturgy. For instance, such was the view of an informant at St.B: "People who do not have a prolonged period of worship are deprived of the chance of losing themselves in God's glory and losing themselves in adoration of God."(CGI) The *Saints in Worship!* training manual identifies a similar benefit:

> The benefit of such extended times is that they allow worshippers space and time to concentrate on God, to be drawn to him and to give ourselves over to him in worship. Equally, if not more importantly, it allows time for God to come close to us to respond as only he can.[117]

---

[115] Hoffman, *Text*, 155.

[116] With regard to this last point, it was interesting to observe that the transition point in the 'block worship' at St.C from proclamation to intimate worship came as a result of a musical change rather than a change in theme in the song text. However, unlike Hoffman's description, I cannot go so far as to say that the words lost all cognitive value, for they, like the secular love songs, are able to convey intimacy.

[117] Howell, *Saints*, 109.

This last statement also illustrates one major difference between the ritual journey of the 'time of worship' and that undertaken by the *yordei merkavah* mystics. For the latter, prayer was designed to allow the worshipper to transcend earthly existence in order to join the heavenly angelic laudators in the presence of God around the chariot of glory.[118] Within the 'time of worship', God comes close to those who worship, and so the sanctuary of divine encounter is within the immanent realities of the worshipping assembly and the space it occupied.

One common way of describing the ritual process of the 'time of worship' was in terms of the cultic life of the Old Testament temple. We have seen above how the vicar at St.E, for example, referred to the 'time of worship' leading from the "outer courts" into the "holy of holies". This cultic model was applied by the musical director at St.C to the *A.S.B.* Rite 'A' Communion liturgy, which he viewed as a journey from praise in the outer courts of the temple (epitomized by the 'block worship' at the beginning of the service) into the presence of God in the "most holy place" (the receiving of Communion, when devotional, intimate songs would be sung). There was evidence that the worship leaders and music groups understood themselves to be exercising a priestly function in this cultic journey. The worship leader at St.B, for example, saw the primary responsibility of the music group as "leading people into the presence of God"(MLI). At St.E, the worship leader spoke of the music group having the role of "leading people into an appreciation of God's presence"(MLI). The cultic role of musicians has been highlighted in the charismatic literature on worship, which has promoted the Levite musicians of 2 Chronicles 5:11-14 as an archetypal role model for music groups and their leaders.[119] As the Levites' offering of praise led to the cloud of the glory of the Lord filling the temple, so church musicians, as the *Saints in Worship!* training manual puts it, 'serve the worship in such a way as to draw the whole congregation into God's presence, so that he may come amongst us in our worship'.[120]

The nature of this experience of God in worship was reflected in the song vocabulary, which reflected an encounter with a 'holy' God, in whose presence worshippers bowed and were struck with awe. For example:

---

[118] Behind this was a cosmology that pictured our world in the centre, with seven heavens surrounding it. In the seventh and furthermost heaven sat God enthroned in his chariot surrounded by angels giving praise in the very words of the Kedushah.

[119] This passage in Chronicles has been a strong influence upon the thinking of charismatics on worship. For example, John Leach uses it to illustrate his theology of charismatic worship. See J. Leach, *Liturgy*, 32-3.

[120] Howell, *Saints*, 50 (Leader's Manual).

At your feet we fall,
Sovereign Lord,
We cry 'Holy, Holy'
At your feet we fall.[121]

Extract taken from the song 'As we seek Your face' by Dave Bilbrough

A sense of awe was evidently the experience of some informants, and, interestingly, it was at St.B and St.E, churches that had the most developed 'time of worship', that informants were more frequently referring to the experience of "awe" in worship. For example, a worship leader at St.E described the experience within a 'time of worship':

There are times when there is a real awesome sense of the Lord's presence and a sense, as it were, of being drawn into the holy of holies and falling before the presence of the Lord. There have been times when that's been there and one has spontaneously dropped to one's knees. It's awe at the Lord's presence, almost tangible. To coin a phrase, you could almost cut the atmosphere with a knife and the sense of the Lord being there brings a tremendous stillness. I've described it to people as being a bit like the sense there is when just before a thunderstorm there is an amazing stillness in the atmosphere. The Lord's presence has pervaded the place in that form and it's been awesome.(MLI)

The most interesting aspect of this expression of traditional numinal vocabulary (God being 'holy') was the way that it was interpreted within the context of romantic intimacy. The first verse of 'As we seek Your face' expressed this intimacy with slow devotional music and lyrics such as 'knowing God's heart', 'feeling' his presence and 'seeking His face':

As we seek Your face,
may we know Your heart,
feel Your presence, acceptance,
as we seek Your face.[122]

Extract taken from the song 'As we seek Your face' by Dave Bilbrough

---

[121] From *SF* (1991), No.30. Copyright © 1990 Thankyou Music*. St.F. Examples of other similar songs sung on fieldwork visits were: 'Holy, holy, holy is the Lord', *MP* (1990), No.239; 'You are the Holy One', *SF* (1991), No.626; 'We see the Lord', *MP* (1990), No.736.
[122] Copyright © 1990 Thankyou Music*.

The most striking example of a romanticized numinal vocabulary was 'When I look into Your holiness'. Again, the music was slow tempo with a ballad-style melody:

When I look into Your holiness,
when I gaze into Your loveliness,
when all things that surround
become shadows in the light of You.
When I've found the joy of reaching Your heart,
when my will becomes enthralled in Your love,
when all things that surround
become shadows in the light of You.[123]

Extract taken from the song 'When I look into Your holiness' by Wayne and Cathy Perrin

I discuss the issue of charismatic numinal vocabulary at greater length at the beginning of Chapter 7. However I conclude this section by acknowledging that the community of worship created by the 'time of worship' and its associated songs is not only expressive and emotional, but also impregnated with a sense of God, known intimately in its midst.

Intimacy and Cultural Trends

Having demonstrated that intimacy is the goal of the ritual process in the 'time of worship' I want to conclude by turning to a broader discussion of how this phenomenon is related to present cultural values. In the interpretative context of the relationship between worship and culture, I want to suggest that the appearance of intimacy as a primary value in public worship is a reflection and expression of dominant cultural norms in the late modern era.

In an illuminating article entitled 'Liturgy and the Present Crisis of Culture', M. Francis Mannion outlines the impact of modern culture on the perception and practice of worship.[124] Among the cultural trends that have most influenced liturgical practice he highlights what he calls the 'intimization of society'. He describes this as the process that is marked by a loss of confidence in social and cultural institutions and an attendant growth of an intimate order which values personal closeness and radical familiarity. The roots of this cultural shift have been outlined by Richard Sennett in *The Fall of Public Man*, where he points to the nineteenth-century emergence of

[123] From SF (1991), No.595. Copyright © 1981 Integrity's Hosanna! Music/ Sovereign Music UK*. St.A (Evening Praise), visit 1.
[124] M.F. Mannion, 'Liturgy and the Present Crisis of Culture', *Worship* 62 (March 1988) 2:98-123.

the idea of personality into social life. The effect of this, as Sennett argues, was that culture began to understand itself in terms of a collective personality, converting all social phenomena into matters of personality in order to have meaning. This emphasis meant that it has become increasingly difficult for people to appreciate social institutions, that embody impersonality, public distance and complex relationships, as meaningful. Thus the development of large, impersonal institutions in the modern world renders a public space that appears to be 'dead' according to Sennett, since it is not recognized as a sphere in which the self can be defined and developed. This alienation from public life leaves society and its institutions in the realm of practical and instrumental necessity, a trend that is mirrored by a growing demand to achieve intimacy in the spheres of life that have not been incorporated into these larger impersonal systems, a demand which some commentators regard as persisting 'to the point where it is virtually compulsive'![125] In this intimate order personal closeness and social unmasking (self-revelation and honesty) provide the matrix for meaning but formality and social distance are regarded as unauthentic. Opinions vary as to the merits of this situation. Sennett is clearly critical of what he calls the 'ideology of intimacy' which threatens to strip public life of codes of civility that foster relationships and bonds that are based upon social distance (such as the encounter between strangers).[126] Giddens, on the other hand, sees the positive benefits that intimacy has brought to friendship and established sexual relationships in the modern world. In particular he observes that intimacy lies at the heart of the quest for self-identity within modern personal relationships (giving rise to a phenomenon that he calls the 'pure relationship'[127]).

The pervasiveness of the ideals of intimacy is illustrated in Mannion's comments on his own native North American Catholicism.[128] Increasingly, Catholics seek 'personal and accessible priests' and 'warmer, more personal parishes'. Popular writing on church and ministry is convinced that 'the ideal structure is community; the ideal relationship, intimate; and the ideal size, small'. There is a corresponding and consequent lack of confidence in ecclesiastical institutions and of the relevance of Gospel values to a complex society. It is not surprising to discover that when the church gathers for worship these values are similarly expressed. Smaller congregations are favoured for their intimacy, closeness and familiarity whereas the large traditional congregation is rejected as 'anonymous, alienating and as a barrier to authentic communal faith and worship'. Traditional liturgical rites

---

[125] Bensman and Lilienfeld, quoted in Giddens, *Modernity and Self-Identity: Self and Society in the Late Modern Age*, 94.

[126] R. Sennett, *The Fall of Public Man*, 259.

[127] Giddens, *Modernity*, 88-98.

[128] Mannion, 'Liturgy', 110-13 (for all quotes in this paragraph).

and symbols lose the scale and complexity needed to engage congregations with society, tradition and history. Spirituality is redefined: Christians identify their deepest religious experiences 'not with public ritual and worship, but with private, personal experiences of intimacy and relationship', and so live with a model of the sacred that is based in intimacy, not liturgy. As Mannion points out, the consequence of this intimization is the loss of the church's sense of the public nature of worship: 'the journey into intimate community is a journey out of the public world', with the result that the church is powerless to transform the public sphere.

Before returning to the intimacy of my case study worship, it is important to acknowledge another cultural development that has intensified the phenomenon of intimacy, namely the subjectification of reality. Mannion describes this development as the assumption that the individual person rather than institutions or traditions is the locus of meaning and values. According to Robert Bellah's *Habits of the Heart*, it embodies the conviction that 'the individual has a primary reality whereas society is a second-order, derived or artificial construct'.[129] Christopher Lasch has written about the same process in terms of the creation of the narcissistic individual who has lost confidence in history, future vision, politics and social and cultural institutions, and who looks instead to find meaning in personal preoccupations, such as psychic and bodily improvements. Lasch notes the attendant rise of a 'therapeutic sensibility' in which ideas and institutions are judged according to their therapeutic or consumer value.[130] It is not difficult to see how this reinforces and informs the assumptions discussed in relation to the intimization of society, or to anticipate its effects upon religion, and Mannion observes a number of related trends.[131] These include the rise of 'experiential-expressive' modes of religion, which celebrate inwardly constituted faith at the expense of more corporate and communal expressions of faith. Liturgy is thus more readily judged according to its therapeutic capacity to meet the needs of individuals than its ability to mediate ecclesiological significance. Studies in Catholic parishes reveal that there has been a corresponding shift in the way that the sense of the sacred is perceived, progressively becoming disengaged from its traditional location in the church's public worship and now located '"inside", in the personal geography of the self'. And so, as Mannion observes, worshippers now 'look for the holy to reveal itself, not in the awe-inspiring rites of Baptism and Eucharist, but in the awesome precincts of the self'.[132]

---

[129] Quoted in Mannion, 'Liturgy', 102.

[130] C. Lasch, *The Culture of Narcissism: American Life in Age of Diminishing Expectations*, quoted in Mannion, 'Liturgy', 103.

[131] Mannion, 'Liturgy', 105-107.

[132] Mannion, 'Liturgy', 106.

This brief excursus into social trends offers an interpretative framework within which it is possible to argue that the dominance of intimacy in the 'time of worship' is a good example of how liturgical piety or consciousness has been influenced by social norms. The character of the intimacy mirrored the trends I have highlighted. The relationship with the divine was defined in terms of closeness, non-complexity (and hence non-rationality), and radical familiarity that had the boldness to reinterpret traditional language of God's otherness (holiness) in terms of romantic intimacy. Worship was characterized by an intensity of feeling and devotion that was an expression of the individual self. The corporate character of worship became invisible as discourse with the divine was conducted in terms of the 'heart' in its transparent openness and longing.

In the light of this, the links I have made with discotheque culture and the ritual intimacy of 'time of worship' become significant. In considering the relationship between the two social situations in the early stages of my observation and reflection I worked by way of analogy: identifying the similarities (or dissimilarities) of the two social situations was a useful means to illuminate the specific characteristics of each. On further reflection I would argue that discotheque culture provided not only a social analogy but also the plausibility structure for the social expression of the intimization of liturgical piety that was so crucial to the 'time of worship'. Consciously or unconsciously, by hosting the secular rituals of discotheque culture, the 'time of worship' had found a suitable ritual form to celebrate the intimate relationship with the divine. As we have seen, the lyrics and music of worship songs and the demeanour of participants mimicked the communal context of the dance floor where the climax of the event is the romantic and intimate encounter between individuals. Interestingly, both environments reflect an intimate private world. Sarah Thornton comments that the experience of discotheques and more recently nightclubs is that of leisure, an otherworldly alternative to the public world of work, college or school. It is rare, for instance, to find a club that has windows through which to look into or out of, and from experience as a participant observer Thornton comments that initiating a conversation about work is taboo.[133] Similarly there was little sense of public space in the 'time of worship', but rather a reinforcement of values that dominate people's private (or leisure) spaces: informality, affectivity, desire, pleasure and intimacy.[134]

---

[133] Thornton, *Club Cultures*, 90-1.

[134] Bryan Turner compares this to the values of modern public spaces, which typically include reason, formality, neutrality, asceticism, universality and production. In similar vein to Mannion, he makes the observation that the transition from Renaissance to the modern world has involved a transition from human existence opened to the public world through ritual and carnival to the more 'closed' existence of the individual consumer. Turner, *The Body and Society*, 66.

For Mannion the impact of the modern trends of intimacy and subjectivity upon Christian worship is a cause of concern. In particular he sees both as a direct threat to the liturgy's proven ability to generate and form a public culture that reflects Christian priorities.[135] I will be conducting my own theological evaluation of the worship observed, which raises similar concerns, in Chapter 7. But for the moment, I conclude this analysis of sung worship by suggesting that the celebration of intimacy in the climax of the 'time of worship' is a good example of the way that contemporary cultural norms have impregnated and shaped charismatic liturgical practice and piety.

---

[135] Mannion draws attention to the work of the cultural historian Christopher Dawson *(Religion and the Rise of Western Culture)* who traces the way that the church's liturgy provided a generative principle of unity for western culture emerging from the ruins of the Roman Empire.

CHAPTER 6

'Prayer Ministry'

Introduction

Along with congregational singing, another common feature of the worship observed was the practice of praying for individual members of the congregation. Unlike public prayers of intercession, this prayer was offered exclusively for the spiritual empowerment, or healing, of individuals present in the worshipping assembly. It invariably involved those praying being in close proximity to the individuals concerned, enabling prayer to be accompanied by the physical gesture of a hand being placed near or upon the recipient, reminiscent of the tradition of praying by laying-on of hands.

In the churches visited this individual prayer took a variety of forms. I observed a number of public commissionings of individuals in which prayer was the focus for congregational attention. At both evening services at St.B individuals who were leaving for Christian work elsewhere were interviewed and then prayed for publicly on the leadership platform. This involved the minister and a small number of friends standing around the individual concerned, offering individual extempore prayer for them. At St.F, the priest commissioned the head server (visit 2) and members of the 'prayer ministry' team (visit 1) in a similar public fashion. Other occasions when prayer for individuals was offered in the public gaze of the congregation were during the instances of public 'prayer ministry' at St.B, St.C, St.D and St.E, and during the administration of Communion. I noticed this latter practice occurring at St.F, where the priest prayed for a number of individuals as they received the sacrament from him at the altar rail, and more formally at St.A's Parish Eucharist, where the priest, seated in the sanctuary, offered prayer with laying-on of hands for those who had received Communion. Unlike the public commissionings, however, these were instances of private prayer within a public setting, for the content of the prayers offered was not audible to the congregation. Prayer was also offered away from the public gaze, both within and outside the context of worship. Within a service this occurred in the more private forms of 'prayer ministry' where recipients moved away from the main assembly to join 'prayer ministers' in a designated prayer area (St.F and St.C, 10.30am Communion). During the preparatory prayer in the vestry at St.C, members of the 'prayer ministry' team would move to stand by significant individuals (the preacher, service leader and worship leader) as prayers were offered for them. Sometimes, prayer for individuals was offered quite spontaneously. For example, on our arrival at our very first church visit (St.B), the Outside Observer and I were greeted and welcomed by a member of the congregation, who, having conversed with us, asked to pray for us as we stood. We obliged, and so found ourselves the recipients of prayer before we had participated in any worship!

Having illustrated the commonality of the practice of prayer for individuals throughout case study worship, this chapter will analyse and interpret the most ritually formalized expression of such prayer, the "prayer ministry" as participants commonly called it. Since my analysis focuses upon the public horizon of worship, I will discuss those occasions when such ministry occurred publicly, namely at St.B, St.C (6.00pm service), St.D and St.E. As with the previous chapter, the discussion is introduced by a description of a particular instance of 'prayer ministry', observed in my first visit to St.D. This occasion was chosen because it contained most of the elements present in other 'prayer ministries' and because it lent itself to a compact description. Drawing also upon my observations at other churches, I will then consider the roles of the three major 'prayer ministry' ritual subjects: those who administered it (the leader and 'prayer ministers'), those who received it (members of the congregation) and the activity of the divine Spirit.

'Prayer Ministry' at St.D.

The congregation was standing, having received Absolution from the priest who faced the congregation as he stood in his presiding position behind the altar. The priest then prayed an extempore prayer:

> Come Holy Spirit, come upon us your people who have known our need of repentance, who have opened our hearts before you, and who have sought your power in our lives to be holy. Come Lord now with your refiner's fire,[1] and pour upon us the precious gift of your Holy Spirit. Come, Holy Spirit, come. Come amongst us now. Come and speak to us, come move among us. Come touch each one of us. Come Holy Spirit, come Holy Spirit.

---

[1]   The priest is drawing upon language used in the song 'Purify my heart', which was used as a part of the Confession that morning (as quoted in Chapter 4).

After a pause, during which the priest could be heard gently speaking in tongues (his voice was amplified by a radio-microphone), individual members of the congregation spoke (C_1, C_2 etc.):

C_1:   I feel there is someone here this morning weighed down by sin, not their sin but sin that has been done to them; it's just weighing them down, I can feel the burden upon them. That burden is upon the Lord's heart too for them. He wants to lift that burden and free them; free them from the guilt and shame.

Priest: We believe that God gives us gifts of his Spirit, and one of those gifts is 'words of knowledge' which speak of our situation. So we believe that the Lord is telling us that there may be someone here who's carrying enormous burdens of sin; not their sin but sin that's been done against them, and the Lord carries that burden too as he wants to lift that burden from us. If that speaks to you then draw near to the Lord today, let him lift that burden. In order to reach out to him, as Father John [the preacher] said, not only do we have to let go of our own sins, but also our brother's, to put our hands into the hands of the Lord.

C_2:   Someone's got a problem in their neck at the top of their spine.

Priest: Someone with a problem in their neck or the top of their spine.

C_3:   A picture of a very old cupboard, dark and dingy, all empty and also a picture of pure liquid flowing through a channel.

Priest: [Contribution is repeated] ... These may speak to you or to others here this morning of the way that the Lord is dealing with us, or wants to deal with us in situations in our lives.

C_4:   I feel the Lord is saying that as we walk, and as our shoes wear down and our feet become blistered, the pain is so tremendous in our hearts and lives; the physical pain of just walking with the Lord is sometimes so much that we can hardly bear it. But he says 'I will put new shoes on your feet, and I will comfort you'.

C_5:   Someone in dark clouds. But there are rays of light coming from Jesus. He wants us to reach out to take his hand.

Priest: [The last contribution is repeated] ... The Lord is reaching out to us with the light of his love. Trevor [C_4] has shared with us how the Lord knows how hard that journey is sometimes. Sometimes we're so worn out. But the Lord today wants to give us new shoes, alleluia! New walking shoes to enable us to walk on that journey and follow him in some comfort. He doesn't want us to be uncomfortable, yet the way of the cross can be painful as well as the joy of the resurrection. So he wants to equip us for that walk.

O.K. The Lord may be giving us some other words and pictures, but we're going to move on to a time of ministry to respond to that; and if the Lord is giving you any other words or pictures, then do either share those by coming to the microphone or by coming to me. We want people to be able to respond to what God may be saying to us this morning and know that the Lord will respond to your longing of him right where you are too. He's moving among us. But if you would like to receive ministry with the laying-on of hands for the assurance of that love which God has for you, I remind you to come forward to receive that special ministry in the power of the Holy Spirit.

As those who are going to minister come forward, we are going to continue to praise the name of Jesus in a very gentle way. We will sing No. 370 [*Mission Praise* (1990)]. I invite you to come and receive that love which God has poured out upon each one of us.

As we were standing, the congregation began to join the music group in singing the quiet devotional chorus, as the priest maintained his position behind the altar:

Jesus, Jesus, Jesus, your love has melted my heart;
Jesus, Jesus, Jesus, your love has melted my heart.[2]

Extract taken from song 'Jesus, Jesus, Jesus' by Chris Bowater

Those on the 'prayer ministry' team (eight people) assembled in the spacious floor area between the front row of seats and the raised sanctuary area,[3] standing in pairs. They prayed together in their pairs before receiving anyone for prayer, and whilst they did so the assistant priest prepared some holy oil on the altar, which was to be used for anointing. After a while, members of the congregation began to move forward, and seated themselves in the vacant front row. Respondents waited there until a 'prayer ministry' pair beckoned them to join them. Each respondent would then briefly explain their need for prayer, after which their 'prayer ministers' (the common designation for those who prayed for others in 'prayer ministry') prayed for them, keeping their eyes open and with hands raised

[2] Copyright © 1979 Sovereign Lifestyle Music* (* denotes address in song index).
[3] As mentioned in Chapter 4, St.D was a modern church with a large square, flat worshipping area; the altar and sanctuary area were raised by only one step above floor level.

above or alongside the respondents, but never touching them. All respondents stood whilst they received prayer, many of them adopting a receptive posture whereby their hands were held out in front of their chests with palms facing upwards. It was not long before one lady respondent collapsed to the ground. Her 'prayer ministers' seemed unperturbed and continued praying for her whilst she lay on the floor (I discovered that falling to the ground, sometimes called 'being slain in the Spirit', was a common occurrence in 'prayer ministry' at St.D). The priest then interjected:

> Let's just continue to praise and worship God. If you'd like to sit or whatever position you'd like to take, as God ministers among us his grace and his love, as God wants to meet you. God wants you to know that there is acceptance of you.

Most of the congregation now sat down and began to sing another devotional song:

> It's Your blood that cleanses me,
> it's Your blood that gives me life,
> it's Your blood that took my place
> in redeeming sacrifice,
> and washes me whiter than the snow, than the snow.
> My Jesus, God's precious sacrifice.[4]

> Extract taken from song 'It's Your blood' by Michael Christ

The assistant priest moved over to the lady lying on the floor and, with her 'prayer ministers' continuing to pray beside her, anointed her with oil (this anointing was a customary practice for those who were 'slain in the Spirit' at St.D). I noticed one 'prayer minister' praying in quite a demonstrative fashion, his fingers moving as if he were spinning fine thread upon his respondent, who appeared to be breathing heavily. Another 'prayer minister' prayed with his hand shaking above their respondent, a female vocalist from the music group. After a while she too collapsed on the floor, and then received an anointing with oil from the assistant priest. As the respondents continued to come forward, the priest directed unoccupied 'prayer ministers' to the waiting respondents as he maintained his presiding position.

When the song finished, the priest spoke again:

---

[4] *Mission Praise* [*MP*], No.351. Copyright © 1985 Mercy/Vineyard Publishing/ CopyCare music@copycare.com*.

As we feel that power of God the Spirit come upon us, sometimes it comes upon us like a surge; we just fall back and just rest in his Spirit. So don't worry that people are on the floor; it's just the Spirit moving and ministering to them. It doesn't happen all the time, but if it does happen don't worry if you see that. God is moving and ministering his love to his people.

The music group began to lead another song, which most of the congregation listened to because the song number had not been announced. The first lady to have collapsed now returned to her seat. Those who fell on the floor appeared to spend a number of minutes lying down after they had been anointed with oil, whilst their 'prayer ministers' continued to pray for them. The priest moved from behind the altar and crouched beside a lady waiting for prayer in the front row. He prayed for her, placing one hand upon her back and the other upon her hands folded in her lap.[5] There was a sound of weeping as she began to sob loudly, the impact of which was lessened by the background music. By now about a dozen respondents had been prayed for, and one or two people were still coming forward. It was noticeable that when prayer ended, the respondents appeared very grateful, and in some cases exchanged a hug or a kiss with their 'prayer ministers'.

As the ministry of prayer continued, the singing finished and the priest led the intercessions to gentle guitar accompaniment from the music group, having resumed his presiding position behind the altar. He used the suggested *A.S.B.* Rite 'A' intercession framework, praying extempore prayers for unity in the church (it was the Week of Prayer for Christian Unity), peace in the nations, the local community, the sick, and the departed. As he concluded the intercessions, one last individual respondent was receiving prayer. The priest then continued the service by introducing the Peace.

Administrators of 'Prayer Ministry'

'Prayer Ministry' Leader

Whenever 'prayer ministry' occurred in worship there was an identifiable leader who presided over the event. At St.D it was the priest, and in other churches the preacher would often lead because 'prayer ministry' always followed, and formed a response to, the sermon. The exceptions to this were the first visit to St.C, when at the 6.00pm service the service leader

---

[5]   I noticed this because it was not typical of the style of prayer in the 'prayer ministry'. The priest moved to her, touched her whilst praying and prayed on his own. He explained afterwards that he intervened because of the lady's particular pastoral needs.

took on the role, and the second visit to St.E when a member of the congregation was selected by the vicar on the basis of being particularly 'anointed' for the role.

There were a number of functions common to 'prayer ministry' leadership, the first of which was the invocation of the divine Spirit. Various forms of the so-called 'Come, Holy Spirit' prayer (a designation popularized by the practice of 'prayer ministry' at Vineyard Conferences) initiated all the observed instances of public 'prayer ministry'.[6] The prayer of the priest at St.D reflected the preceding act of Confession and, in his request for the Spirit to "speak to us" and "move among us", anticipated the forthcoming events of 'prayer ministry'. Other case study 'Come Holy Spirit' prayers often included a brief request that reflected the preceding sermon. For example, following a sermon on the Annunciation at St.C, in which the preacher had encouraged us to follow the example of Mary by saying 'yes' to God, the prayer was as follows:

> Lord, we ask you through your Son to send your Holy Spirit upon us in great power. We want you to come and do all that you want to do. Break the power of fear that is stopping us from saying 'yes' to God tonight. Come Holy Spirit.[7]

At St.B, following a sermon on the need for passionate intercession, the preacher prayed:

> Holy Spirit, you are so welcome, giver of life, author of life, pour down upon us. Let it come Lord. Let the spirit of grace and intercession come on people. Stir up our hearts, O God, for the honour of your name. Just pour into this place, Holy Spirit. Come, come Holy Spirit ... now! [8]

Having called upon the Spirit, the leader also presided over the events of 'prayer ministry'. This meant a clear visible presence, as the vicar of St.E explained when referring to a Wimber conference he had attended:

> I remember one occasion the Spirit spontaneously started moving at a big conference where John Wimber was on the stage. He stood there at the microphone and didn't say a word for twenty minutes. That was very strong leadership ... everyone in the place knew he was there and that he could step in if needs be.(LI)

---

[6] When 'prayer ministry' occurred privately (i.e. away from the gaze of the congregation), such as at St.F and in the morning Communion at St.C, there was no associated public prayer for the Spirit.

[7] 6.00pm service, visit 1.

[8] 6.30pm service, visit 2.

The position of 'prayer ministry' leaders was a very important element of their authority. At St.D, the priest had located himself in the westward presiding position at the altar, the place of authority in the worshipping assembly. The leaders at St.B, St.E and St.C established their authority by being located at the front of church, reflecting the 'platform' approach to positional authority in the example of Wimber quoted above.[9]

Exercising leadership was also dependant upon the sound privilege afforded by the use of microphones. For example, with the aid of a radio-microphone, the priest at St.D very effectively directed the events. His spoken contributions formed the transition points between each of the three main phases of the ritual: the offering of spoken 'words of knowledge', the 'prayer ministry' with background music, and 'prayer ministry' with intercessions. In the first phase, he was able to repeat the spoken contributions offered by members of the congregation, which had the two-fold purpose of confirming their validity (as he said in interview, "If I don't repeat it, it's because I don't think it is of God."[LI]) and including the hard-of-hearing. In the second phase he gave brief directions both to those who wished to receive prayer and to those who remained in the body of the congregation. He also became the interpreter of God's involvement in the 'prayer ministry', expressing God's desires ("God wants to meet you ... God wants you to know that there is acceptance of you") and reassuring the congregation of God's loving purposes through the ecstatic phenomena. We were not to worry when we saw respondents falling on the floor, because it was a sign that God "is moving and ministering his love to his people". Announcing 'words of knowledge', giving directions and offering theological interpretation were common elements of other 'prayer ministry' leadership. At St.B, St.C and St.E, I observed more developed strategies of linking ecstatic behaviour with God's activity. Leaders reinforced their explanations that such behaviour was the work of the Holy Spirit by using accompanying prayers of blessing, most commonly, "We bless you Lord, for what you are doing". 'Prayer ministry' leaders at St.B, St.C, and St.E were also observed to encourage ecstatic behaviour by the way they prayed for further divine action after the initial 'Come Holy Spirit' prayer. "Increase your presence", "increase your power", "more of your power", "increase what you are doing" were typical phrases that the leaders used to address God during the 'prayer ministry'.[10] With ecstatic behaviour thus

---

[9]   See Walker and Atherton's exposition of the authority of the 'platform' in their study of a Pentecostal Convention: 'An Easter Pentecostal Convention: The Successful Management of a "Time of Blessing" ' in *Sociological Review* (August 1971), 372-75. Of the case study churches, only St.B used a raised platform. On one occasion at St.C, the leader stayed in the pulpit to lead 'prayer ministry' (6.00pm service, visit 2).

[10]   Although this kind of prayer was most noticeable on my second 'post-Toronto' visits to St.B and St.E, it was not original to the 'Toronto Blessing'. I first observed it in

implicitly linked to the Spirit's presence, such prayers could also convey the leader's wish for an increase in ecstatic phenomena. In my second visit to St.E, this was illustrated by the contrast of leadership in the 11.00am and 6.30pm services: in the 11.00am service, where there was little ecstatic behaviour, the leader prayed repeatedly for an "increase" in God's power, whereas in the 6.30pm service, where there was a riot of ecstatic behaviour, there was need only for one request for an increase in power.

These prayers also represented a remarkably high degree of control consciously exercised by the leaders over the action of God. Perhaps the most striking example of this was the way the leader at St.C called upon the Spirit to begin the 'prayer ministry' at the 6.00pm service on the second visit: "Father, we give you permission to send your Spirit, to show us whatever you want to do tonight." The nature of this ritual function of leaders is comparable to the traditional role of shamans in ecstatic religions.[11] I.M. Lewis in his sociological study of ecstatic religions understands the main vocation of the shaman as being a 'master of spirits'.[12] Among the Siberian Tungus people from whose language the word shaman derives, the shamans are essential to each clan's well-being, controlling the clan's own ancestral spirits and other foreign spirits which, in their free state, are believed to be hostile and the source of diseases. For the Tungus, the core of a shaman's activity is the séance. It is within this ritual setting that the shaman demonstrates his control over the spirits by incarnating them in his own body. These 'mastered' spirits can thus be applied to fight off, or overcome, other hostile spirits which have not yet been rendered harmless by human incarnation. Shamans therefore regulate the intercourse between mankind and the gods. Lewis summarizes the role of shamans among the Tungus and other shamanistic religions:

> Through [the shaman] the otherwise unfettered power of the world beyond human society is harnessed purposefully and applied to minister to the needs of the community. If by incarnating spirits he embodies the most profound intrusion of the gods into the realm of human society, his mastering of these powers dramatically asserts man's claim to control his spiritual environment and to treat with the gods on terms of equality. In

the Ministry at Wimber conferences in the 1980s, and it was used at St.C, which had not been affected by the 'Toronto Blessing'.

[11] The similarities between shamanic religion and Pentecostalism have also been explored with relation to Korean Pentecostalism by Harvey Cox in *Fire From Heaven: The Rise of Pentecostal Spirituality and the Reshaping of Religion in the Twenty-first Century*, Ch.11: 'Shamans and Entrepreneurs: Primal Spirituality on the Asian Run'. Cox however does not specifically identify the element of control that is central to my comparison.

[12] I.M. Lewis, *Ecstatic Religion: An Anthropological Study of Spirit Possession and Shamanism*, 56.

the person of the shaman, man triumphantly proclaims his supremacy over elemental power which he has mastered and transformed into a socially beneficial force. And this hard-won control over the grounds of affliction is re-enacted in every shamanistic séance. This, rather than the repetition of any personal crisis, is the message of the séance. For at the séance the gods enter the shaman at his bidding, and are thus brought into direct confrontation with society and its problems. It is by dragging the gods down to his own level, as much by soaring aloft to meet them, that the shaman enables man to deal with his deities on an equal footing.[13]

From this description, we can also see how the 'prayer ministry' leaders demonstrated shaman-like qualities by being identifiable agents of control in an ecstatic religious setting which was designed to bring therapeutic relief to the gathered community. However, there were significant differences in the way that control was mediated, for, unlike the shaman, leaders exercised their mastery of the divine Spirit by simply addressing God in prayer. They deliberately did not abandon themselves to the action of the divine Spirit, but encouraged participants in the congregation to do so, and thus congregational ecstatic behaviour became the public authentication of the leaders' role. For example, on the much anticipated occasion of the 'prayer ministry' following the vicar's return from Toronto at St.E, the vicar announced to the congregation that he had chosen a leader who seemed to be especially 'anointed' for the task.[14] The vicar informed me afterwards that it was generally recognized that when that particular leader asked the Spirit to come "a lot of good things happened"(LI). Like a shaman, this 'prayer ministry' leader was recognized as someone who was skilled at regulating the divine-human intercourse in such a way that the community was blessed.

'Prayer Ministers'

Apart from St.A where public prayer for healing was administered by clergy, each case study church had teams of trained lay people who administered prayer to individual respondents during the 'prayer ministry', the so called 'prayer ministers'. The seriousness with which such ministry was undertaken was evident in the regular programmes of training for 'prayer ministers' and well-defined selection processes for members at each church. At St.D, for example, the 'prayer ministers' had been selected and trained by the priest with help from a neighbouring charismatic evangelical

---

[13] Lewis, *Ecstatic*, 189.

[14] 6.30pm 'Come Holy Spirit' Service, visit 2.

church and a team from St. Andrew's, Chorleywood.[15] Even at St.F, where there was no public 'prayer ministry', the 'prayer ministry' team's annual commissioning made it clear that the members' selection had been authorized by the P.C.C. and priest, and that it was understood that members would continue to be involved in further training.[16] At St.C and St.E the formalization of such ministry was evident in the special badges that were worn by 'prayer ministers', and like the music group, the 'prayer ministers' on duty would take part in a prayer meeting before a service (observed at St.C and St.D).

In all the instances of public 'prayer ministry' observed, the style of gesture used for prayer follows the Vineyard pattern of not touching the respondents but raising hands above or alongside them. The only exception to this was the Parish Eucharist at St.A where prayer for healing took a more conventional form with the priest laying hands upon respondents. Percy states that the Vineyard practice of not touching respondents is an accident of history which arose out of the particular climatic conditions in California. It was too hot and sweaty to lay hands on people in buildings that were not air-conditioned (Wimber's original meetings were often held in vacant warehouses), and so the practice of 'almost touching' developed and spread over the world through Wimber meetings, irrespective of climatic conditions.[17] Informants who were in the 'prayer ministry' team at St.D had rationalized the practice of not touching on the basis that it was immune to the accusation of pushing people over, and because it was less invasive for the respondent. These informants also explained that the reason they kept their eyes open was partly so that they could avert injury in the case of a respondent falling down, and partly so that they could see the Spirit at work. When asked what they were looking for, one informant replied:

It's very difficult to describe ... I mean it's not like the dove that came down on Christ; yet it is, because it's almost a gentleness on them. I see the manifestations of the Spirit, the shakings and the things, but it's not always like that. And with some people there's peace, and you can almost see it and touch it.(CI)

Literature written by charismatics on 'prayer ministry' makes similar observations. David Pytches, for instance, in his book *Come Holy Spirit,*

---

[15] Examples of material written by Anglican charismatics for use in training in 'prayer ministry' include: D. Pytches, *Come Holy Spirit: Learning How to Minister in Power*, P. Lawrence, *Signs and Blunders!* and R. Vaughan, *Saints for Healing.*

[16] St.F, visit 1.

[17] M. Percy, *Words, Wonders and Power: Understanding Contemporary Christian Fundamentalism and Revivalism*, 176, n.42.

describes typical signs of the Spirit as fluttering of the eyelashes, 'sheen' on the face, flushes around the neck, feeling of heat, shaking or trembling, deep breathing, weeping, laughing, falling and even bouncing on the floor and a general demeanour of peace and engagement with God.[18]

The main role of the 'prayer ministers' was to focus the action of the Spirit upon their respondents. This focusing of divine presence was ritualized by the bodily posture and gestures of the 'prayer ministers'. Hands that shake or 'spin' invisible thread give the impression of being channels, or conduits, of an invisible force. One of the informants at St.E described a family service where the children, acting as 'prayer ministers', took on the posture of a drain-pipe! "Drain-piping", as the informant called it, was when the 'prayer minister' extended a hand vertically to receive the Spirit 'from above', and the other hand horizontally towards the respondents. The Spirit is thus ritually channelled onto the respondents. This focusing is also demonstrated in the prayers of the 'prayer ministers', which reflected the language used by the 'prayer ministry' leader. They too were heard to pray for the Spirit to come upon their respondents, asking for an "increase" in power, and "blessing" God "for what he is doing". These prayers tended to be the standard ones used when the 'prayer minister' had no information about their respondent's situation, which occurred frequently when they moved among a crowd of respondents.[19] At St.D, where respondents offered information before prayer (as was also the case in the more private 'prayer ministry' at St.F and St.C's 10.30am service), the 'prayer ministers' were able to pray more specifically, although they nearly always began with a prayer calling upon the Spirit, and during the course of prayer used the standard prayers quoted above, particularly if ecstatic behaviour developed.[20] When a respondent exhibited ecstatic behaviour, such as falling to the ground, it became a dramatic demonstration of the way that 'prayer ministers' were perceived to focus the work of the divine Spirit. Indeed, in 'prayer ministry' settings where the 'prayer ministers' approached respondents who were already exhibiting ecstatic behaviour, the presence of the former usually resulted in an intensification of the behaviour.[21]

---

[18] Pytches, *Holy Spirit*, 142.

[19] Observed at St.C, St.B, and St.E.

[20] It is to my regret that the Outside Observer and I were not able to organize ourselves in a way that enabled one of us to become a respondent in 'prayer ministry'. The information on the prayer language was obtained from informants and also from occasions when 'prayer ministers' were in close proximity to us.

[21] This was observed at St.C, St.B and St.E.

The Congregation

The role of those who administer the 'prayer ministry' can be summarized as controlling and focusing the divine action. The congregation had the different role of being compliant recipients of the divine action. In this next section of the discussion, I analyse the way in which different ritual subjects and actions facilitated congregational responsiveness to the divine action in the 'prayer ministry'.

The Sermon

As we have seen in the overview of liturgies in Chapter 4, churches that had public 'prayer ministry' followed the standard Vineyard pattern of preceding the 'prayer ministry' with the sermon. One of the consequences of this was that the sermon played an important part in preparing for the 'prayer ministry'. In the instance described at St.D, the sermon that preceded 'prayer ministry' was on the theme of the burden of sin, repentance and forgiveness, which was reflected in the subsequent prayer of invocation of the Spirit, one of the 'words of knowledge' (C_1), and the song, 'It's Your blood that cleanses me'. Other sermons functioned by highlighting particular kinds of people who needed prayer. For example, following a sermon on evangelism at St.B, the leader of the 'prayer ministry' invited forward those who "longed to share their faith".[22] At a 6.00pm service at St.C,[23] the 'prayer ministry' leader applied aspects of his sermon on Jacob to those present. So, after calling upon the Spirit, he suggested to the standing congregation that there might be some present, who like Jacob, were manipulating others, wrestling with God, or needed to be reconciled to family. Similarly, after a Lent sermon on the nature of confession, repentance and forgiveness at St.E, the preacher in the 'prayer ministry' highlighted a series of spiritual problems that he had mentioned in his sermon: sexual sins, hatred towards neighbours, compromise of Christian witness, and the inability to forgive others.[24]

Sermons also functioned by instructing the congregation in how they should respond to the Spirit. In the sermon on the Annunciation at St.C, which, as we have seen, influenced the invocation of the Spirit, the preacher related Mary's example to the 'prayer ministry': "What are we doing when we say 'Come Holy Spirit'? We are saying 'yes' to God. Mary had no idea what was in store for her, but she was still prepared to say 'Yes, Lord. Do whatever you want to with my life'".[25] In recommending Mary as the paradigmatic respondent to 'prayer ministry', the preacher highlighted the

---

[22] 10.30am service, visit 1.
[23] Visit 2.
[24] 6.30pm service, visit 1.
[25] Extract from sermon; St.C, 6.00pm service, visit 1.

key quality of being open to God, which was defined by complete abandonment to God's purposes. Equally important was the ambiguity associated with these purposes: "Mary had no idea what was in store for her".[26] Within the context of the subsequent 'prayer ministry' this meant being open to *anything* that the Spirit might do to us, an attitude reinforced in a phrase used in the invocation of the Spirit, "We want you to come and do all that you want to do."[27] Confirmation that this open passivity was part of the public horizon mediated by the sermon and 'prayer ministry' came from the Outside Observer in interview after the service:

> I felt distinctly uncomfortable tonight because I didn't know what I was letting myself in for. There was a lot of talk about saying 'yes' to God, but the question that arose in my mind was that Christian commitment is a conscious commitment where we voluntarily and consciously, with our mind engaged, give ourselves to God. I felt uncomfortable because I thought that somebody might come round and pray for me and that I might be letting myself in for something for which I wasn't quite in control of my senses.(OI) [28]

It was anxious people like the Outside Observer that the 'prayer ministry' leader had included in her invocation of the Spirit: "Break the power of fear that is stopping us from saying 'yes' to God tonight."

'Words of Knowledge'

The practice of offering 'words of knowledge' and its management by leadership varied in case study worship. As we have seen, at St.D the words were both received and offered by the congregation within the 'prayer ministry'. At St.E they were received by the 'prayer ministry' team in their pre-service prayer meeting, and then announced in the 'prayer ministry'.[29] I witnessed a combination of both approaches at St.C, where the 'words of knowledge' offered were received in the pre-service prayer meeting and by members of the congregation within the 'prayer ministry'.[30] At St.B there were no 'words of knowledge' observed.

---

[26] This is of course a misreading of the Annunciation. The point of the angel's visit was that she should know what was in store for her, and then respond in faith!

[27] The full version of the invocatory prayer was quoted above in the section on the 'prayer ministry' leader.

[28] This, incidentally, is further confirmation of my earlier observation that the presence and prayer of 'prayer ministers' is associated with spontaneous ecstatic behaviour.

[29] Visit 2, all services.

[30] St.C, 6.00pm service, visit 1.

The function of the 'words of knowledge' within the 'prayer ministry' was to evoke response on the part of individual members of the congregation. They were offered with the understanding that they were revelations from God about the specific conditions of individuals present. Their divine origin is illustrated in the 'prayer ministry' narrated at St.D where they followed the invocation of the Spirit. The priest reinforced this belief by quietly speaking in tongues as a prelude to the words, and by repeating each contribution, which was understood by the congregation as his confirmation of their divine authenticity.

Appendix C of this book is a collection of the 'words of knowledge' recorded on church visits. The variety of communication styles used for the 'words of knowledge' that were recorded in the St.D 'prayer ministry' were typical of those offered in other churches. Two used the medium of image (C_3 and C_5), one with an element of interpretation (C_5), and the other without (C_3). One related to a specific bodily ailment (C_2). I was told by one of the 'prayer ministers' at St.D that this kind of word could be recognized through the experience of discomfort in an area of their body: "The word that I gave was that someone had something wrong with their toe, like an in-growing toe nail. I had excruciating pain in my toe which went as soon as I said the word."(CGI) This corresponds with advice given by David Pytches to 'prayer ministers': 'We may feel that another person is afflicted in some way by feeling an unaccustomed pain or strange physical sensation in our own body.'[31] The other word (C_1) identified with a burden of sin, and then promised liberation. The common element of all these contributions was the recipient's identification with the condition of someone present in the congregation (all but C_3 make this explicit). The odd-one-out is C_4 which appears to be more characteristic of what informants would call a prophecy, in that it addressed a corporate experience that may well have been the experience of that congregation.

The public offering of the 'words of knowledge' encouraged those individuals who recognized themselves in the words to believe that God had turned his face to them, was aware of their condition, and wanted to 'minister' to them (God was always understood to be the chief minister in the 'prayer ministry' observed). Although the means of communication had been public, its impact was highly personal and individual; not even those who received the words knew the identity of those whom they were describing. Thus 'words of knowledge' become a powerful means to encourage individuals to avail themselves of prayer, as each potential respondent became aware of both God's intimate knowledge of their needs and also of his desire to minister to those needs.[32] And so, as witnessed

---

[31] Pytches, *Holy Spirit*, 101.

[32] Percy's concern is that they may be an abuse of power by not evoking a genuinely free response from the respondent (*Words, Wonders, and Power*, 23-4). His concern is

above, the priest at St.D encouraged his congregation for the forthcoming
'prayer ministry': "We want people to be able to respond to what God may
be saying to us this morning and know that the Lord will respond to your
longing of him right where you are too."

This focus upon the individual is typical of revivalism. As Andrew
Walker points out, revivalism, by definition, involves the notion of like-
minded crowds as the matrix within which God visits his people individually.[33] In 'prayer ministry', it is the individual within the crowd of the
gathered worshipping assembly who is the beneficiary of God's action; the
'words of knowledge', the intimate devotional songs, and the personal
attention of 'prayer ministers' all focus upon the individual. On the
occasion when congregational chairs were cleared to the side of the hall at
St.E in preparation for the 'prayer ministry', the last visible symbol of
corporate identity was removed.[34] An empty space had been created within
which the individual, within the context of a crowd, was free to express
their ecstatic self and, as participants understood it, receive God's blessing.

From observation at other churches, on the occasions when a 'prayer
ministry' functioned without 'words of knowledge' there were other factors
encouraging congregational response, such as the sermon, a testimony[35] or
the heightened corporate expectancy generated by the 'Toronto Blessing'.
In the 'prayer ministry' at St.B and St.E on the second post-Toronto visits
there were no 'words of knowledge' at St.B, and those given at St.E seemed
to have been eclipsed by the overwhelming sense that the 'Blessing' was
for everyone. As already mentioned, the 6.30pm service at St.E was
particularly significant in this respect because it marked the return of the
vicar from a week's visit to the Vineyard church in Toronto. This special
occasion generated an immense amount of corporate expectation, as was
evident in the comments of the group of informants after the service:

I think there was a sense of expectancy, because with the vicar having
been to Toronto this week, you sensed people coming hungry with that
expectancy that God was going to do something tonight.(CGI)

Bernard [the worship leader] was lively tonight wasn't he? The moment
he started talking you knew that he was expecting things to happen
tonight.(CGI)

---

valid, but just as significant for my purpose is his recognition of the power inherent in
this mode of communication within the ritual context of 'prayer ministry'.

[33] A. Walker, *Telling the Story: Gospel, Mission and Culture*, 64.

[34] 6.30pm 'Come Holy Spirit' Service, visit 2.

[35] The one occasion a testimony was used was at St.B, 6.30pm service, visit 2, when
a member of the congregation was invited by the preacher to relate a recent healing she
had received through 'prayer ministry'.

A lot of people came that I haven't seen for a while. They had come from other churches, so the news must have got around, mustn't it, about Toronto? I think it shows that people are hungry for the Spirit.(CGI)

The 'prayer ministry' that evening was characterized by the indiscriminate way in which members of the congregation were moved to ecstatic behaviour. As one informant commented, "God seems to have been moving all over the room in all kinds of ways tonight."(CGI) Under circumstances like this, the role of 'words of knowledge' had become subsidiary to the reality that all members of the congregation were potential respondents to the divine Spirit.

Musical Accompaniment

The music groups provided a background accompaniment to the 'prayer ministry' at St.B, St.D and St.E. Unlike their role in the 'time of worship', the music groups were no longer the focus for congregational gaze, which had now shifted to the 'prayer ministry'. As a worship leader at St.B said, "During the 'prayer ministry' the band relax because they feel that they are not 'on show'; the focus is off the band and upon what God is doing."(LGI) Although some of the songs at St.D were announced, songs sung during the 'prayer ministry' at St.E and St.B were not provided on the O.H.P. screen, which was a further indication of the music groups' background function.

Returning to the social analogy of the discotheque already referred to in Chapter 5, the music groups fulfilled a role that is analogous to the DJ. Unlike live pop performers, the DJs tend to be unseen, tucked away in their mixing booths, and Thornton comments that as cultural figures they are known by name rather than face. Through this 'face-less' interaction with the dancing crowd, the DJ's chief role is to construct a musical experience that communicates the authentic 'buzz', 'vibe' or 'atmosphere' of disco culture.[36] Similarly the significance of the musical contribution to the 'prayer ministry' lies in the atmosphere mediated by the music and the accompanying song lyrics. Virtually all the 'prayer ministry' songs were characteristic of those used in the devotional climax of the 'time of worship'. Their soft tone, slow rhythms and ballad-style melodies conveyed an intimate atmosphere, as reviewed in Chapter 5. This intimate atmosphere signalled the closeness of God, and therefore reinforced the reality of God's presence initiated ritually by the invocation of the Spirit. They also facilitated congregational response by suggesting that in such an intimate context, respondents are able to relax and abandon themselves in the hands of God. The lyrics of the songs suggest this by using a variety of dominant metaphors or images that assure participants of security. One song used in

---

[36] S. Thornton, *Club Cultures: Music, Media and Subcultural Capital*, 58-66.

'prayer ministry' at St.B, St.D and St.E proclaimed God to be the 'Faithful One' upon whom the worshipper could depend.[37] Other songs portrayed worshippers as children who find security in a fatherly God. At St.C, although there was no music during the 'prayer ministry', the leader prepared us for the invocation of the Spirit by playing a recorded song which included the following refrain:

> Father me, for ever You'll father me;
> and in Your embrace I'll be for ever secure.
> I love the way You father me,
> I love the way You father me.[38]

Extract taken from the song 'Father of the fatherless' by Graham Kendrick

A song with a similar theme was sung at St.E during 'prayer ministry':

> Show me, dear Lord, how You see me in Your eyes,
> so that I can realize Your great love for me.
> Teach me, O Lord, that I am precious in Your sight,
> that as a father loves his child, so You love me.
>
> I am Yours because You have chosen me.
> I'm Your child because You've called my name,
> and Your steadfast love will never change;
> I will always be Your precious child.[39]

Extract taken from the song 'Precious child' by Andy Park

The worship leader at St.E said that by singing such songs about the Fatherhood of God we, as his children, were saying that we were "wanting to allow him to do what he wants to do in our lives"(LGI). That abandonment is made attractive because as worshippers we were trusting children who knew we were 'precious' to our heavenly Father.

A romantic conception of Jesus was also used to the same effect, as illustrated by the following song which was used at St.E during the 'prayer ministry'. Note how the beloved's embrace mediates a sense of security:

---

[37] 'Faithful One, so unchanging', *New Mission Praise* [*NMP*], No.27.

[38] From *NMP*, No.108. Copyright © 1992 Make Way Music*. All rights reserved. International copyright secured. Used by permission. St.C, 6.00pm service, visit 2.

[39] *Songs of Fellowship* [*SF*] (1994) No.147. Copyright © 1989 Mercy/Vineyard Publishing/CopyCare music@copycare.com*. St.E, 6.30pm service, visit 2.

I sing a simple song of love to my Saviour, to my Jesus.
I'm grateful for the things You've done,
my loving Saviour, O precious Jesus.
My heart is glad that You've called me Your own,
there's no place I'd rather be, then in Your arms of love,
in Your arms of love,
holding me still, holding me near in Your arms of love
holding me still, holding me near
holding me still, holding me near in Your arms of love.[40]

Extract taken from the song 'Arms of love' by Craig Musseau

A similar sentiment is conveyed through John Wimber's 'Spirit Song', which encourages the essential qualities of a respondent, such as submissiveness, trust, and receptiveness:

O let the Son of God enfold you
With His Spirit and His love,
Let Him fill your heart and satisfy your soul.
O let him have the things that hold you,
And His Spirit, like a dove,
Will descend upon your life and make you whole.

Jesus, O Jesus,
Come and fill Your lambs;
Jesus, O Jesus,
Come and fill Your lambs.

O come and sing this song with gladness,
as your hearts are filled with joy;
lift your hands in sweet surrender to His name.
O give Him all your tears and sadness,
give Him all your years of pain,
and you'll enter into life in Jesus' name.[41]

Extract taken from the song 'Spirit song' by John Wimber

---

[40] *NMP* No.57. Copyright © 1991 Mercy/Vineyard Publishing/CopyCare music@copycare.com*. St.E, 6.30pm service, visit 2.

[41] *MP* (1990) No.502. Copyright © 1979 Mercy/Vineyard Publishing/CopyCare music@copycare.com*. This was sung at St.C, 6.00pm service, visit 1 and St.F visit 1, but not in the context of 'prayer ministry'.

The song invites the worshipper, cast as needing to be 'whole', to entrust their emotional pain to Jesus. In so doing they become the recipients of the Holy Spirit (the descent of the Spirit 'like a dove' is consonant with the ritual of the invocation of the Spirit). The reference to Jesus 'enfolding' the worshipper conveys a sense of security, enabling them to 'surrender' themselves into his hands. Percy argues that this is typical of Vineyard songs which function by recapitulating the nineteenth-century Gospel hymns' rhetoric of passivity and passion: worshippers surrender them-selves, and especially their emotions, and in return are the passive recipients of God's love and power.[42] This stress on emotional, or 'inner' healing reflects John Goldingay's remark that 'nearly all the charismatic "healing" one comes across is a matter of the resolution of interwoven spiritual-emotional-physical questions rather than the miraculous reversal of purely physical illness such as makes the medics scratch their heads in astonishment.'[43]

The abandonment of the respondent was also represented in the text of songs that encouraged the malleability of the worshipper, a common metaphor being that of the potter and clay. In 'Jesus, You are changing me' Jesus is the potter and the worshipper is the clay who is willing to let Jesus have his way.[44] The Pentecostal chorus 'Spirit of the living God', that has been used in Charismatic Renewal since the 1960s, is the classic expression of this malleability, of "allowing God to do whatever he wants to do" in the respondents' lives:

> Spirit of the living God,
> fall afresh on me;
> Spirit of the living God,
> fall afresh on me;
> break me, melt me,
> mould me, fill me;
> Spirit of the living God,
> fall afresh on me.[45]

Extract taken from the song 'Spirit of the Living God' by Daniel Iverson (d.1977)

---

[42] Percy, *Words*, 62-8. Percy's discussion makes similar points to mine with regard to the textual function of Vineyard songs.

[43] J. Goldingay, 'Charismatic Spirituality: Some Theological Reflections', *Theology* XCIX (May/June 1996), 789:182.

[44] 'Jesus, You are changing me', *MP* (1990) No.389; St.D visit 2. Similarly, 'Change my heart, O God', *MP* (1990) No.69; St.F visit 2.

[45] *MP* (1990) No.613. Copyright © 1963 Birdwing Music/EMI Christian Music Publishing/CopyCare music@copycare.com*.

The 'Prayer Ministry' Space and Respondent Posture

I observed a variety of ways in which 'prayer ministry' and its respondents related to liturgical space. Often, respondents were invited to enter a designated area for the 'prayer ministry'. This could mean moving during the course of a service to a public area in front of congregational seating, (St.D and St.B) or to the more private setting of a side chapel (St.F and St.C's 10.30am service). Alternatively, one could choose to stay after a service's conclusion when the main body of the church became the designated area. At St.E, for example, between the sermon and the 'prayer ministry' at the 'Come Holy Spirit' Service there was an interlude during which congregational chairs were moved to the side of the hall.[46] Some of the congregation chose to leave, whilst those who remained were invited to stand in the cleared space as the Spirit was called upon. Similarly, after the end of an evening service at St.C, people gathered in the front pews of the nave for the 'prayer ministry'.[47] However, there were also occasions when respondents did not need to move to a designated area because the whole assembly became the 'prayer ministry' area. This occurred at St.C (6.00pm service, visit 2), St.B (6.30pm service, visit 2), and St.E (6.30pm service, visit 1 and 11.00am service, visit 2). On these occasions the Spirit was called upon the whole congregation during the course of the service, enabling my participant observation to occur spatially within 'prayer ministry'. On two of these occasions (St.B and St.E at 11.00am) individuals could also respond by coming to the front for prayer, usually for specified reasons that had been announced by the leader.[48]

The spatial arrangement of the public 'prayer ministry' was an important factor in determining the character of congregational response. First, when 'prayer ministry' took place within a designated public area within the assembly, the physical movement of individuals into that space symbolized their spiritual response, rather like an 'altar call' at a revival meeting. Secondly, on those occasions when 'prayer ministry' was conducted in an area clear of obstructions, such as the cleared hall at St.E or the front area at St.B and St.D, informants suggested this was a definite advantage both for the 'prayer ministers', who could move freely amongst the respondents, and also for the respondents themselves, who were relieved of the worry of falling on a chair or pew or even someone else if they were to fall to the floor.[49] At St.E, the clearing of congregational chairs was viewed as a

---

[46] 6.30pm, visit 2.

[47] Visit 1 only.

[48] At St.E, for example, those who had been identified as having prophetic and healing gifts came to the front for prayer, as did, subsequently, those who were seeking physical healing.

[49] The vicar at St.E informed me that the Vineyard Toronto church had taken to positioning the respondents in rows six and a half feet apart so as to avoid people

means of enhancing greater 'blessing', as the vicar explained:

> Some of our housegroups went to a local Christian fellowship where they were holding Toronto style meetings and most of them ended up on the floor and got blessed and so on. When I started saying things like "Ellie Mumford[50] has been here but not much is happening. Why do you think it is?", they said that it's because you don't move the chairs back, that being the one thing that we did not do that this local fellowship did ... so when people here began saying "we think you should move the chairs back", I thought, "Alright, we'll move the chairs back", and I think they are probably right.(LGI)

Such an approach is typical of the pragmatism and technique of revivalism, which Susan White summarizes as an approach which presupposes that 'whatever *worked* was necessarily right'.[51]

The posture of respondents within the 'prayer ministry' area was also a significant reflection of their role. As we observed at St.D, and at all other occasions of 'prayer ministry', many respondents adopted a receptive posture with their hands held out and palms facing upwards, a practice that symbolized the individual's openness to the divine Spirit.[52] It was also significant that respondents always *stood* for public 'prayer ministry'.[53] The priest at St.D rationalized the practice of standing, as opposed to sitting or kneeling, on the basis that it made respondents more vulnerable to ecstatic behaviour, and therefore more reliant upon and open to the Spirit. I became aware of this vulnerability when participating in 'prayer ministry' at St.C. Along with others gathered in the front nave seats, I had stood for the invocation of the Spirit at the invitation of the 'prayer ministry' leader. In the subsequent 'prayer ministry' I felt uneasy all the while I was standing, half expecting to fall over in an involuntary manner as one or two near me had done. Eventually I sat down and from that moment felt secure and in control; existentially, I had discovered that standing was indeed a way of

---

hurting one another. This is an interesting example of a Weberian 'routinization of charisma'.

[50] As noted in my historical overview, Elleanor Mumford received fame by being associated with the outbreak of the 'Toronto Blessing' in this country. In May 1994 she was responsible for introducing the 'Blessing' to Holy Trinity, Brompton, which then attracted the first media coverage of the phenomenon.

[51] S.J. White, *Christian Worship and Technological Change*, 96.

[52] I can remember attending a Vineyard conference in which we were specifically encouraged to hold out our hands in this receptive posture in preparation for the leader's invocation of the Spirit.

[53] The one exception to this was when the congregation remained seated at St.E, 6.30pm service, visit 1. The vicar admitted that this was a "half-blown" attempt at a 'prayer ministry'.

making oneself an available candidate for public ecstatic behaviour.

Summary of Congregational Response as a Romantic Narrative

James Hopewell, in his work on the social and religious nature of Christian congregations, *Congregations: Stories and Structures*, identifies spiritual worldviews that correspond to Northrop Frye's four narrative settings: comic tales, romantic tales, tragic tales and ironic tales.[54] The charismatic Christian, so Hopewell argues, inhabits a universe that is dominated by a romantic narrative. According to Frye, a romantic tale typically involves a quest for a desirable object (such as the beloved in gothic novels) in which the hero or heroine leaves familiar surroundings and embarks on a dangerous journey in which strange things happen, but in the end gains a priceless reward for their endeavours. When coming to terms with diagnosed cancer, Hopewell observed that charismatic friends encouraged him to leave behind his domestic religious routine and wholeheartedly yield to the promise of God's healing love. According to these friends, God's Spirit would fill and empower Hopewell on a spiritual adventure in which he would persist in the face of evil and discouragement and eventually receive the gift of healing.

Hopewell's romantic narrative is a helpful and insightful way of inter-preting the nature of congregational response promoted by the public horizon of 'prayer ministry'. Making oneself available for 'prayer ministry' was the beginning of an adventure in which one moved from the routine into an exciting though uncertain world. This was represented by the movement to the 'prayer ministry' area from one's seat in the congregation, or the decision to stay after the regular service for 'prayer ministry'.

There were a variety of ways in which encouragement was given to make this journey. Through sermons and 'words of knowledge', the invitation was given with a voice which was received as authentically divine; God was the one calling respondents to a spiritual encounter. One preacher at St.E used the story of Peter walking on the water to prepare the congregation for 'prayer ministry'.[55] This is a story that has many of the elements of a romantic narrative: Peter leaves the routine of his boat and embarks on the dangerous journey of walking on the water towards Jesus. For a time Peter becomes a typical romantic hero, the character in Frye's romantic tales who 'moves in a world in which the ordinary laws of nature are suspended: prodigies of courage and endurance unnatural to us are natural to him'.[56] In the 'prayer ministry' following this sermon, the preacher encouraged us to be like Peter and be courageous enough to "step

---

[54] N. Frye, *The Anatomy of Criticism*.

[55] Matthew 14:22-33. Used at the 11.00am service, visit 2.

[56] Frye, *Anatomy* 33, quoted in Hopewell, *Congregation: Stories and Structures*, 59.

out of the boat" and come to the front for 'prayer ministry'. A similar call to adventure was observed in a 'picture' offered during the 'prayer ministry' at the 'Come Holy Spirit' Service at St.E.[57] The 'prayer ministers' had already begun to move among the standing respondents in the hall when a thirteen-year-old girl walked to the leader's microphone:

> I was given a picture by God [the microphone is turned up to drown the noise of a laughing man] and it was of a rushing river and it was so blue and clear, and on the bottom there were shiny pebbles that you could see and they would sparkle in your eyes. And in the river there were just so many people with their arms waving high up to the sky with smiles on their faces. And there were a few people on the riverbank and they looked so sad and they were looking into the river, and they were so scared that if they jumped in they would drown. And I just feel that some people here tonight, they are those people on the riverbanks, and they are so scared that they are going to drown. But they are not, because the river is Jesus Christ [the girl almost bursts into tears]. [58]

Leader: Thank you Tina. If that's you [addressing congregation], jump in!

The people on the banks of the river were people like myself, observing the 'prayer ministry' from the side of the cleared hall (as mentioned, the congregational chairs had been moved to the side of the hall). We were called to leave the 'sadness' of our routine and abandon ourselves to the 'blessing' and adventure of being in the river (the 'prayer ministry' in the middle of the hall), depicted in the beauty of the pebbles and the joy of those in the river. Our fear of losing control ("drowning") in this uncertain world was confronted with the reality that we were placing ourselves into God's hands ("the river is Jesus Christ"), who was the source of our security, as the song lyrics continually reminded us. Hopewell comments that God's constancy and faithfulness is the source of integrity in the charismatic world in which the self launches out towards God in exciting adventure.

Having started the romantic journey, the respondent waits upon the Spirit, standing in a receptive posture, open to "whatever God might want to do". In some cases, nothing observable happened. But for many respondents, strange things began to happen. The events during the 'prayer ministry' at St.D narrated above were relatively routine and orderly

---

[57] 6.30pm service, visit 2.

[58] It was interesting to note that the vicar had made a connection between the Toronto Blessing and the River Jordon in the sermon earlier in the service: Naaman the Syrian, travelling to the Jordan River was the archetypal pilgrim travelling to Toronto to receive the 'Blessing'.

compared with the riot of ecstatic behaviour observed in the post-Toronto visits at St.B and St.E. Bodies not only fell to the ground but shook and twitched as if in an uncontrolled convulsion. Some ran on the spot and others bounced up and down as if they were on a pogo stick. There was uncontrollable laughter (ranging from polite giggles to hysterical fits of mirth), wailing and weeping. Some made animal sounds, the most common being roaring like lions.[59] However, even in this strange world there was reassurance from 'prayer ministry' leaders for respondents and those who were observing: "Don't worry about the bouncing or shaking or things like that ... that's the work of the Holy Spirit (St.E)"; "Let's keep our attention on Jesus. He's the Lord who comes to bless us and refresh us ... don't focus on any of the phenomena things that people may be doing. We bless you Lord (St.B)."

The reward for embarking on the adventure of 'prayer ministry' was primarily spiritual empowerment. At St.D, for example, the priest recommended the ministry to respondents as a means of gaining assurance of God's love (see above). "God is going to do good things tonight" the 'prayer ministry' leader at St.C confidently affirmed. Wimber's 'Spirit Song', referred to above, promises an infilling of the Spirit that brings wholeness and satisfaction to the soul. One informant at St.B explained that when she goes to the front to receive 'prayer ministry' she visualizes a woman putting out empty pots that are then filled with the 'oil' of the Holy Spirit. Other informants spoke about the benefits in terms of a deep sense of peace, or a cleansing from guilt, or being filled with a sense of God's love. All this confirms Hopewell's observation that in the world of the charismatic, 'the floodgates of God's blessing are thrown open wide to those who venture beyond religious convention'.[60]

The Divine Action: God as 'Live Performer'

Having analysed the respective roles of those who administer and receive the 'prayer ministry', I turn now to consider the relationship of God to 'prayer ministry'. There were a variety of images used of God, who was variously described in active terms such as 'ministering to', 'moving among', or 'visiting' the congregation, or by attributes such as 'presence' or 'power'. Whilst acknowledging work that has already been done on these images, most notably Martyn Percy's work on 'power' within the context of Wimber's Vineyard worship,[61] I wanted to find a metaphor that would do

---

[59] One young man I sat behind at St.B shook up and down with increasing intensity as the service progressed. When the 'prayer ministry' began, he bent over double as if in great pain, fell on his knees, and let out enormous roars (6.30pm service, visit 2).
[60] Hopewell, *Congregation*, 78.
[61] Percy, *Words*, 60-81.

justice to the performative dynamics of God's activity that was mediated in 'prayer ministry'. Here I return to Thornton's notion of the 'live performer', understood in three categories of presence, visibility, and spontaneity, and in this section I will demonstrate how each of these categories can be adequately applied to the divine involvement in 'prayer ministry'.

God's Presence

The invocation of the Holy Spirit that marks the beginning of 'prayer ministry' also defined the character of 'prayer ministry' as an arena where God's presence is revealed. The mode of activity of the Spirit, who was understood as the bearer of divine presence, was represented in a number of ways. In the language of 'prayer ministry' leaders, the Spirit was described as "filling", or being "poured upon", "coming upon" or "resting upon" respondents. The point of such metaphors was to signal the reality of the divine made present in and among the worshipping assembly. As we have seen, in calling upon the Spirit the 'prayer ministry' leaders also assured participants of the reality of the divine presence, thanking God for his presence and on occasions asking for an increase in its intensity. The devotional style of background music also created an intimacy of presence which was reinforced by the physical presence of the 'prayer ministers' to individual respondents and the 'words of knowledge', which conveyed God's intimate knowledge of individuals present.

God's Visibility

The fact that most instances of 'prayer ministry' were in public view is a significant phenomenon, illustrative of a preference for the public display of ecstatic behaviour. This contrasts with classical Pentecostal tradition, which has maintained a boundary between public worship and private ecstatic religious expression on the basis of the Pauline injunction that worship should be conducted 'decently and in order' (1 Cor.14:40). This can be illustrated by Walker and Atherton's ethnographic study of a classic Pentecostal Convention, referred to earlier. They observed that at the end of each main Convention meeting there was the opportunity for individuals to seek baptism in the Spirit or some other spiritual advancement, usually in response to an appeal from the preacher. Respondents would identify themselves publicly by walking forward to the platform, and then after a prayer they were ushered into a smaller back room. It was in this comparatively private context that they were free to 'get to grips with the Lord' in highly demonstrative ways; some cried and moaned, others chanted in tongues. Walker and Atherton comment that in this way 'the emotional expression of this self-selected group was channelled out of the main service, and did not disrupt the organized event'.[62]

The Wimber ideology however, reinforced by the 'Toronto Blessing' gave a specifically theological rationale for the public display of ecstatic behaviour: it was the evidence of God's activity among the assembly. Thus bodies that fell to the ground in the 'prayer ministry' were signs of the power of God at work, as we were assured, for example, in the 'prayer ministry' at St.D by the priest's public explanation, and by the action of sacramental anointing of those who had fallen to the floor. This was also reflected in the way participants named the phenomenon as being 'slain in the Spirit' ('falling under the Power' is another expression used in charismatic literature[63]). As I have discussed, 'prayer ministers' were encouraged to pray with their eyes open as they watched for somatic signs of God's Spirit at work in their respondents. Songs celebrated a visibly active God, such as the petition in the following Vineyard song refrain:

Show Your power, O Lord our God;
show Your power, O Lord our God,
our God![64]

Extract taken from the song 'Show Your power' by Kevin Prosch

This attention to the visible activity of God was also illustrated in shift of congregational gaze away from leadership at the front to the public 'prayer ministry' area which in all cases observed was situated within what could be termed 'congregational space' (when 'prayer ministry' occurred in front of congregational seating, the areas used were physically and symbolically distinct from the leadership space occupied by music groups and service leaders, and by all appearances were an extension of congregational space). This shift is analogous to the contrast between the social arrangements of the live 'gig' and the discotheque. Unlike the stage of a live performance, in a disco it is the dance-floor that becomes the focus for gaze. As Thornton comments, 'In the absence of visually commanding performers the gaze of the audience has turned back upon itself. Watching and being seen are key pleasures of discotheques.'[65] Similarly, in contrast to the 'time of worship' where congregational gaze focused upon the music groups, in 'prayer ministry' the congregational gaze turned in upon itself and focused upon the 'prayer ministry' area. Despite the occasional encouragement from leaders not to concentrate on the ecstatic phenomena, it was clear that there

---

[62] Walker and Atherton, 'Easter Pentecostal Convention', 382.

[63] For example, Pytches, *Holy Spirit*, Ch.18: 'Falling under the Power of God'.

[64] From *SF* (1994) No.48. Copyright © 1991 Mercy/Vineyard Publishing/CopyCare music@copycare.com*. St.B, 10.30am service, visit 1 and St.E, 11.00am service, visit 1.

[65] Thornton, *Club*, 65.

were a significant number of individuals within the congregation who, like me, were simply watching what was going on.

This emphasis upon the visibility of God's activity is by no means new to charismatic worship. Joy Hillyer in her study of a Cambridge charismatic church in the early 1970s observed that the prayers of members of the congregation frequently expressed the desire to "see the Lord really working in our midst", a desire that was satiated by the public use of charismatic gifts.[66] This charismatic expectation has been revived through Wimber's conferences and by theological argument in his addresses, books and teaching tapes.[67] Visibility has been a crucial aspect of Wimber's presentation of the 'signs and wonders' that accompany the preaching of the Kingdom of God. Their purpose, as Wimber writes, is to *'demonstrate the kingdom of God'.*[68] Wimber insists that the power of God is a visible, tangible phenomenon, and so in keeping with this, 'prayer ministry' has been promoted as a kind of showroom of God's activity. Here again we are reminded of one of the defining aspects of revival culture, succinctly summarized by Susan White:

> For the later revivalists, salvation was a commodity to be 'promoted', and worship was the principal 'showroom' in which that commodity was marketed and sold (as well as the means of production by which that salvation was 'manufactured').[69]

God's Spontaneity

The spontaneity of God's action, like that of a live performer, is linked with notions of liveness, authenticity and excitement. One of the key metaphors describing this spontaneity is the 'movement' of God among the gathered assembly, as can be illustrated by the following two comments from informants:

> We've come to recognize that God does move among us, and because of that we have visitors now at our new monthly evening service. People come and they recognize that God is working, that God is alive. People do

---

[66] J.V Hillyer, *Liturgical Change in Cambridge: Attitudes to Liturgy with Special Reference to Charismatic Gifts*, 117.

[67] For example, *Power Evangelism: Signs and Wonders Today*; *Power Healing*; *Power Points* (manual with tapes).

[68] Wimber, *Power Evangelism*, 95 (italics original).

[69] White, *Christian Worship*, 96. In relation to this comment, it was interesting to observe participants at a conference on the 'Toronto Blessing' in 1996 ('Waves Of The Spirit', Bournemouth, February 1996) being encouraged to introduce the 'Blessing' to their sponsoring churches through the visual medium of the recorded videos of the conference.

recognize that we have got something special here, because God moves.(CGI)[70]

I find it exciting here. There is a real sense that God is on the move and that he has lots for us to do. It's fun!(CI)[71]

The metaphor was also present in extempore language used by 'prayer ministry' leaders. For example, in his invocatory prayer recorded above, the priest at St.D asked that the Holy Spirit would come and "move among us now". Songs used the same language:

Move among us now,
come reveal Your power,
show Your presence, acceptance,
move among us now.[72]

Extract taken from the song 'As we seek Your face' by Dave Bilbrough

As Your Spirit moves upon me now,
You meet my deepest need.[73]

Extract taken from the song 'I worship You' by Carl Tuttle

Holy Spirit, we welcome You.
Holy Spirit, we welcome You.
Move among us with holy fire,
as we lay aside all earthly desires.[74]

Extract taken from the song 'Holy Spirit, we welcome You' by Chris Bowater

The appropriate respondent posture towards this movement of the divine Spirit was 'openness' to God. As we have seen, in allowing God "to do whatever he wants to do", respondents enacted Hopewell's romantic narrative in which they engaged in a ritual adventure characterized by an abandonment to the spontaneous divine movement. This emphasis upon the

---

[70] St.D

[71] St.B

[72] From *SF* (1991) No.30. Copyright © 1990 Thankyou Music*. St.F, visit 1. Notice how this song also reflects the theme of God's visibility.

[73] From *MP* (1990) No.271. Copyright © 1982 Mercy/Vineyard Publishing/ CopyCare music@copycare.com*. St.F visit 1 and St.A visit 2.

[74] From *SF* (1991) No. 188. Copyright © 1986 Sovereign Lifestyle Music Ltd*. St.A, visit 2.

divine spontaneity also led to a characteristically open-ended texture of time in 'prayer ministry', which explains the preference we have seen at St.B, St.C and St.E for placing 'prayer ministry' at the end of a service where, in theory, leaders could afford the luxury of letting 'prayer ministry' go on for as long as was needed. The post-Toronto visits to St.B and St.E were characterized by lengthy 'prayer ministries', which appeared to have no proper public ending.

It also became apparent that one of the main ways in which participants interpreted God's movement was in terms of its effect upon the human body. As we have seen, sensations within the body were perceived as an authentic means of receiving revelation from God in the exercise of 'words of knowledge'. At a 'prayer ministry' at St.E, the leader associated bodily sensations with the divine gifting of individual respondents. He told us that those being "anointed" with a prophetic gift had a "tingling on the tongue, around the lips, or the mouth" and those with a healing gift would be able to see "white blobs" appear on their hands.[75] Typically, participants saw ecstatic somatic behaviour as a "manifestation" of God's movement among respondents, which led in some cases to the search for interpretations of such activity. For example, the leader at a 'prayer ministry' at St.B identified the phenomenon of groaning amongst the congregation with the "labour-pains" associated with the birth of a deeper and more passionate form of intercession.[76] An informant at St.B told me how in one 'prayer ministry' he found himself boxing, which as well as reminding him of the Pauline athletic metaphors describing discipleship, spoke to him of how God was restoring his masculine identity. The literature written by participants of the 'Toronto Blessing' is full of similar attempts to see in somatic expression a prophetic message, either for the individuals concerned, or for the wider church. For example, Michael Mitton, when he was the Director of Anglican Renewal Ministries, used the experience of falling onto the floor during 'prayer ministry' at the New Wine summer convention as a way of interpreting the spirituality of the 'Toronto Blessing'.[77] However, for most participants interviewed, interpretation of ecstatic behaviour was unnecessary; for them it was enough to believe that such behaviour was a sign that God was working and moving among the assembly.

In conclusion, I have suggested that the categories of presence, visibility

---

[75] He informed us that the plurality of 'blobs' meant that the respondents had more than one gift of healing, but he failed to explain what he meant by that! In the event, three people identified themselves as 'prophetic' and six as 'healers'; 11.00am service, visit 2.

[76] 6.30pm Visit 2.

[77] M. Mitton, *The Heart of Toronto: Exploring the Spirituality of the 'Toronto Blessing'*.

and spontaneity characterize God as the 'live performer' in the 'prayer ministry'. Whilst for the sake of exposition each category has been analysed separately, clearly they are inter-dependent and interpret each other: God's movement is discerned when he is perceived to be present and visible, the arena within which God is visible is where he is present in spontaneous acts, and God's presence issues in visible spontaneous events.

A song that summarizes this understanding of the divine involvement in 'prayer ministry' is 'Be still, for the presence of the Lord', which, although not sung in case study worship, is one of the more well known charismatic songs. Its composer, David Evans, wrote it with the purpose of evoking a sense of awe, wonder and mystery.[78] It also celebrates a God who is present (verse 1), visible (verse 2) and spontaneously at work (verse 3) among the gathered assembly:

> Be still, for the presence of the Lord, the Holy One is here;
> come bow before Him now with reverence and fear;
> in Him no sin is found – we stand on holy ground.
> Be still, for the presence of the Lord, the Holy One is here.
>
> Be still, for the glory of the Lord is shining all around;
> He burns with holy fire, with splendour he is crowned:
> how awesome is the sight – our radiant king of light!
> Be still, for the glory of the Lord is shining all around.
>
> Be still, for the power of the Lord is moving in this place;
> He comes to cleanse and heal, to minister His grace.
> No work too hard for Him, in faith receive from Him;
> Be still, for the power of the Lord is moving in this place.[79]

Extract taken from the song 'Be still, for the presence of the Lord' by David J Evans

Looking back upon the analysis of this chapter we can see a number of important stories that were played out in the practice of 'prayer ministry' which mirror my analysis of the 'time of worship'. First, in both in-stances we have witnessed the power of ritual to embody a transforma-tion for participants. In the 'time of worship' participants were drawn into an encounter with God framed in terms of intimacy. The 'prayer ministry' invited all present into what I have described as a romantic adventure of therapeutic encounter with God. Both recipients and ad-ministrators of 'prayer ministry' shared in this ritual journey, either ministering or receiving God's therapeutic power. Secondly, we have

---

[78] D. Evans, 'Be still...' in *Deo: Today's Music & Worship* (Summer 1993), 32-3.
[79] *MP* (1990) No.50. Copyright © 1986 Thankyou Music*.

seen how these two ritual contexts drew upon traditions of worship, most especially the Pentecostal-Charismatic tradition. The transformation through song in the 'time of worship' is an established feature of the Pentecostal-Charismatic tradition, and the specific instance that I used to illustrate this was the Black gospel song tradition. The revivalist features of the 'prayer ministry' that I have highlighted were evidence of the continuing dependence of the Pentecostal-Charismatic tradition upon forms of worship practice that owe their origin to the American revivalism of the eighteenth and nineteenth centuries, particularly the American camp meeting tradition and the American Holiness movement. Finally, the story of these two contexts is also one of worship absorbing cultural norms to express theological and ritual priorities. At the conclusion of the last chapter I argued that the intimate encounter with God in the 'time of worship' was a reflection of the growth in an intimate social order that prized personal closeness and familiarity. Elements of discotheque culture, evident in the 'time of worship', provided an admirably suitable plausibility structure and ritual expression for this intimacy. Similarly, the culture of popular live performance has provided a framework for the expression of God's involvement in the 'prayer ministry'. For charismatic celebration to be authentic it has to be an encounter with God who acts, as we might say, 'in the present tense'; what matters is what God is doing *now* in this worshipping assembly. As I have demonstrated, the chief authenticities of a live event (presence, visibility and spontaneity) have each informed the 'prayer ministry' in such a way as to make it a ritual that celebrates this active and dynamic action of God within the worshipping assembly. The therapeutic dimension of this divine action in 'prayer ministry' also resonates with a feature of our late modern culture that Lasch calls a 'therapeutic sensibility',[80] whereby personal growth and maturation is understood as being achieved through therapeutic means rather than through moral development. In other words, the focus is more upon individuals' needs being met than their growth in character. Evaluating the impact of these cultural norms is one of the issues that I address in the final main chapter in which I consider the adequacy of the theological dimensions of the worship observed. It is to this task that I now turn.

---

[80] C. Lasch, *The Culture of Narcissism: American Life in Age of Diminishing Expectations*, quoted in Mannion, 'Liturgy and the Present Crisis of Culture', *Worship* 62 (March 1988), 2:103.

CHAPTER 7

A Theological Appraisal

In keeping with the methodological strategy outlined in Chapter 3, this final chapter explores the theological adequacy of the public horizons of worship that have been presented in previous chapters. After a preliminary summary of the ways in which the divine was conveyed in these public horizons, the main extended discussion focuses upon the presence and adequacy of the trinitarian theology mediated by the worship observed.

A Summary of the Numinous in Case Study Worship

As a preliminary to the main theological analysis of this chapter, I shall attempt to summarize the ways in which the divine was encountered in the worship I observed with reference to a term often used in sociological descriptions of religion, the 'numinous'. I am indebted in particular to Lawrence Hoffman's discussion of the role of the numinous in his book *Beyond The Text* in which he provides a framework for conceptualizing the numinous within liturgical celebrations.[1]

Hoffman builds upon the work of Rudolf Otto, whose work *The Idea of the Holy* first popularized the term 'numinous'. By using the term, Otto attempted to transcend the nineteenth-century rationalism that had reduced religion to ethics; he intended the term 'to stand for the holy minus its moral factor...and...minus its "rational" aspect altogether'.[2] Otto described the numinous as the *mysterium tremendum*, summarizing the *tremendum* as the absolute unapproachability of God in his overpowering majesty before whom mere creatures stand in open-mouthed awe,[3] and the *mysterium* as the God who is 'Wholly Other', always beyond us, but who also evokes a

---

[1] L.A. Hoffman, *Beyond the Text: A Holistic Approach to Liturgy*, Ch.7: 'The Numinous'.

[2] R. Otto, *The Idea of the Holy*, 20.

[3] Abraham's statement in Genesis 18:27 that he is 'nothing but dust and ashes' before God is for Otto a supreme example of this 'creature consciousness'. Otto, *Idea*, 24.

strong element of fascination (*fascinans*) in the worshipper. The numinous consciousness therefore has the dual characteristic of being daunted by the *tremendum* and fascinated by the *mysterium*. As Otto himself summarizes, 'the creature, who trembles before it [the numen], utterly cowed and cast down, has always at the same time the impulse to turn to it, even to make it somehow his own'.[4] Otto also recognized that the chief means by which the experience of the numinous is awakened in the human spirit is in the ritual of worship:

> More of the experience lives in reverent attitude and gesture, in tone and voice and demeanour, expressing its momentousness, and in the solemn devotional assembly of a congregation at prayer, than in all the phrases and negative nomenclature which we have found to designate it.[5]

Hoffman follows in the tradition of Otto by arguing for the necessity of the numinous aspect of religion to be accorded appropriate academic attention in its own right, particularly in his own field of liturgical studies. Hoffman is critical of the way that academic liturgical study has traditionally concentrated on the relationship between worshippers and their texts to the relative neglect of the way in which, as he puts it, worshippers 'intuit' a relationship with the divine. However Hoffman rejects Otto's claim that the *mysterium tremendum* is a description of the universal experience of the numinous. Despite Otto's attempts in *The Idea of the Holy* to discern the *mysterium tremendum* in other world religions, Hoffman argues that his description is particular to the numinous consciousness of early twentieth-century German Protestantism. Hoffman states that to make Otto's account a universal description of religious experience 'is to make the critical error of confusing the numinous *per se* with a specific culturally bound example of the way in which the numinous was apprehended'.[6] Hoffman illustrates his argument by using a cross-cultural comparison: the use of the Kedushah in the liturgy of the Jewish mystics, the *yordei merkavah*, whom I discussed in Chapter 5. The way the mystics used this prayer, which was a classic text for Otto's exposition of the numinous, reveals a very different apprehension of the numinous to that of Otto, one in which God was not totally Other, but quite approachable, even desirous of being approached.[7]

In order to avoid Otto's error of limiting the experience of the numinous to a particular cultural manifestation, Hoffman develops a framework that provides a conceptualization of the numinous as it operates in any liturgical setting. The three items that constitute this framework are 'synecdotal

---

4   Otto, *Idea*, 45.
5   Otto, *Idea*, 75.
6   Hoffman, *Beyond the Text*, 154.
7   Hoffman, *Beyond the Text*,154-64.

vocabulary', a 'master image' and 'cultural backdrop'. By 'synecdotal vocabulary' Hoffman means the most basic units of communication within a liturgical celebration, which includes language, dress, gesture, and spatial arrangement of objects. In the Ottonian system, the features of such vocabulary include the following: language that emphasizes majesty, awe, reverence and 'otherness'; the use of silence (such as that which accompanies the moment of consecration in the Mass); cathedral architecture, art and musical style emphasizing grandeur and transcendence (typically Gothic[8]) and worship choreography emphasizing the social distance between the laity and the clergy who are the sacred representatives of the divine.[9] The 'master image' is the whole of which the 'synecdotal vocabulary' is the part, and to which the 'synecdotal vocabulary' points. In the Ottonian system the 'master image' is the transcendent deity whose chief characteristic is summed up in the phrase *mysterium tremendum*. The 'cultural backdrop' contains the assumptions about reality that inform the 'master image' and also provide the parameters according to which the expression of worship is judged as authentic or unauthentic. The 'cultural backdrop' to the Ottonian system is post-Enlightenment Europe with its post-Kantian philosophy emphasizing the unknowable deity, a German social system emphasizing social space between classes, and a cultural heritage of classical music, particularly the nineteenth-century discovery of romanticism and emotionality.

The importance of Hoffman's framework to my analysis of the apprehension of the divine in charismatic worship is its recognition of the cultural relativity of numinal vocabulary. The temptation for critics of charismatic worship is to confuse the absence of specifically Ottonian language for the absence of the experience of the numinous itself. The critic Peter Mullen, for example, scorns those who claim that charismatic celebration is inspired by the Spirit. He regards the music to be fifth rate and characterized by 'the trivial argot of pop-culture', and the style of leadership aping television's games shows, effectively transposing *Game for a Laugh* to the sanctuary.[10] However his criticism of the aesthetics of charismatic celebration is highly Ottonian, assuming that high culture (for Mullen represented by Tallis, Gibbons, Cranmer, the *Parish Psalter*, the *English Hymnal* and the King James Bible) is the privileged medium for the numinous. What he cannot accept is the claim implicit within charismatic celebration that the numinous can be experienced within the aesthetics of

---

[8]   Gothic architecture was for Otto the 'most numinous of all types of art'. Otto, *Idea*, 83.

[9]   Many of these elements are discussed by Otto in a chapter entitled 'Means of Expression of the Numinous', *Idea*, 75-86.

[10]   P. Mullen, 'Confusion Worse Confounded' in D. Martin and P. Mullen (eds.), *Strange Gifts: A Guide to Charismatic Renewal*, esp. 103-4.

popular culture. Of course the religious validity of such an expression needs to be questioned from a theological point of view, which is the purpose of this final chapter, but to make the *a priori* judgement that the numinous cannot be expressed through popular culture is to make an aesthetic judgement not a religious one.

The way in which the numinous was represented in the worship I observed could be described and summarized with reference to Hoffman's framework. The 'synecdotal vocabulary' was characterized by some typical Ottonian categories, for example in the language of songs which addressed God as the 'Holy One' and encouraged associated responses ('reverence', 'awe', 'bowing down'). However, unlike the Ottonian system this was a holiness experienced as immanence, not transcendence. The immanence was expressed by a language of intimacy (such as 'presence' and 'touch'). Worshippers addressed God as the personal 'You', which would have been inconceivable within the Ottonian system. The choreography of worship minimized social distance, emphasizing that God was discovered in the midst of the worshipping assembly, in and through the active participation of the congregation. Participants discovered each other in liturgical celebration, and sacred roles were democratized so that any individual becomes the potential bearer of spiritual grace, particularly through the exercise of charismatic gifts. The musical style was popular, enhancing full participation. Regal melodies and rhythms emphasizing triumph and kingship were mingled with a ballad-style that conveyed the intimacy of encounter between the worshipper and God.

The 'master image' was God as holy king who was both exalted and also dynamically present among the worshipping assembly. As we have seen, and as will be illustrated later in this chapter, this had a characteristic trinitarian expression in the Son as the ascended and victorious king, the Spirit as the empowering presence, and the Father as the benevolent source of security and good gifts for his children.

The 'cultural backdrop' to charismatic worship is the popular culture that developed from the 1960s counter-culture with its emphasis on individual participation and expressiveness, impatience with formality and institutional life, and willingness to experiment with new forms of community life.[11] We have seen how two elements of this culture, intimacy in relationships and therapeutic concerns, have informed the worship observed. Writing from a post-Toronto perspective it is also possible to recognize elements of the consumer culture of late modernity in which one is expected to be permanently unsatiated and 'seething with desire for new

---

[11]   This cultural change is charted in T. Roszak, *The Making of a Counter Culture* and B. Martin, *A Sociology of Contemporary Cultural Change*.

things and experiences',[12] reflected, as commentators have identified, in the prayers of 'prayer ministry' that ask for 'more power, more of You, Lord'.[13] Within this late modern environment, the body takes on fresh importance as a servant of consumption, and a mediator of desire and emotional intensity,[14] elements of which we have witnessed in respondent behaviour in 'prayer ministry'.

The musical 'cultural backdrop' is the popular dance and live performance culture which, as we have seen, has influenced the performance of case study worship and notions of divine action within worship. As I have demonstrated, the sung worship also has an ecclesial 'cultural backdrop' in the Black gospel tradition. Similarly, the public 'prayer ministry' exhibits core elements of the nineteenth-century revivalist tradition. These include the way in which the gathered assembly becomes the arena for God's visitation of individuals, accompanied by the use of technique and promotion through public demonstration.

The Trinitarian Expression in Case Study Worship

Having summarized the relationship with the divine in terms of the numinous, I turn to consider the theological understandings mediated by the worship observed. In order to keep the subsequent discussion manageable and focused, I have selected for appraisal what may be described as an 'instinctive trinitarianism' in worship, an instinct born of the worshipful relationship with God the Holy Spirit. One of the chief features of the early charismatics' testimony to their baptism in the Spirit, as Peter Hocken has documented, was a greater awareness of the trinitarian nature of God.[15] Central to many of these testimonies was a new level of knowledge of Jesus Christ, a fresh appreciation of the love of the Father and the distinctiveness of the Holy Spirit, whom, as one participant put it, 'we feel that we know ... as a person in his own right.'[16] Michael Mitton confirmed this perspective when, following his appointment to the directorship of Anglican Renewal Ministries in the late 1980s, he wrote in *Renewal* magazine: 'At the heart of the charismatic renewal is a personal experience of the Holy Spirit bringing an awareness of the love and holiness of our Father, and equipping us to

---

[12] J.H. Simpson, 'Religion and the Body: Sociological Themes and Prospects' in W.H Swatos, *A Future for Religion? New Paradigms for Social Analysis*, 156.

[13] P. Richter, 'God is not a Gentleman! The Sociology of the Toronto Blessing' in S.E. Porter and P.J. Richter (ed.) *The Toronto Blessing - Or Is It?*, 26.

[14] B.S. Turner, *The Body & Society: Explorations in Social Theory*, 4.

[15] P. Hocken, *Streams of Renewal: The Origins and Early Development of the Charismatic Renewal in Great Britain*, 154-5.

[16] George Forester, quoted by Hocken, *Streams*,77.

serve our Lord Jesus.'[17]

The writings of one of the more theologically articulate leaders of the Fountain Trust, Tom Smail, also reflect a dialogue with this trinitarian experience. Smail's initial book, *Reflected Glory*, focused upon the relationship between the Son and the Spirit. Then *The Forgotten Father* concentrated on the Father and the Son, and in the last of his main studies, *The Giving Gift*, he explored the place of the Spirit within the life of the Trinity.[18] It is also significant that two recent theological interpretations of charismatic worship and celebration develop their analysis in trinitarian terms. The first is Jean-Jacques Suurmond's *Word and Spirit at Play*, which draws upon the anthropologist Huizinga's definition of play and describes charismatic celebration as the play of the Word and the Spirit in a sabbath game. The Word represents order, the rules of the game, and the Spirit the dynamism and interchange, the enthusiasm which brings the church to life. The second is the attempt by the Anglican Chris Russell in articles in successive editions of *Anglicans for Renewal* magazine to formulate a theology of charismatic worship, which leads him from pneumatology into a re-appropriation of an orthodox trinitarian theology of worship.[19] These two approaches are not without their problems, but they are further confirmation that the interpretation of charismatic worship and spirituality invites an engagement with trinitarian concerns. [20]

What then of the instinctive trinitarianism in case study worship? Given that the authorized liturgical provision used by churches visited contained prayer that was shaped by trinitarian concerns,[21] I will illustrate the instinctive trinitarianism by focusing upon the presence of trinitarian language in the non-authorized forms of prayer, most notably the extem-

---

[17] *Renewal*, 1 (January 1989), 152.

[18] These books were published in 1975, 1980, and 1988 respectively.

[19] C. Russell, 'Skepsis: A Theological Viewpoint', *Anglicans for Renewal* 70 (Autumn 1997) and 71 (Winter 1997).

[20] Suurmond's concept of 'play' is too general a concept to be readily employed as an interpretative tool for the case study data, and it tends to reduce the Trinity to a theologized anthropology. Though theologically more orthodox, Russell's work lacks the necessary grounding in field data to test his own claim that the distinctive understanding of the Spirit generated in worship is consistent with the doctrine of the Trinity.

[21] For an overview of trinitarian language within the Rite 'A' of the *A.S.B.* and other contemporary eucharistic liturgies, see Archimandrite Ephrem's 'The Trinity in Contemporary Eucharistic Liturgy' in A.I.C.Heron (ed.), *The Forgotten Trinity: 3. A Selection of Papers presented to the B.C.C. Study Commission on Trinitarian Doctrine Today*, 47-61.

pore prayers of service leaders and congregational songs.[22]

Extempore Prayers of Leaders

Evidence to support the claim that the core relationship with the Holy Spirit in charismatic worship has generated a trinitarian consciousness is provided by prayers addressed to or for the Spirit within case study worship. The epicletic prayers that initiated public 'prayer ministry' provided ample illustration of the way that prayer to, or for, the Spirit included prayer to the Father and the Son. I observed the following examples:

> Holy Spirit, you are so welcome. Giver of life author of life, pour down upon us ... Let it come Lord Jesus; pour it out now. More Lord.[23]

> O come Holy Spirit, in Jesus' name. Father, as we stand, and as the Spirit comes, we admit to our doubts, deliberately and purposefully before you now in the heavenly places ... Lord Jesus, send down the Spirit we pray. Lord Jesus, be with us today.[24]

> Father, I ask you now that you would come and minister to all your people. Holy Spirit, come, and Lord I ask that you would renew in us, Lord, our first love ... Come Holy Spirit.[25]

> Father God, we ask you through your Son to send your Holy Spirit upon us in great power ... Come Holy Spirit.[26]

Prayers calling upon the Spirit outside the context of public 'prayer ministry' also had a trinitarian dimension. At St.D, whereas in 'prayer ministry' the priest prayed only to the Spirit in a simple 'Come Holy Spirit' prayer, at other stages in the Mass he offered extempore prayers for the gift of the Spirit which would be addressed either to the Father, Jesus, or 'the Lord' as the origin of the gift.[27] At St.A and St.F, where there had been no public 'prayer ministry', prayers for the Spirit included references to other persons of the Trinity. At Evening Praise at St.A, the leader offered the following prayer before a period of devotional worship:

---

[22] Unlike other Reformation churches, the Church of England has never made provision for authorized hymnody, with the result that all hymn and song collections are technically non-authorized!

[23] St.B, 6.30pm service, visit 2.

[24] St.E, 11.00am service, visit 2.

[25] St.E, 6.30pm service, visit 2.

[26] St.C, 6.00pm service, visit 1.

[27] Typically such prayers were prompted by songs describing the Spirit's ministry.

Holy Spirit, we pray that you'd come and melt our hearts. Spirit of Jesus, break through those barriers, those hurts. Clothe us with yourself ... come Lord Jesus.[28]

At St.F in the commissioning of the 'prayer ministry' team, the priest prayed first for the assembled team in trinitarian terms and then addressed the Spirit alone when he prayed for individual members:

> May the Almighty God and Father of our Lord Jesus Christ fill you with all grace to fulfil his ministry into which you have been called, and may his Holy Spirit come upon you with healing power, that those who you will be led to pray for will receive from his most gracious hand all that he desires for the wholeness of body, mind and spirit. We make this prayer in the name of Jesus.
> [As the priest laid his hands upon each individual member of the group, he prayed:] Come Holy Spirit upon your servant [name] with all your gifts of healing and love.[29]

Staying with St.F, I also observed an extempore variation on authorized liturgical provision which was a more formalized example of prayer addressed to all three persons of the Trinity. Within the traditional three-fold versicle and response structure of the *Kyrie* the priest composed prayers to each person of the Trinity, and in the following instance introduced and concluded the Confession with prayers to the Spirit (congregational response in bold):[30]

> Now we ask for God's mercy upon us, and forgiveness of all our sins:
>
> [Prayer] Holy Spirit, reveal to us God as our Father.
> [To congregation] Today we are thinking of practical ways of showing love and the overwhelming generosity of God.
> [Prayer] Heavenly Father, there are so many times when we are self-centred and want to keep things for ourselves. That makes us blind to the needs of the people around. Yet you say that you love the wicked as well as the righteous. For our shortcomings,
> Lord have mercy.
> **Lord have mercy.**

---

[28] St.A, Evening Praise, visit 1.
[29] St.F, visit 1.
[30] This is not without precedent, for in recent official supplementary liturgical texts, provision has been made for similar trinitarian *Kyries*. See the Trinity season prayers in *Enriching the Christian Year*.

Lord Jesus Christ, you came and gave up your life for the whole world. We pray that you would help us to give our lives too, to you and to one another;
Christ have mercy.
Christ have mercy.

Holy Spirit of God, you come and empower your people to be generous and loving. For the times that we use that gift for ourselves, we're sorry. Lord have mercy.
Lord have mercy.

Holy Spirit of God, now come upon each one of us with your cleansing and absolving power. Cleanse your people so that we might be free to sing your praise, Father, Son and Holy Spirit.
Amen.

Finally, I observed service leaders pray extempore preparatory prayers that established a trinitarian context for the subsequent act of worship. Two examples are quoted here, the first from the non-liturgical setting of St.B and the second from the more liturgical Mass at St.D:

Father, we thank you so much for gathering us together this morning. We thank you for your great love towards us. We thank you Lord Jesus that you've come to us. We thank you that you send your Spirit upon us. We ask you this morning that we may draw close to you, to worship you with our hearts, our lips our lives; all of ourselves. For Jesus Christ's sake.[31]

Father, as we come into this your Temple this morning, may we do so with hearts full of thanksgiving. Father, may we give you the glory for all you have done for us. And Father, as we come to gather around your altar, to celebrate your love and the death of your Son, may our hearts be filled with praise for all that you are. Father, pour out your Spirit upon us this morning. Come among us and have your way among us. May you be Lord here, in all that we do and say. We ask this in Jesus' name.[32]

Congregational Songs

Reviewing the lyrical content of songs provided further evidence for the instinctive trinitarianism of charismatic prayer. Many of the songs that were

---

[31] St.B, visit 1, the vicar at 11.00am service. It was interesting to note that although that St.B was the least liturgical of the case study churches, the vicar ended each service with an orthodox trinitarian blessing.

[32] St.D, visit 2, assistant priest at the Parish Mass.

sung, as has been illustrated in Chapter 5, were addressed to God the Son. Alongside these were a smaller number of songs addressed to the Father (for example, 'Father God, I wonder',[33] 'O Father of the fatherless'[34] and 'Father in heaven, how we love You'[35]) and the Spirit (for example, 'Spirit of the living God'[36] and 'Holy Spirit we welcome You'[37]). There were also songs that had an explicit trinitarian shape. At St.D we sang 'Father we adore You', a song originally popularized through the Fisherfolk collection *Sounds of Living Water*:[38]

> Father, we adore You,
> lay our lives before You:
> how we love You!
>
> Jesus, we adore You,
> lay our lives before You:
> how we love You!
>
> Spirit, we adore You,
> lay our lives before You:
> how we love You![39]

> Extract taken from the song 'Father we adore You' by Terrye Coelho

The Vineyard song 'Father we adore You' follows a similar pattern with successive verses beginning 'Father we adore You ... Jesus we love You ... Spirit we need You'.[40] An interesting example of a more developed trinitarian song was sung as a solo item at the end of an evening service at St.B (visit 1). This had been composed by a member of the congregation:

> One bread, one body, one Jesus, one hope to which we are all called.
> One Lord, one faith and one baptism, one God and Father of us all.
> God bids us to love one another, to be bound in unity,
> for the Holy Spirit of love in Jesus is a love which sets us free.

---

[33] *Mission Praise* [*MP*] (1990) No.128; St.E, visit 1.

[34] *New Mission Praise* [*NMP*], No.108; St.E, visit 1; St.C, visit 2.

[35] *MP* (1990) No.135; St.E, visit 1.

[36] *MP* (1990) No.612; St.D, visit 2.

[37] *Songs of Fellowship* [*SF*] (1991) No.188; St.A (Evening Praise), visit 2.

[38] Other Fisherfolk songs with a similar trinitarian shape are 'Holy, holy, holy, holy' (*MP* [1990] No.238)], and 'Father we love You' (*MP* [1990] No.142).

[39] *MP* (1990) No.139. Copyright © 1972 Maranatha! Music/Copycare music@copycare.com* (* denotes address in song index).

[40] *MP* (1990) No.140: St.B, visit 1.

He sent one Holy Spirit to guide us, one Saviour Jesus Christ is here.
One Father in heaven, our God Almighty, one blessed Trinity.
Our God he has brought us all together, His Holy Spirit to release,
that we may show a dying world His heaven, His joy and His peace. [41]

The trinitarian consciousness articulated in the extempore prayers and songs quoted above gives legitimate grounds for conducting a theological appraisal of case study worship with reference to the doctrine of the Trinity. Christopher Cocksworth has also recognized this line of theological investigation in a recent article in which he suggests that the 'apparent instinctive trinitarianism of charismatic worship is a field wide open for proper research and exploration'.[42] He argues for the need of a dialogue between charismatic worship and the liturgical tradition with respect to the two classic Christian doxologies which give 'Glory to the Father and to the Son, and to the Holy Spirit' and which offers praise and prayer 'to the Father, through the Son, in the Spirit'.[43] The remainder of this chapter will appraise the trinitarian characteristics of the worship observed by engaging with the trinitarian concerns represented by these orthodox formulations of Christian worship. I will argue that there were features of worship that represent a renewal of an orthodox trinitarian understanding of worship 'in the Spirit'. I will then discuss the problematic features of worship exhibited in sung worship and 'prayer ministry' in terms of the dislocation from the christological heart of trinitarian worship, namely worship that is offered through the Son.

Worship 'In The Spirit'

As the title of this book suggests, the main claim of the praxis of charismatic worship is that it is 'worship in the Spirit'. The Charismatic Movement, rooted in the experience of the 'personal epiclesis'[44] of baptism in the Spirit, has naturally developed styles of worship that have sought to reflect the dynamic involvement of the Holy Spirit among the worshipping assembly. In the worship observed the most obvious example of this was the epiclesis initiating public 'prayer ministry', a liturgical moment whose significance was such that some participants defined 'prayer ministry' as a

---

[41] The lady concerned explained to the congregation that she had been 'given' the words when praying on the previous day, and that she had 'received' the tune whilst playing her guitar at home earlier that day!

[42] C. Cocksworth, 'The Trinity Today: Opportunities and Challenges for Liturgical Study', *Studia Liturgica* 27 (1997), 1:61-78.

[43] Cocksworth, 'Trinity Today', 74.

[44] A phrase used by J. Fenwick and B. Spinks in their description of charismatic experience: *Worship in Transition: the Twentieth Century Liturgical Movement*, 112.

"'Come Holy Spirit' time".[45] But as we have seen, there were plenty of
other instances of prayer to, or for, the Spirit, giving liturgical expression to
the nature of the church, which, according to the Anglican-Orthodox
dialogue, is 'that Community which lives by continually invoking the Holy
Spirit'.[46] Worship 'in the Spirit' was also symbolized by the simple bodily
posture of hands held in front of the chest with palms cupped upwards,
indicating an openness or readiness on behalf of participants for receiving
the Holy Spirit. As the minister at St.B told the children just before calling
upon the Spirit at 'prayer ministry', "stand with your hands out as I start to
pray – that's saying to the Lord that you want to receive a gift from him". [47]

There were three main features of worship that reflected a trinitarian
understanding of worship 'in the Spirit': the celebration of the Spirit as a
divine person, or hypostasis, in his own right, the freedom and enabling
bestowed by the Spirit upon participants to fulfil a vocation to worship, and
the creation of a community in which participants relate to one another in
the giving and receiving of gifts.

Celebrating God the Holy Spirit

The 'common-sense' understanding of participants was that, with reference
to the Spirit, it was God who was being addressed and God who acted
among the worshipping congregation. The interchangeable way in which
divine names were used in prayer, as seen above, indicates the ease with
which the Spirit was included as an intrinsic part of the divine being.
Requests for his presence were understood unambiguously as invitations for
God to reveal himself and 'work' among the assembly, and I have already
demonstrated how this understanding was publicly reinforced in 'prayer
ministry'. As we have seen, both the use of charismatic gifts and the
presence of ecstatic behaviour were visible signs to participants of the
dynamic presence and activity of God among the worshipping assembly.

This has important trinitarian implications, for the understanding mediated by the worship observed assumed that the Spirit is a distinct person, or
in Eastern trinitarian language, hypostasis, within the Godhead. This is an
understanding which is consistent with the creedal formula on the nature of
the Spirit agreed by the early church fathers who met in Constantinople in
381AD: 'We believe in the Holy Spirit, the Lord, the Giver of Life, who
proceeds from the Father; who with the Father and the Son together is

---

[45] For example, at St.C (MLI). At St.E, the 6.30pm service with 'prayer ministry'
was advertised as a 'Come Holy Spirit' Service (visit 2).
[46] K. Ware and C. Davey (eds.), *Anglican-Orthodox Dialogue: The Moscow Agreed
Statement*, 91; quoted in C. Cocksworth, *Holy, Holy, Holy: Worshipping the Trinitarian
God*, 186.
[47] St.B, 10.30am service, visit 2.

worshipped and glorified'. The Council of Constantinople had confirmed the doctrines of the Council of Nicaea in 325AD, and extended Nicaea's belief in the deity of the Son (expressed as *homoousios*, or 'of the same essence' as the Father) to include the Holy Spirit, who in 325AD had been mentioned almost as an afterthought: 'We believe in the Holy Spirit.'

The theological formulation for the Spirit at the Council of Constantinople was to a great degree the result of the work of the Cappadocian fathers, Basil of Caesarea, Gregory of Nyssa and Gregory of Nazianzus, who in establishing the deity of the Spirit also created a new theological language for expressing the unity and the trinity of God. They spoke of the Father, Son and Spirit as being three distinct *hypostases*, and all sharing in the one *ousia*, or divine 'essence', which is derived from the Father. The particularity of each hypostasis is defined in relational terms: the Father is the source of the divine essence, possessing it in and from himself alone; the Son possesses the divine essence from the Father, and is begotten eternally; and the Spirit possesses the divine nature from the Father by eternally proceeding from him, as the everlasting breath of his mouth. Thus, as the creed of Constantinople states, by fully sharing the divine essence the Spirit is to be worshipped and glorified with the Father and the Son, and in his particularity, he is spoken of as proceeding from the Father.

It was the defence of the liturgical and theological appropriateness of giving glory to the Spirit, along with the Father and the Son, that prompted Basil's work, *On the Holy Spirit* (375AD). His treatise defends his use of a 'co-ordinated' form of doxology within the Eucharist ('Glory to God the Father with [*meta*] the Son, with [*sun*] the Holy Spirit'), in response to the charge of innovation by the Pneumatochians. The customary form in Greek speaking churches at the time was the traditional 'Glory to the Father through (*dia*) the Son in (*en*) the Holy Spirit', a formula that receives New Testament expression in Ephesians 2:18. Basil's treatise is dominated by lengthy grammatical discussions in which he draws upon scripture and the wider worshipping tradition of the church to argue for the appropriateness of both formulas in Christian worship. He understood the more traditional formula to be appropriate for describing God's economy of salvation (and hence it is often called the 'economic' formula), and the 'co-ordinated' form appropriate for the adoration and contemplation of God as he is in himself (the so called 'immanent' formula). Specifically, in regard to the Spirit, Basil argues that when his rank is considered, 'we think of Him as present with the Father and the Son', and when the working of his grace is considered upon recipients, 'we say that the Spirit is in us'.[48] But, as Basil argued, it was crucial for worship that the indwelling Spirit be God, for it was only on account of the Spirit sharing in the divine glory that worshippers could participate in the saving knowledge of God the Son and the

---

[48]   Basil of Ceasarea, *St Basil the Great On the Holy Spirit*, 26.63. , 96.

Father. Or as Basil was to put it, 'If you are outside the Spirit, you cannot worship at all.'[49]

The relevance of Basil's work to the present discussion is two-fold. First, in theological method, charismatics share a similar orientation to working out their theology of the Spirit from within the experience of public worship. Songs, prayers, leadership explanations, ritual process, liturgical actions and ecstatic phenomena all create a living theology of the Spirit. As Chris Russell has succinctly described it: 'Distinctive charismatic pneumatology is fashioned within and from corporate worship; it is pneumatology-through-doxology.'[50] Secondly, by celebrating the presence of God the Holy Spirit within worship, charismatics are led, like Basil, to an understanding of worship as a transforming event, or to put it more theologically, a redemptive event. As we have seen, the ritual of songs was designed to lead to communion with God and the 'prayer ministry' invited individuals to a healing encounter with God.

In many ways, by celebrating the Spirit in a way that draws attention to his dynamic relationship as a distinct divine hypostasis to the worshipping community, the worship observed (and charismatic worship in general) stands much closer to the Eastern theological tradition of the Cappadocians than its native Western tradition. The latter has found it more difficult to celebrate the distinct hypostasis of the Spirit, particularly within the economy of God's action in the world. As has been highlighted by Colin Gunton, the theological roots of this difficulty lie in the trinitarian formulations of the father of Western theology, Augustine of Hippo, expounded in his treatise *De Trinitate*.[51] With regard to Augustine's understanding of the Spirit, Gunton identifies a failure to relate adequately the Spirit of the immanent Trinity (what God is in himself eternally) to the economy of God (his action in Christ and with the Spirit in time). As Gunton argues, the way that Augustine conceives of the Spirit as 'bond of love' between the Father and the Son tends to be in Platonic terms, emphasizing the unitative function of love (relating the Father to the Son, and the believer to God), rather than the outgoing nature of love rooted in the concrete realities of the incarnation. The Spirit thus tends to be conceived as 'a link in an inward-turned circle',[52] which contrasts significantly with the Eastern tradition, as the thirteenth-century Bonaventura summarized: 'The Greeks have compared the Spirit to the breathing forth of

---

[49] Basil, *On the Holy Spirit*, 26.64. , 97.

[50] C. Russell, 'Skepsis' in *Anglicans for Renewal*, 70 (Autumn 1997), 2.

[51] C.E. Gunton, 'Augustine, the Trinity and the Theological Crisis of the West' in *The Promise of Trinitarian Theology*, 31-57.

[52] C.E. Gunton, 'The Spirit in the Trinity' in A.I.C. Heron (ed.), *The Forgotten Trinity: 3. A Selection of Papers Presented to the BCC Study Commission on Trinitarian Doctrine Today*, 131.

an "outer breath", the Latins to the breathing forth of an "inner love".[53]
The outcome is that far from being in some respect an implication of the
economy, Augustine's immanent Trinity is in effect conceived in terms
contradictory to the economy, which in turn undermines the theological
weight of the economy of the Spirit.

The texts of the Western liturgical tradition are symptomatic of this
weakness with their hesitant acknowledgement of the economy of the
Spirit. Take, for instance, the Holy Communion rite of the *Book of Common
Prayer*, a foundational liturgy for Anglicanism. Apart from the Nicene
Creed, the only clear mention of the economy of the Spirit is in the Collect
for Purity, with its petition to Almighty God to 'cleanse the thoughts of our
hearts by the inspiration of thy Holy Spirit'. The other references to the
Spirit are in concluding doxologies to the immanent Trinity, such as
'through Jesus Christ our Lord, who with thee and the Holy Ghost liveth
and reigneth, ever one God, world without end',[54] or the characteristic
Augustinian formula of 'through Jesus Christ our Lord; by whom, and with
whom, in the unity of the Holy Ghost, all honour and glory be to thee, O
Father Almighty, world without end'.[55] The eucharistic prayer, following
the pattern of prayer in the Roman *canon missae*, is strictly binitarian in
form, addressing the Father and celebrating the death of Christ; the Spirit is
only mentioned on three occasions in the year when the Proper Prefaces
celebrate Christmas Day, Whit Sunday and Trinity Sunday. This truncated
form of trinitarian prayer was not unique to the *Book of Common Prayer*.
As Bryan Spinks comments, such prayer was a common feature of Western
eucharistic liturgies of the Reformation period, which meant that these
liturgies were 'ill-suited to nurture a spirituality which could long withstand
the inroads of Socinianism and Deism with their antipathy to the doctrine of
the incarnation and the Trinity'.[56] Spinks continues, 'it is salutary to
remember that eighteenth and nineteenth-century Anglican Deists produced
revised Prayer Books with only minor omissions from the standard text,
showing just how marginal this belief [in the Trinity] is in terms of prayer
texts.[57]

In the light of this tradition, it was little surprise to discover the more
liturgically aware charismatic Anglicans, such as John Gunstone, welcoming the revisions to the *Book of Common Prayer* found in the *Alternative*

---

[53] Bonaventura's *Commentary* on Bk.1 of Lombard's *Sentences*, quoted in A.I.C.
Heron, *The Holy Spirit: The Holy Spirit in the Bible, in the History of Christian Thought
and in Recent Theology*, 83.

[54] The first prayer for the Sovereign.

[55] The first collect after Communion.

[56] B.D. Spinks, 'Trinitarian Theology and the Eucharistic Prayer', *Studia Liturgica*
26 (1996), 212.

[57] Spinks, 'Trinitarian Theology', 212.

Service Book, particularly the eucharistic rites.[58] These eucharistic rites allowed the worshipping assembly to affirm confidently the presence of the Spirit in their gathering. The eucharistic prayers had more explicitly trinitarian language than Cranmer's, notably the extended praise to the Father in the Preface which outlined the economy of the Trinity (in the incarnation of the Son and the mission of the Spirit), and invocations of the Spirit upon the eucharistic elements, and upon communicants.[59]

By affirming the divine person of the Spirit, the worship observed also celebrated what is best described as the freedom of the Spirit. As we have seen, this is represented in charismatic liturgical time by the key element of openness to the Spirit's action within the assembly: leaders encouraged participants to allow God 'to do whatever he wants to do', and moments of silence were characterized by a waiting upon the Spirit to 'move' among the assembly. For some participants, liturgical celebration could negate such freedom. "Does your liturgy allow God in?", asked one informant when in conversation with me about the quality of the worship in my own parish.[60] Other participants, most notably at St.B and among some of the Evening Praise congregation at St.A, expressed their frustration with their experience of Anglican liturgy, which they regarded as too structured, predictable, leaving "no space for God to work or speak".[61] This has been a common complaint of charismatics. Michael Harper, in the course of writing about the central elements of charismatic worship, is unsparing in his criticism of Anglican liturgical celebration:

> [T]he Holy Spirit has been tamed and domesticated, imprisoned and encapsulated by dry liturgy, ancient forms, Victoriana galore and Anglo-Saxon phlegm ... We have been so obsessed with divine *order* that we have been blinded to the Spirit's freedom.[62]

This protest on behalf of the Spirit's freedom is another indication of the way that charismatic understanding of worship stands over against the Western tradition, and nearer the Eastern. The problem with the West has been its inability to give adequate theological weight to the free personhood of the Spirit, a problem that has its roots in Augustine's treatment of the

---

[58] See further, comments on worship at St.D in Ch. 4.
[59] Rite 'A', Eucharistic Prayers 1,2 and 3. Prayer 4, and the first Rite 'B' prayer were an updating of the Cranmerian rite with an invocation of the Spirit in the post-Sanctus position. The second Rite 'B' prayer followed the Rite 'A' shape, but included only an invocation upon the elements.
[60] Informal conversation, St.C.
[61] CI, St.B.
[62] M. Harper, 'Principles of Congregational Worship', *One in Christ: A Catholic Ecumenical Review* 13 (1977), 1&2:37 (italics original).

Spirit in *De Trinitate*, where he describes the Spirit as the 'Gift' and 'bond of Love' between the Father and the Son, and from them to the world.[63] But gift and love is the language of substance, not persons. As Tom Smail puts it, the Augustinian approach tends 'to dissolve the Spirit into a relationship or an attitude rather than affirm him as distinct person.'[64] Because Augustine is not able to establish personhood as constitutive of the Spirit's existence convincingly, there is a tendency for the Spirit to be conceived in terms of a divine substance belonging to and given by the Father and the Son. This, together with Augustine's insistence that in origin the Spirit proceeded from both the Son and the Father, though not himself involved in the origination of any divine person, tends to subordinate the Spirit to the Son. The logic of this position led in due time to the *filioque* controversy with the East, and the associated Eastern accusations of Western theology that by subordinating the Spirit to the Son, the West fails to do justice to the particular realities of the economy of the Spirit in his divine freedom.[65] Symptomatic of this has been the Western subordination of the Spirit's economy to a spiritual grace, which, as Tom Torrance has highlighted, has been conceived either in terms of the ministry of the institution of the church (Catholicism) or as an indwelling vivifying force within the individual soul (Protestant piety).[66] Both positions compromise the divine freedom of the Spirit in his particular hypostasis by making the Spirit a function of the institution (which is the particular criticism of charismatics with respect to the liturgy), or individual spirit.

Celebrating a Vocation to Worship

The second main element of worship 'in the Spirit' was that it affirmed the Spirit's role as the enabler of the human vocation to worship. This was particularly evident in the acts of congregational singing, where, as we have seen from Chapter 5, participation was understood as being enabled by the Spirit, 'releasing' participants for the offering of worship.

The texts of case study charismatic songs leave worshippers in little doubt as to their primary vocation. Epitomizing this is a song by Graham Kendrick:

---

[63] See *De Trinitate*, XV for Augustine's main discussion in J. Burnaby (tr.), *Augustine: Later Works*, Library of Christian Classics, VIII.

[64] T. Smail, *The Giving Gift: The Holy Spirit in Person*, 153.

[65] The history of the debate has been exhaustively outlined by R.P.C. Hanson in *The Search for the Christian Doctrine of God*.

[66] T.F. Torrance, 'Come Creator Spirit, for the Renewal of Worship and Witness' in *Theology in Reconstruction*, 240-58.

> We are here to praise You,
> lift our hearts and sing;
> we are here to give You
> the best that we can bring.[67]

Extract taken from the song 'We are here to praise You' by Graham Kendrick

The long periods of confident congregational singing reflected the spirit of this vocation. These were extended acts of thanksgiving, witnessing to the eucharistic nature of humanity. As Alexander Schmemann writes, 'thanksgiving is truly the first and the essential act of man, the act by which he fulfils himself as man'.[68] Or, as the Preface in the Holy Communion liturgy of the *Book of Common Prayer* puts it, 'It is very meet, right, and our bounden duty, that we should at all times, and in all places, give thanks unto thee, O Lord, Holy Father, Almighty, Everlasting God'. Or again, to the question 'What is the chief end of man?', the Westminster Shorter Catechism (1647-48) answers 'Man's chief end is to glorify God, and to enjoy him for ever.[69]

The theological basis for this vocation is trinitarian, as revealed in the economy of God's action in the incarnation. As Tom Smail points out, the earthly life of the Son is encompassed by the Spirit's action, at his conception (Luke 1:35), baptism (Luke 3:22 and parallels), and resurrection (Romans 1:4).[70] Thus, in the Spirit, who is the gift from the Father, the Son in his humanity offers himself to the Father, and so fulfils the worshipful response of creation as the new Adam.[71] This trinitarian pattern is reflected liturgically in the New Testament by the Pauline references to the distinctive prayer '*Abba*, Father' in use in the early church.[72] The content of such prayer draws directly upon Jesus' own prayer, which, as New Testament scholars such as Jeremias and Dunn have argued, was characteristically addressed to God as *Abba*, or 'Father'.[73] The mode of prayer is in the Spirit, for 'God sent the Spirit of his Son into our hearts' to enable the prayer '*Abba*, Father' (Galatians 4:6). Thus, as John Zizioulas argues with regard to ecclesial existence in general, Christian worship is instituted

---

[67] From *MP* (1990), No.717. Copyright © 1985 Thankyou Music*.

[68] A. Schmemann, *Of Water and The Spirit: A Liturgical Study of Baptism*, 46.

[69] Quoted in G. Wainwright, *Doxology: The Praise of God in Worship, Doctrine, and Life*, 17.

[70] Smail, *The Giving Gift*, 99-107.

[71] See Romans 5:12-21 and 1 Corinthians 15:20-28, 45-47.

[72] See Romans 8:15 and Galatians 4:6.

[73] J. Jeremias, *The Prayers of Jesus*, 11-65; J.D.G. Dunn, *Jesus and the Spirit: A Study of the Religious Charismatic Experience of Jesus and the First Christians as Reflected in the New Testament*, 21-26.

by Christ and constituted by the Spirit.[74] Christ embodies the reality of Christian worship, in which we participate through the power of the Spirit, or as the economic trinitarian doxology puts it, prayer is offered to the Father through the Son, and in the Spirit.

It is important to recognize that the trinitarian offering of the Son in the Spirit is not only a pattern for Christian worship, but also its redemptive foundation. Through the atoning death of the Son, the vocation to worship is restored to mankind. Writing on the death of Christ in an essay on eucharistic sacrifice, Rowan Williams argues that 'the effect of Christ's sacrifice is precisely to make us "liturgical" beings, capable of offering ourselves, our praises and our symbolic gifts to a God who we know will receive us in Christ.'[75] In the Orthodox tradition this is expressed in more pneumatological terms as the freedom given by the Spirit to face God with unveiled face, summed up in the New Testament word *parrhesia*.[76] The Orthodox commentator Paul Verghese summarizes this grace of the Spirit as the 'joy of freedom'.[77] This same freedom to approach God boldly was evident in the manner of celebration of the worship observed, which led the worshippers into communion, or 'intimacy', with God. The texts of some songs reflected this ethos, most notably a song sung at St.D (visit 1) which combined both the christological and pneumatological dimensions of celebrating the 'joy of freedom':

Jesus, we celebrate Your victory,
Jesus, we revel in Your love,
Jesus, we rejoice You've set us free,
Jesus, Your death has brought us life.

His Spirit in us releases us from fear,
the way to Him is open,
with boldness we draw near.[78]

Extract taken from the song 'Jesus we celebrate Your victory' by John Gibson

Thus worship not only witnessed to the divine freedom of the Spirit, but also to the nature of the Spirit as the grounds of freedom for participants'

---

[74] J.D. Zizioulas, *Being as Communion: Studies in Personhood and the Church*, 140.

[75] R. Williams, *Eucharistic Sacrifice: The Roots of a Metaphor*, 27.

[76] For example, it is used in 2 Cor. 3:12 as a comparison between the bold, open and confident nature of Paul's ministry and the 'veiled' nature of Moses' ministry. For a more liturgical expression, see Eph. 3:12.

[77] P. Verghese, *The Joy of Freedom: Eastern Worship and Modern Man*, 23 and 82.

[78] From *MP* (1990), No. 387. Copyright © 1987 Thankyou Music*.

worship. This reflects the concerns of Colin Gunton who argues that only by correctly establishing the Spirit's divine 'Otherness' can human freedom be guaranteed.[79] Worship 'in the Spirit' gives us the freedom to live according to the 'law of our own being',[80] which in liturgical terms, as the sung worship repeatedly reminded its participants, is our creaturely sacrificial self offering of praise to the Father as eucharistic beings.

Celebrating the Community at Worship

The third aspect of worship 'in the Spirit' that was highlighted in the worship observed was the creation of communities in which participants were encouraged to relate to one another (which I have described as becoming present *to* one another), and through the inspiration of the Spirit, give to and receive from one another. This was most obvious at St.A's Evening Praise and St.F where there were high levels of personal interaction between worshippers. However, in each church visited there were examples of participants offering and receiving gifts 'in the Spirit'. As we have seen, this could be inspired utterances in a 'time of worship' (St.A, St.B and St.E), or 'words of knowledge' in public 'prayer ministry' (St.C, St.D, and St.E). Through various commissionings, gifts and ministries were celebrated as being 'in the Spirit' by prayer which invoked the Spirit's power or presence upon the relevant practitioners. At St.F the chief server and 'prayer ministry' team were commissioned with prayer for the Spirit. During a 'prayer ministry' at St.E, the leader, having identified those in the congregation with a gift of prophecy and others with healing gifts, prayed that the Spirit would come upon them to empower them for ministry.[81] On another occasion at St.E the Spirit was called upon the 'prayer ministry' team just before they prayed for respondents.[82] At St.B I witnessed two occasions when individual members of the congregation were publicly commissioned for service in the church overseas by prayer for the Spirit and laying on of hands.[83]

Once again, we witness a contrast with the nature of liturgical community that has been characteristic of the Western tradition, where public worship has been dominated by a sacred officiant who ministers to the people, whose role it is to receive the grace mediated to them. In Catholi-

---

[79] Gunton, 'Immanence and Otherness: Divine Sovereignty and Human Freedom in the Theology of Robert W Jenson' in *The Promise of Trinitarian Theology*, 122-41, and 'The Spirit as Lord: Christianity, Modernity and Freedom' in A. Walker (ed.), *Different Gospels: Christian Orthodoxy and Modern Theologies*, 169-82.

[80] Gunton, 'The Spirit as Lord', 177.

[81] St.E, 11.00am service, visit 2.

[82] St.E, 6.30pm service, visit 2.

[83] St.B, 6.30pm service, visit 1 and 10.30am service, visit 2.

cism this has traditionally been focused in the priestly administration of the sacrament, and in Protestantism in the faithful ministry of the preaching of the word of God. Michael Harper's criticism of this tradition is in terms of the arrangements of church furniture, 'before the Reformation in extensive sanctuaries and since the Reformation in pulpits and pews',[84] which Harper sees as reflecting the absence of a communitarian understanding of the Body of Christ. In charismatic worship, as illustrated in the case studies, individual participants in the worshipping assembly were encouraged and permitted to become present to each other in ways not previously enabled by the tradition. As mentioned in Chapter 4, this has been described as the removal of individual masks in the stately masked ball of traditional worship. Each participant was potentially a minister of, as well as being a recipient of, spiritual grace.

This kind of community represents a recovery of the ministry of the Spirit as the creator of *koinonia*, or fellowship, the reality of which is illustrated in the communal life of the early church in the book of Acts, (such as Acts 2:42-7) and identified as a particular characteristic of the Spirit in the trinitarian greeting of 2 Corinthians 13:14. As already mentioned, Paul's instruction on worship in 1 Corinthians 12 – 14 has been the classic biblical passage used by charismatics in the shaping of common life, or *koinonia*, in worship. An assembly is envisaged in which each participant is the minister of spiritual gifts, by virtue of their common participation in the Spirit. The Pauline community of the body of Christ is realized in the exercise of the particular gifts of the Spirit: to each person 'the manifestation of the Spirit is given for the common good' (1 Cor. 12:7). There are two points to be made here. The first is that despite the reservations that have been expressed with regard to the place of the Spirit in Augustine's trinitarian formulation, his emphasis upon the Spirit as the gift of love between the Father and the Son does enable the economic reality of the *koinonia* of the Spirit to be rooted within the life of the immanent Trinity. Tom Smail, for example, develops the Western tradition in writing of the giving that is in God, and describes the Spirit as the Gift of the Father's very own self to the Son, and the Son's responsive Gift of himself to the Father.[85] These two movements in the eternal life of God can be seen to correspond to historical events in the life of the incarnate Son, such as Jesus' baptism (the Father's gift to the Son) and Jesus' self-offering upon the cross (the Son's offering to the Father; Heb. 9:14). This mutual self-giving, constituted by the Spirit, is the foundation for the life of the mutual self-giving in the charismatic assembly.

Another point to mention is that the charismatic assembly of 1 Corinthians 12 – 14, which to varying degrees the worship observed reflected, witnesses to the Spirit as honouring and establishing the particularity of each contribution. The Pauline metaphor of the body of Christ celebrates the particularity of gifts within the communal unity. Gunton has argued that this is the distinctive role of the Spirit, who by relating us to the Father through Christ, establishes us in our true relationality to God and to others:

> It is not a spirit of merging or assimilation – of homogenisation – but of relation in otherness, relation which does not subvert but establishes the other in its true reality ... as the liberating Other, the Spirit respects the otherness and so particularity of those he elects.[86]

This was represented by the culture of charismatic liturgical time, which as we have seen was open to the particular presentations of individual selves offering gifts but quite different from what participants called the 'formality' of traditional worship which rendered the individual invisible, assimilated within the liturgical act behind the mask of corporate orderliness.

It is time, however, to test the adequacy of the trinitarianism of the worship observed by considering the critical question of whether the worship represents an activity that by virtue of being offered in the Spirit is *therefore* also located through the Son, to the Father, as the trinitarian pattern of the economic doxology reminds us. Within the economy of salvation, the chief function of the Spirit is to lead us to the Son, and through the Son to the Father. As Gunton puts it, the Spirit is the 'self-effacing' person of the Trinity,[87] or in the words of Yves Congar, 'the person without a face',[88] who points us beyond himself to the Son and the Father. In order to root the discussion in the realities of worship in the case study churches the discussion will focus upon the two main charismatic elements of congregational singing and 'prayer ministry'.

The Place of Christ in Congregational Sung Worship

As I have demonstrated, the dominant metaphor used of Christ in songs was the ascended and glorified Lord and king. Regal music and bodily expressions, such as triumphantly raised hands, were consonant with the language of songs that celebrated Jesus as the majestic king. His name was 'magnified', 'exalted' or 'lifted up' and before him worshippers 'bowed down'. The divinity of Christ in these songs was powerfully celebrated, for he was the recipient of prayer and praise, and as Lord claimed victory over

---

[86] Gunton, *The One, the Three and the Many: God, Creation and the Culture of Modernity*, 182-3.

[87] Gunton, *The Promise of Trinitarian Theology*, 168.

[88] Y. Congar, *I Believe in the Holy Spirit*, III, 5.

evil and sin, exercising authority over the world.[89] The theological emphasis of these songs was reminiscent of the early Christian hymns that celebrate the divinity of Christ. Two examples that have an established place within the liturgy of the Church of England are the *Gloria in excelsis* and the *Te Deum*, both of which date from the fourth century, the time when the church was establishing the divinity of the Son in opposition to Arianism.[90] In the *Gloria*, which has an established place in the eucharistic liturgy, the Son is addressed directly and petitioned to 'have mercy upon us' and 'receive our prayer', and also worshipped as the 'Holy One', the 'Lord', the 'Most High', who is 'with the Holy Spirit in the glory of the Father'. The second stanza of the *Te Deum*, used as a canticle in Morning Prayer, similarly addresses the Son who is petitioned to 'help your servants' and 'save your people' and worshipped as the 'everlasting Son of the Father', the 'King of Glory' who shares in the glory of the Father.[91]

There is, however, a dilemma posed by this concentration upon the divine majestic Christ, namely the way that it obscured his humanity. What I had observed in worship is reflected in an article written by Ian Traynor for *Anglicans for Renewal* magazine in which he identified the fact that in charismatic hymnody the exalted Christ has almost completely overshadowed the gospel accounts of Jesus of Nazareth.[92] Traynor comments, 'It seems to me that if you want to sing about Jesus' humanity you have to go to the children's department where we can sing about Zacchaeus up a tree, or building one's house upon the rock!'[93] This struck me most forcibly on the visits to St.E, which coincided with the season of Lent. Of the fifty-two songs that were sung during the course of my two visits, those addressed to Jesus exclusively praised him as the risen and ascended king. Thus, instead of singing to a Jesus who in his humanity faced temptation, conflict and suffering, we sang to a triumphant Christ who in his majesty and power defeats the powers of evil.

Celebrating Christ's majesty in a way that obscures his humanity is by no means a new dilemma for Christian worship, as Tom Torrance indicates in his essay 'The Mind of Christ in Worship: The Problem of Apollinarianism in the Liturgy'.[94] Building upon Jungman's thesis in *The Place of Christ in Liturgical Prayer*, Torrance argues that by trying to counter the influence of Arianism and by simultaneously colluding with Apollinarianism, the public liturgy of the church in the fourth and succeeding centuries

---

[89] Such language of kingship is also used more generally of 'God' in songs.

[90] Wainwright, *Doxology*, 53.

[91] Quotations from versions in *A.S.B.*, 92-4.

[92] I. Traynor, 'Pure Religion – True Worship', *Anglicans for Renewal* 54, 20-4.

[93] Traynor, 'Pure Religion', 22.

[94] T.F. Torrance, *Theology in Reconciliation: Essays towards Evangelical and Catholic Unity in East and West*, 139-214.

tended to exalt the divinity of Christ at the expense of his human mediatorial role. The result was a gradual change in liturgical piety in which the
stress was now placed not on what united Christians to God (Christ as one
of us in his human nature, Christ as our brother), but on what separates
them from God (Christ in God's infinite majesty). Or, as Torrance puts it,
'the effect was to thrust Christ up into the majesty and grandeur of the
Godhead in such a way that it seriously diminished, and sometimes almost
entirely eliminated, the ancient Biblical and Patristic stress upon the High
Priesthood of Christ and his human mediation of prayer to the Father'.[95]
These themes of Christ's priesthood are elaborated upon in the Letter to the
Hebrews, where as our High Priest, Christ was appointed by God in his
humanity (Heb. 2:11-18; 5:1-10), offered the once for all sacrifice for sin
through his death (Heb. 10:9-18), and now appears in heaven as our
forerunner (Heb. 6:19,20) exercising a perpetual priesthood in the order of
Melchizedek (Heb. 7:1-28). On account of this priestly mediation, the
Letter to the Hebrews encourages the early Christians to 'draw near' to God
through Christ (Heb. 7:25; 10:19-22; 13:15). In the patristic era, the
mediatorial role was celebrated with the use of expanded prepositional
imagery, so that prayer was offered 'through', 'with' and 'in' Christ. For
example (as Torrance demonstrates) Cyril of Jerusalem saw the teaching of
Apollinaris, who had taught that Jesus had the divine Mind of the Logos, as
a direct threat to the efficacy of Christ's priesthood because of its failure to
affirm his full humanity.[96] This led Cyril to emphasize the mediatorial
pronoun 'with', along with the conventional 'through', in describing the
priestly function of Christ within worship. By so doing he was drawing
attention to the fact that Christian prayer was made with Christ who, as one
of us, offered prayer and mediation to the Father. Christopher Cocksworth
neatly summarizes the nature of the biblical and patristic concerns: 'Our
worship is *with* Christ our brother, *in* Christ our priest, but always *through*
Christ our sacrifice, whose death for us is the means of our cleansing,
renewing and perfecting.'[97]

Within the West, the historical consequences of this eclipse of the
mediatorship and humanity of Christ are marked, as Torrance outlines. The
Eucharist became the mediation of the saving and sanctifying grace, rather
than a participation through and with Christ in the worship he offers to God
on behalf of all mankind. Holy fear accompanied the presence of the divine
victim on the altar. The concept of Christ's priesthood changed, evident in
the change in language from *pontifex* to *sacerdos*, that is, away from being
a bridge between humanity and God to being a mediator of divine gifts
from God to humanity, and who as such attracted liturgical prayer directed

---

[95] T.F. Torrance, *Theology in Reconciliation*, 142.

[96] T.F. Torrance, *Theology in Reconciliation*, 170-85.

[97] Cocksworth, *Holy,Holy,Holy*, 162 (italics original).

to him as God. Even when prayer was officially offered in the traditional manner of 'through Jesus Christ our Lord', it was the majesty and Godhead of the Mediator and High Priest that was envisaged. This resulted in the rise of other mediatorial functionaries to make up for the human priesthood of Christ, notably the Virgin Mary and the saints associated with her mediation of prayer. This also affected the function of priesthood within the church, which tended towards a mediation between the sinner and Christ.[98]

As James Torrance outlines, the Reformers sought to restore the mediatorial role of Christ.[99] They spoke of the threefold office (*triplex munus*) of Christ as king, priest and prophet, and in these terms expounded not only the once and for all ministry of Christ, but also his continuing ministry. Calvin, for example, in his *Institutes of the Christian Religion* and in his commentary on the Letter to the Hebrews, reaffirmed the mediatorial priesthood of Christ, teaching that the worship of Christ gathers up the worship of Israel, replaces it, and is the substance of all Christian worship.[100] However, as James Torrance points out, subsequent Protestant tradition, whilst affirming the continuing prophetic office of Christ in preaching, and his continuing kingship over church and state, has neglected his continuing priesthood, though still strongly affirming his once for all priestly offering upon the cross. The horizons of worship conveyed by sung worship in the case study churches stand within this Protestant tradition, for they affirmed Christ's kingship, his prophetic ministry (for example in 'words' given to members of the congregation), and his victory on the cross, but fail to do justice to his continuing priesthood in his risen humanity. I observed no reference to the ascended Christ's priesthood in songs sung on my visits, and a careful look through the hymnbook collections of charismatic hymnody revealed an almost complete absence of such songs.[101] The symptoms of this neglect of Christ's priestly mediation were evident in a series of inter-related characteristics present in case study sung worship.

Christ as the Exalted Dispenser of the Spirit

The almost exclusive focus upon the exalted and majestic Christ had the effect of defining his place in worship as the authority called upon to establish spiritual presence or power within the worshipping assembly. We have witnessed, for example, that the internal ritual logic of the 'time of worship' began with a proclamation of the majestic God and his Christ, so

---

[98] T.F. Torrance, *Theology in Reconciliation*, 202-4.

[99] J. Torrance, *Worship, Community and the Triune God of Grace*, 5.

[100] J.T. McNeill (ed.), *Calvin: Institutes of the Christian Religion*, Book2, Chs.9-11; Book 4, Chs.14-17.

[101] 'Jesus is King and I will extol Him', *MP* (1990) No.366 is a notable exception.

as to establish the ground for the Spirit to become present in the midst of the worshipping assembly. As Jesus is enthroned,[102] and the kingdom established in the peoples' praise,[103] so the congregation experienced the blessings of the Spirit. This was epitomized by a prayer used as a preparation for worship by the service leader at St.E:

> We want to acknowledge you, Lord Jesus, as our risen Lord and Saviour. There's no other God but you. And I want to pray now Lord, that as we place our lives in submission to you, you would send your Holy Spirit upon us now, in power.[104]

The problem with this is not with what it affirms, namely the New Testament's teaching that the Spirit is given as a fruit of the ascension (John 16:5-7; Acts 2:33), but in what it tends to deny, for there was little sense of the Spirit dynamically incorporating the worshippers into the priestly Christ in his risen humanity. Using Tom Torrance's terms, Christ's mediation in sung worship was understood primarily in terms of *sacerdos*, the dispenser of the divine blessing of the Spirit, and his role as the bridge between worshippers and God, as *pontifex*, was located solely in the past event of his atoning death upon the cross. The result of this was an experience of worship that had its centre of gravity located with the worshippers, who invite the Spirit to join them in their worship, as witnessed in leaders' prayers and in song lyrics, in contrast to worship that is offered with its centre of gravity located in, with and through the priestly Christ in his offering to the Father. The invitation that remained unarticulated in sung worship was Christ's invitation to join him in his life of worship, an invitation identified by Christopher Cocksworth as a central theme of early apostolic witness in the New Testament: 'Christ invites us into the redeemed humanity which he bears, the new creation which he brings to birth and the holy city which he has entered. The invitation is to accompany him into the glory of God.'[105]

In his book *A Kingdom of Priests*, the Anglican charismatic Mark Stibbe makes a promising attempt to rectify this tendency for the priesthood of Christ to be overwhelmed by concepts of kingship. Reflecting on his

---

[102] See 'Jesus we enthrone You' in my earlier discussion on the transformation of place in Ch.5.

[103] 'May your kingdom be established in our praises' from 'Father in heaven how we love You', *MP* (1990), No. 135; St.E, visit 2 (as quoted in Ch.5).

[104] St.E, 11.00am service, visit 1.

[105] Cocksworth, 'Trinity Today', 67. See also Cocksworth, *Holy, Holy, Holy*, Ch.6: 'The Invitation of Christ'. A classic Anglican liturgical expression of this is Christ's invitation from Matthew 11:28 placed at the beginning of the Comfortable Words in the *Book of Common Prayer* Communion Service.

experience of Charismatic Renewal, Stibbe admits that 'we have heard a lot about preaching the kingdom, healing the sick and delivering the demonized. We have heard less about ministering to God as priests in the Holy Temple of his presence.'[106] Stibbe locates the life of prayer within the journey from the temple's outer courts to the holy of holies, a ritual metaphor that participants had referred to in connection with the ritual process of the 'time of worship'.[107] The significance of this priestly journey is that it provides an invitation to shape worship according to the priestly ministry of Christ, a link which Stibbe makes at various stages in the journey. However, it is disappointing that Stibbe does not make more of the possible implications of the journey being made with, in and through Christ as the Great High Priest. For instance, the very first liturgical act recommended by Stibbe is an invocation of the Holy Spirit: 'The most important act of 'warming up' is to ask the Holy Spirit to empower us for our ministry as priests of the kingdom.'[108] The problem with this is not with the act of invocation itself, which as I have already indicated, is an essential witness to worship 'in the Spirit', but in the way that no explicit link is made with this empowerment and its primary purpose, namely enabling a response to the invitation of Jesus as our High Priest to join him in *his* offering of worship to the Father.

The Spirit-Inspired Congregation as Sole Subject of Worship

We have already seen how the worship observed highlighted our vocation as liturgical beings, those who offer thanksgiving in the Spirit. However, one of the features of its estrangement from a dynamic relationship with Christ's offering of worship is the way that it drew attention to itself. Song lyrics tended to celebrate the act of worship itself as much as the object of worship. Worshippers typically 'celebrate' and 'revel' in God's love,[109] speak often of their desire and wish to worship[110] and take delight in describing its material expression.[111] Even God was invited to 'take joy' in what was sung: 'may it be a sweet, sweet sound in Your ear' was the prayer of the song 'I love you, Lord'.[112] Estranged from a dynamic relationship to

---

[106] M. Stibbe, *A Kingdom of Priests: Deeper into God in Prayer*, 10.

[107] See the section on 'Intimacy, Prayer and God' in Ch.5.

[108] Stibbe, *Kingdom*, 12.

[109] Words from 'Jesus, we celebrate Your victory', *MP* (1990), No.387.

[110] 'I just want to praise You', *MP* (1990) No.276; St.C visit 1. For other examples see Ch.5: 'The Songs as Liturgical Text'.

[111] For example, 'I lift my hands, I raise my voice' *MP* (1990) No.280; St.E visit 2. See also the text of 'When the Spirit of the Lord' *SF* (1991) No.598, quoted in Ch.5, at the end of the section on 'Transformation of Personae'.

[112] Also quoted in Ch.5, in the section on 'The Goal of Ritual Process: "Intimacy" in Worship'.

Christ's worship, the worshipping assembly, believing itself to be the only subject of true worship, has appeared to have fallen into the temptation of gazing upon itself as it worships 'in the Spirit'. As Tom Torrance comments, if there is no consciousness of our offering of worship being in, with, and through Christ, then 'we are inevitably thrown back upon ourselves to offer worship to the Father, worship of our own devising, although it may be worship for the sake of Christ, motivated by him and patterned on his earthly example.'[113] Case study sung worship may have been inspired by the Spirit, and offered in response to Christ's saving work upon the cross, his present reign and the blessings of his presence, but it remained all too self-consciously 'our' worship, with its centre of gravity located within the worshipping congregation. This also created difficulties for the inclusivity of the worship, for once a particular style of worship 'in the Spirit' is allowed to protrude so obviously and thus dominate the public horizon of worship, there is a greater likelihood of excluding those who do not, or cannot, express worship in a similar way. We have noted, for example, how a participant at St.A found Evening Praise too emotionally charged for her comfort, as did the Outside Observer in the 'time of worship' experienced in different churches.[114]

The Collapse of Worship into Immanentism

In the light of the sustained emphasis upon the exalted Christ and majestic Godhead in songs, judging sung worship as falling into immanentism appears at first to be rather a contradiction. However, when analysing the practice of sung worship, there is an important distinction to be made between its object, the transcendent majestic God, and its ritual destination, the encounter with the immanent presence of the Spirit. As I have described, the climax of the 'time of worship' was experienced as an intimate encounter, often romantically conceived, with signs such as gifts of utterance which confirmed the close presence of the divine among the worshipping assembly. Within such an environment there was no affirmation of the goal of worship being participation with Christ in the worship of the heavenly sanctuary, of which the Letter to the Hebrews describes Christ as leader (Heb. 8:2). This lack of reference to the transcendent and eschatological reality of heavenly worship becomes evident when charismatic songs are compared with the hymns of Charles Wesley.

As I have discussed elsewhere, though charismatic and early Methodist hymnody are similar in a number of respects, one fundamental difference is Wesley's celebration of the risen Christ as the ascended High Priest and

---

[113] T.F. Torrance, *Theology In Reconciliation*, 204.

[114] See Ch.5, in the discussion on 'The Goal of Ritual Process: "Intimacy" in Worship'.

sacrificial Lamb.[115] This is particularly marked in Wesley's hymns for the Ascension and Eucharist, which draw worshippers into the transcendent and eschatological reality of worship around the throne of God in the presence of the wounded and interceding Priest, and the company of the saints. For the Wesleys, this vision of heavenly worship was the goal of all earthly worship. For example, Charles Wesley's hymn on Christian fellowship, 'All praise to our redeeming Lord' celebrates many charismatic themes, such as supporting one another, delighting in one another's gifts, harmony in Jesus' name, peace and joy, but concludes with a verse that captures a vision of future perfection and ecstasy that was noticeably absent in case study songs:

> And if our fellowship below
> in Jesus be so sweet,
> what heights of rapture shall we know,
> when round His throne we meet! [116]

In this connection it is interesting to observe that angels, traditionally an important feature of exploring the transcendence of God in worship, feature prominently in the hymns of Charles Wesley. In Wesley's hymns angels very often heighten the sense of wonder at the mystery of God's love and salvation for mankind. Charles' famous hymn 'And can it be', celebrating his newly found assurance and wonder of God's salvation, includes this verse:

> 'Tis mystery all! The Immortal dies:
> who can explore His strange design?
> In vain the first-born seraph tries
> to sound the depths of love divine.
> 'Tis mercy all! Let earth adore,
> let angel minds inquire no more. [117]

By contrast, in the songs of Charismatic Renewal angels are a rare species, only appearing in some of Graham Kendrick's Christmas songs, and the Fisherfolk song that is based on Isaiah's vision in the temple narrated in Isaiah 6, 'We see the Lord', which we sang at the conclusion of Mass at St.D.[118]

---

[115] J.H.S. Steven, 'Charismatic Hymnody in the Light of Early Methodist Hymnody', *Studia Liturgica* 27 (1997), 2:217-34.

[116] *A Collection of Hymns for the Use of the People called Methodists* (1780), No.500.

[117] *Collection* (1780), No.201.

[118] *MP* (1990), No.736, quoted in Ch.4, in the section on St.D.

Another indicator of this impoverished sense of participation in heavenly
worship was the lack of genuinely ecstatic language in the songs. The
Wesley's hymns, at their most ecstatic, celebrate a movement beyond
ourselves and into the unfathomable depths of the life of God, where, we
are 'lost in wonder, love and praise'.[119] Witness the language in one of
Charles Wesley's hymns for Pentecost which starts with a charismatic
intensity which then leads to an ecstatic movement into God:

> Come, Holy Ghost, all-quickening fire,
> come, and in me delight to rest;
> drawn by the lure of strong desire,
> O come and consecrate my breast;
> the temple of my soul prepare,
> and fix Thy sacred presence there.
>
> Eager for Thee I ask and pant;
> so strong, the principle divine
> carries me out, with sweet constraint,
> 'till all my hallow'd soul is Thine;
> plunged in the Godhead's deepest sea,
> and lost in Thine immensity. [120]

The ecstasy expressed within the 'times of worship' was different. Placed
within the context of intimacy, with associated romantic overtones, it was
more to do with losing oneself in amorous feelings for the divine and the
experience of closeness with the divine, than the experience of being drawn
into a reality in which we are lost by virtue of its transcendence. Transformation in the 'time of worship' occurred in an intense and intimate
encounter with the Spirit of God being with us and among us, rather than by
worshippers being drawn by the same Spirit through Christ into the life of
heavenly worship. Liturgical space reflected this, as the music groups faced
the congregation and thereby enclosed a space within which the encounter
was experienced, and into which God was invited. As we have seen,
musical style also reinforced this intimate environment with its resonance
with the sounds of the secular discotheque dance-floor. This failure of the
'time of worship' to mediate an ecstatic movement is confirmed by the
Outside Observer who on a number of occasions summarized the experience of such worship as spiritually "claustrophobic".[121]

---

[119] From Charles Wesley's hymn, 'Love divine, all loves excelling', *Collection*
(1780), No.385.
[120] *Collection* (1780), No.374, verses 1 and 3.
[121] At St.A (Evening Praise), St.B, St.C and St.E.

Individualism and the Climax of Worship

Another aspect of the climax of the 'time of worship' that betrayed its disconnection with the eschatological goal of worship in Christ was the individualism of its romantic intimacy. The journey into God's presence mediated through song and music had the effect of nullifying the corporate consciousness of the charismatic assembly, turning the body of Christ into a single 'I' in its communion with God. This is an obvious casualty of the pervasive influence of two cultural trends I highlighted at the end of Chapter 5, the intimization and subjectification of social reality. Even during the administration of Communion in the churches visited, a liturgical context in which one would expect a corporate voice of praise, participating in the heavenly feast of the redeemed, devotional songs were persistently sung in the first person singular.[122] Typically these were expressions of individual love for Jesus,[123] individual thanksgiving for the blessings of his salvation and presence[124] and petitions for transformation and sanctification in the individual's heart.[125] This again contrasts with the way that Charles Wesley's hymns depict the goal of Christian worship as an essentially corporate activity, standing with the redeemed community before the throne of God. For example, the last verse of 'All praise to our redeeming Lord', quoted above, evokes the thought of worship in heaven being an everlasting Methodist Class Meeting! Because worship for the Wesleys was offered through, in and with the ascended High Priest, their hymns avoid the individualism of the charismatic vision of communion with God. In Charles Wesley's lyrical theology, wherever Jesus is, there too are his people:

See where our great High Priest
before the Lord appears,
and on His loving breast
The tribes of Israel bears,
never without His people seen,
the Head of all believing men![126]

---

[122] This was common to St.C, St.D, St.E and St.F. At St.A there was no singing during the administration of Communion, and I did not observe Holy Communion at St.B.

[123] 'I just want to praise You', *MP* (1990) No.276; St.C, visit 2; 'Lord, You are so precious to me', *SF* (1991) No.369; St.D, visit 1.

[124] 'It's Your blood that cleanses me', *MP* (1990) No.351; St.D visit 1; 'To be in Your presence', *SF* (1991) No.167; St.F, visit 1 (and quoted in Ch.5 in the section 'The Goal of Ritual Process: "Intimacy" with God').

[125] 'Change my heart, O God', *MP* (1990) No.276; St.C visit 2 and St.F visit 1.

[126] *Hymns and Psalms: A Methodist and Ecumenical Hymn Book*, No.622, verse 1.

The Priestly Character of Worship

Alongside affirming the transcendent and the corporate nature of Christian worship, worship that is offered through Christ is also inescapably related to the created order. As James Torrance writes, 'Jesus comes as our brother to be our High Priest, to carry on his heart the joys, the sorrows, the prayers, the conflicts of all his creatures, to reconcile all things to God, and to intercede for all nations as our eternal Mediator and advocate'.[127] In case study worship, however, one of the effects of the large emphasis upon Christ as king, without reference to his priestly ministry, has led to a view of the world as a godless environment which needs to be conquered in the name of Christ. The songs from the *Songs of Fellowship* stable, as we have seen, have particularly promoted this understanding, as have some of the more militaristic songs that Graham Kendrick has written for the Praise Marches. The popular 'Rejoice, rejoice' reflects Old Testament conquest themes and has the congregation singing that it is time for them 'to march upon the land' in the confidence that Christ 'will give the ground' they claim.[128] Not only is this far from the New Testament portrayal of the kingdom of God, but it also obscures the priestly role of the worshipping church, which in the Spirit participates in the priestly work of Christ.

The non-priestly relationship with creation can also be detected in the relative absence of songs in the churches visited that connected the worshipper with the realities of daily life. This contrasts with the hymns of Charles Wesley, in which a wide range of worldly concerns are represented, such as the workplace (masters of households and physicians), travelling (journeying and visiting friends) and domestic life (women in childbirth, and even a child when teething!).[129] It is true that in case study worship daily concerns were addressed at other points in services, such as in sermons, and occasionally in intercession, but their absence in sung worship, which in participants' understanding tended to be seen as the primary act of worship, is a serious omission.

Related to this lack of engagement with the larger realities of created life in songs is a failure to do justice to our created humanity at worship. This, again, can be illustrated with reference to early Methodist hymnody. Charles Wesley's hymns encompassed a wide range of Christian experience and thus articulated the breadth of redeemed creaturely response to God. For example, in the Wesleys' celebrated hymnbook the 1780 *Collection of Hymns for the use of the People called Methodists*, the section on the life of the Christian believer (Part IV) includes hymns for believers rejoicing, praying, watching, working, suffering, and groaning for full redemption. Bernard Manning writes that the 1780 *Collection* reflects the breadth of the

---

[127] J. Torrance, *Worship, Community*, 2.
[128] *MP* (1990) No.572; St.F, visit 1.
[129] Steven, 'Charismatic Hymnody', 228.

Old Testament Psalms in being a 'treasury for the expression of every state of mind and every condition of the soul'.[130] The songs sung in case study worship, however, whilst able to celebrate Christian joy, victory and confidence, did not articulate other themes of Christian life, such as the cost of discipleship (suffering, endurance, and patience in face of opposition), and lament for human sinfulness. This can also be said of charismatic hymnody in general, as Jeremy Begbie pointed out in his study of charismatic songs.[131] In many ways this is just what would be expected within a horizon of worship in which the humanity of Christ has been overshadowed by his exalted divine glory. In the singing during Lenten visits to St.E mentioned above, a victorious Christian life seeking power from on high had swept away any Lenten notions of penitence or spiritual discipline. The consequences of this for the church's worship can be best summarized in Tom Torrance's criticism of the effect of Apollinarianism on the church's worship: 'A mutilated humanity in Christ could not but result in a mutilated Christian worship of God.'[132] Gone is the Christian theme of hope in the face of suffering, which, ironically, was an integral part of the Black gospel musical tradition from which Pentecostal and charismatic music has derived.[133] Gone therefore is the ability to link with the pain and suffering of the created world, for in celebrating the victory of Jesus, as one song put it, 'in His presence all our problems disappear'.[134]

Weakened also is the articulation of human sinfulness, the failure to live according to the new humanity that Christ invites us into. This is reflected in the tendency for the 'heart' to be conceived romantically in charismatic hymnody, rather than the more biblical view of the heart as a moral centre, which in Anglican tradition is given liturgical expression in Cranmer's Collect for Purity.[135] This may explain why on the occasions in case study worship when authorized liturgy was disregarded (thereby making worship more dependent upon a liturgy provided by songs), a corporate confession of sin would be omitted. So in St.A's Evening Praise and in the services at

---

[130] B. Manning, *The Hymns of Wesley and Watts: Five Informal Papers*, 13.

[131] J. Begbie, 'The Spirituality of Renewal Music' in *Anvil: An Anglican Evangelical Journal for Theology and Mission* 8 (1991) 3:234-36.

[132] T.F. Torrance, *Theology in Reconciliation*, 150.

[133] See further, Graham Cray, 'Justice, Rock and the Renewal of Worship' in R. Sheldon (ed.), *In Spirit and in Truth: Exploring Directions in Music and Worship Today*, 3-27.

[134] From 'Jesus, we celebrate Your victory', *MP* (1990), No.387; St.D, visits 1 and 2. At St.B this was regarded as erroneous, and so they had changed the line to read 'in His presence all our darkness disappears' (CI).

[135] See further, S.W. Sykes, 'Cranmer on the Open Heart' in *Unashamed Anglicanism*, 24-48.

St.B there was no corporate act of confession observed.[136] At St.E the
retention of elements of authorized liturgy meant that it was included in
every service, and the same was true of all services at St.C, St.D, and St.F.

This enquiry into the priestly character of case study worship can be
extended to include the content of public intercession, a liturgical action
which ought to reflect clearly the priesthood of Christ. After many years of
experience in Charismatic Renewal, Tom Smail makes the observation that
genuine intercession that identifies with the needs of others is often
neglected in charismatic worship.[137] In what ways was this true of the
worship observed? As with corporate confession, I discovered that the
content of intercession was least priestly in settings of worship where
authorized liturgy had been disregarded. In Evening Praise at St.A there
was little or no intercession for others outside the worshipping assembly
and yet plenty of prayers for the spiritual advancement of those present.
Those who led prayers at St.B varied between rather intense prayers for
individual sanctification to those which demonstrated more of a genuine
engagement with the needs of the world. One of the sermons at St.B was
about the desperation and passion of genuine prayer, but this tended to be
focused upon the subjective experience of prayer rather than the need for
prayer to be identifying with a broken world.[138] There was more evidence
of intercessory prayer at St.E where, for example, those who led prayers in
Holy Communion used the *A.S.B.* intercessory guidelines that embrace the
needs of the world, local community and the suffering. However, in the
relatively non-liturgical 'Come Holy Spirit' Service, there were no public
intercessions at all.[139] Intercessory prayer featured in every service I
attended at the more liturgical churches (St.C, St.D and St.F), the worship
at St.F being particularly permeated by a priestly consciousness, evident in
the way that the needs and brokenness of the estate were naturally
incorporated and articulated within worship, not only in intercession but
also in the dialogue sermons, notices, and even in song.[140] This was the
result not just of the liturgy but, as we have indicated in Chapter 4, of the
parish priest's theology and style of liturgical leadership.

These observations with regard to corporate confession and intercession
illustrate the different worshipping environments, or what might be called
'ecologies', particular to Anglican liturgy on the one hand, and a charis-

---

[136] I was informed at St.B, however, that there would be a Confession used in Holy
Communion.
[137] T. Smail, A. Walker and N. Wright, *Charismatic Renewal: The Search for a
Theology*, 113.
[138] St.B, 6.30pm service, visit 2.
[139] St.E, 6.30pm service, visit 2.
[140] As mentioned in Ch.4, St.F was the only church where I observed the local
community named in the course of a song.

matic worship culture as evidenced in case study worship on the other hand. The former has been shaped by the wisdom of a trinitarian theology of worship, providing an ecology of worship that locates worship in the Spirit through Christ to the Father, whereas the latter, conveyed through song within the non-liturgical contexts of conferences or small groups, has spawned worship with an ecological imbalance, celebrating the triumph of Christ but failing to do justice to the dynamic priestly pattern of Christ's worship in his risen humanity.

Receiving the Spirit in 'Prayer Ministry'

Earlier in this chapter I indicated how prayer for the Holy Spirit, the liturgical initiatory event in 'prayer ministry', was an example of the instinctive trinitarianism of case study worship. I argued that within this liturgical context the Spirit was celebrated in Eastern rather than Western trinitarian terms as a distinct divine hypostasis. However, the critical question that remains to be answered is how adequately did the under-standing of the Spirit's presence and activity mediated by 'prayer ministry' relate the worshipping community to the Son's receiving of the Spirit? This is a fundamental question given the trinitarian shape of Christian worship, where by the Spirit we approach the Father through the Son, who, as Chris Cocksworth puts it, invites us not only into his worship of the Father but also into his receiving of the Spirit from the Father.[141] It is also a question evoked by the fact that 'prayer ministry' is presented as a means of spiritual empowerment. A Christian theologian must ask whether the role of the Spirit adequately reflects the pattern of the economy of the Spirit's empowerment of Jesus of Nazareth. I will discuss three characteristics of the pneumatological dimensions of 'prayer ministry' that appeared to be dislocated from these christological concerns.

The Spirit as Divine Performer

I suggested in Chapter 6 that 'performance', understood as the combination of presence, visibility and spontaneity, was a dominant metaphor for the divine action in the public 'prayer ministry'. The authenticity of the initial prayer to the Spirit was demonstrated by the way in which the Spirit could be seen to be 'doing things'. Indeed, it appears that the reason for the adoption of the 'Come Holy Spirit' prayer is not on account of any theological conclusion but because it has proved to be the necessary liturgical and ritual trigger for ecstatic behaviour associated with the Spirit's presence. However, this performance culture creates a number of inherent tensions for leadership, not least the need to ensure that the Spirit

---

[141] Cocksworth, *Holy, Holy, Holy*, 162.

'shows-up'.[142] This tension was, to a certain degree, resolved by a technique driven style of presiding, which, as we have seen, functioned through the dynamic of the shaman-like control of the leader coupled with rhetoric that emphasized the need for participants to be open to the sovereign and free Spirit.

The danger of this technique, however, is two-fold. First, the character of the control exercised by leaders inevitably involved some notion of control in relation to the Spirit, which had the effect of undermining the freedom and divine personhood of the Spirit. Requests for 'more power', or 'more presence' had the effect of depersonalizing the Spirit into a 'power' or 'presence' which could be increased at request. Therefore, despite signs in case study worship of an alignment with an Eastern view of the Spirit, as discussed earlier, the pneumatology mediated by the public 'prayer ministry' exhibits a subordination of the Spirit, which the Eastern Church would regard as typically Western in its formulation. Alasdair Heron summarizes the more forthright accusations of Eastern theologians in describing Western trinitarianism as involving

> a subordination of the Holy Spirit to the person of Jesus Christ which tends towards a 'depersonalisation' of the Spirit, a reduction of him to a mere 'power' flowing from Christ, and so loses sight of his sovereign freedom and initiative as the Spirit, who like the Word, is one of what Iranaeus called 'the two hands of God'. No longer does 'he blow where he wills', but 'it goes where it is sent'.[143]

It is tempting to suggest that a liturgical practice dominated by the worship of the exalted Christ as the source of divine authority is fertile ground for such a subordination of the Spirit. It is also ironic that a movement that was initially fuelled by a protest on behalf of the freedom on the Spirit should be showing tendencies of imprisoning the Spirit within a depersonalized, functional and performative role.

The second danger of the techniques observed in public 'prayer ministry' is their threat to the integrity of human creatureliness. In compromising the freedom and 'otherness' of the Spirit, the 'prayer ministry' has the effect of undermining the free response of participants. The Spirit is the active subject who does things *to* respondents, who willingly and passively 'open' themselves as objects of such action. The problem with this is the lack of affirmation of the prayer recipient as an authentic moral actor. Indeed, it is

---

[142] A phrase used by John Leach in an article on worship, 'Hitting The Target', in *Christian Music*, Summer 1992, 4.

[143] A.I.C. Heron, 'The *filioque* in recent Reformed theology', in *Spirit of God, Spirit of Christ*, Lucas Vischer (ed.) (Geneva: W.C.C., 1981), 113; quoted in T.Smail, *The Giving Gift*, 134.

precisely the powers of self-determination that one relinquishes in order to become available for the Spirit's action; one has to be open to *whatever* the Spirit may do. The result, particularly in the post-Toronto 'prayer ministries' observed, is that the recipient appears to be so overwhelmed by the Spirit, epitomized in forms of ecstatic behaviour, that very little account can be given of their own active response. This verges towards what Buber called an I-It relationship, in which the Spirit as the active subject does things to passive and malleable participants, a version of the Hegelian concept of self-realization through the other.[144] Much of the problem lies in the way that the Spirit was defined repeatedly as 'presence', which not only tends to depersonalize the Spirit ('presence' is a definition of substance rather than relation), but also threatens the reality of participant space, their own otherness and particular unique freedom. This was the experience of David Runcorn, an ordained Anglican and charismatic, for whom this repeated ritualized form of realizing the presence of God became a tyranny: 'I remember how I often heard people praying for God's presence to be real to me. I didn't know how to tell them that that was exactly what I didn't want. His presence had become a total burden. I wanted his absence. I wanted space.'[145] By contrast, the Spirit's relationship with Jesus of Nazareth was such that Jesus was freed to be himself in relationship to others. As Gunton writes, '[W]e must put out of our minds the popular view that the Spirit was a homogeneous possession of Jesus, like a built in soul-stuff. The Spirit is the one, the personal other, by whom Jesus is related to his Father and to those with whom he had to do.'[146] This is illustrated in the sequence of Jesus' baptism leading to his temptation. Having received the Spirit from his Father, the Spirit leads Jesus into a space in which he is to define his particular self as the Son of God; in the face of temptation in the wilderness, he defines and asserts his true identity in relation to the material world, and spiritual and political power. By participating in Jesus' receiving of the Spirit, Christian worshippers are freed to be moral actors 'in Christ', defining themselves in relation to God, the Christian community and the wider world.

The Therapeutic Spirit

With the suppression of the moral integrity of participants comes a more modern and subtle role for the Spirit, the therapist. Interweaved with the notion of 'performer' is the notion that the Spirit engages in therapeutic

---

[144] Most famously expressed in Hegel's use of the parable of the Lord and Bondsman. See R. Roberts, 'Lord, Bondsman and Churchman' in C.E. Gunton and D.W. Hardy (eds.), *On Being the Church: Essays on the Christian Community*, 163-69.
[145] D. Runcorn, *Rumours of Life: Reflections on the Resurrection Appearances*, 21.
[146] C.E. Gunton, *The One, the Three and the Many*, 182.

work, resolving individual need. Hopewell's romantic adventure into which participants were invited was a therapeutic adventure, a search for a promised divine blessing. For instance, in Wimber's 'Spirit Song', quoted in Chapter 6, participants bring to consciousness their 'tears and sadness' and 'years of pain', and in presenting them to Jesus are promised that the descending Spirit will make them whole.[147] In the Vineyard song 'I give You all the honour', the Spirit moves upon participants, meeting their 'deepest need'.[148] Many 'words of knowledge' were focused upon the personal needs of individuals in the worshipping assembly.[149] Within this therapeutic framework, these 'words of knowledge' can be viewed as the means by which the Spirit searches for presenting problems, which participants are invited to recognize within themselves and consequently make themselves available for divine therapy. As regards the therapeutic content of the ministry in its more overt Toronto style, what was observed would correspond to I.M. Lewis' description of the therapy of a shamanistic séance:

> The atmosphere, though controlled and not as anarchic as it may seem, is essentially permissive and comforting. Everything takes on the tone and character of modern psychodrama or group therapy. Abreaction is the order of the day. Repressed urges and desires, the idiosyncratic as well as the socially conditioned, are given full public rein. No holds barred. No interests or demands are too unseemly in this setting not to receive sympathetic attention.[150]

The dominance of the therapeutic over the moral is further illustrated in the way that God the Father was viewed. We have witnessed in the 'prayer ministry' that the Fatherhood of God was portrayed in song as the source of existential security, thereby encouraging participant response as one launches on the romantic adventure of being open to the Spirit's work. A similar model of paternal care could be seen informing the language of some of the inspired utterances offered in the 'time of worship' when those in the congregation were addressed as 'children'.[151] However, this portrayal of the Father is only a partial representation of New Testament teaching, for whilst we may indeed be secure in the love of God the Father (1 Jn. 3:1), this is not the love of an indulgent parent but of the one who has authorita-

---

[147] *MP* (1990) No.502.

[148] *MP* (1990) No.271; quoted in Ch.6 in the section 'The Divine Action: God as "Live Performer" (God's Spontaneity)'.

[149] See Appendix C.

[150] I.M. Lewis, *Ecstatic Religion: An Anthropological Study of Spirit Possession and Shamanism*, 195.

[151] Most notably at St.E; See Ch.4.

tive and absolute rights to the obedience of his children. In his book *The Forgotten Father*, Tom Smail argues that there has been a tendency in Charismatic Renewal to lose sight of the moral demands of being children of the Father. He reminds his readers that the only place in the gospels when we hear the word *Abba* upon the lips of Jesus is in his prayer in the Garden of Gethsemane, the place of costly obedience (Mark 14:36).

> *Abba* is a Gethsemane word spoken by the Son made man who trusts his Father so absolutely that he can obey him completely. His call to sonship is a call to total trust and radical obedience. The sonship of the eternal Son consists of a divine obedience; the sonship of the adopted sons of a human obedience.[152]

Therefore, by participating in Jesus' receiving of the Spirit from the Father, Christian worshippers are invited into a life of trusting obedience, the shape of which is defined by Jesus' example, and the glory of which goes to the Father.[153] A good example of how this trinitarian pattern of life was represented in case study worship was the priest's commissioning prayer for the head server at St.F.

> Our Heavenly Father, we want to thank you for Anna and her love for you. And I pray for her, remembering how Jesus served at the Last Supper, taking off his robe, and with cloth and water, washing his disciples feet. We pray that the same Spirit of humility may come upon your child Anna [the priest places his hand over Anna's head], and that she may be filled with the Holy Spirit in this work that you have ordained for her to do. We pray this in the name of our Lord Jesus Christ.[154]

There were other indications in 'prayer ministry' that the moral had not completely been eclipsed, thanks to the practice of linking the sermon to such ministry. I have already drawn attention to three occasions when 'prayer ministry' was a response to the moral demands of a sermon.[155] However, in all other 'prayer ministries' an attitude of trustful obedience to the promptings of the Spirit, defined as abandonment to a ritual therapeutic adventure, had replaced the invitation of Christ to a moral or ethical life. In essence, the participants were not required to repent of sin but instead to offer their 'years of pain'. Graham Cray, who succeeded David Watson at

---

[152] T. Smail, *The Forgotten Father*, 103.

[153] The ethical instructions in the New Testament letters, for instance, are rooted in the example of Christ, for example, Col. 3:1-25 and Eph. 4:17-32.

[154] St.F, visit 2.

[155] See the discussion of the place of the sermon in the section on 'The Congregation' in Ch.6.

St. Michael-le-Belfry in York, recognized this tendency.

> When I was vicar of St. Michael's, we could stand in church on a
> Saturday or Sunday night with large numbers, particularly of young
> people and students, and I, or my colleague, could say 'Come Holy Spirit'
> and we could see young people all around the church having the most
> profound encounters with the Spirit of the living God ... but those
> encounters seemed to make little or no difference whatsoever to the way a
> lot of those people led their lives from Monday to Saturday ... David
> Wells, the American evangelical theologian, has written 'The modern
> culture has secured the triumph of the therapeutic over the moral, even in
> the church.' Feeling whole is more important than being good ... Being
> good comes out of knowing what is right and finding in Jesus Christ the
> power of the Spirit to live that way. The satisfaction of our psychological
> needs pales in significance when compared with the enduring value of
> doing what is right.[156]

The Spirit for the Individual

One of the traits of revivalism in the public 'prayer ministries', as we have
seen, was the focus upon the individual as the recipient of God's visitation
within the context of a crowd. 'Words of knowledge', by definition, were
addressed to individuals. Liturgical space was arranged so as to enhance
individual response. For example, the removal of the rows of chairs at St.E
in preparation for 'prayer ministry' signalled the physical and symbolic
removal of corporate restraint and discipline.[157] However, on the occasions
when 'prayer ministries' occurred at the end of services, this focus upon the
individual led to a marked fragmentation of the gathered assembly into a
collection of individuals 'doing their own thing'.[158] The particular meanings
of each ecstatic expression were individually interpreted, for the only
interpretation available to the public assembly was the blanket assurance of
the 'prayer ministry' leader that God was 'moving', or 'ministering' to
people. The disintegration of the public assembly was further confirmed by
the marginalization of the final public dismissal, which was either relegated
to a blessing which signalled that non-participants could leave,[159] or was
ignored altogether.[160]

This kind of social gathering is, of course, a contradiction of the com-

---

[156] G. Cray, 'Back to the Future' in *Anglicans for Renewal* 64 (Spring 1996), 13.
[157] 6.30pm service, visit 2.
[158] St.B, St.C and St.E.
[159] St.B, 10.30am service (visit 1); St.C, 6.00pm service (visits 1 and 2); St.E,
11.00am service (visit 2).
[160] St.B, 6.30pm service (visit 2); St.E, 6.30pm service (visit 2).

munity life outlined by Paul in his description of the Corinthian church as the body of Christ, aspects of which we have seen modelled elsewhere in worship. As I have discussed, according to Paul, the gift of the Spirit establishes the Christian community by inspiring particular gifts that through use relate participants to one another as one body. In the same way that the Spirit enables Jesus to be himself, so it is with the Christian community. As Paul argues, to each individual 'the manifestation of the Spirit is given for the common good' (1 Cor. 12:7). Hence, in 1 Corinthians 14, Paul argues that the gift of prophecy is superior to the gift of tongues on the basis of its public intelligibility and hence its power to edify and build up the church (1 Cor. 14:5).[161] Like speaking in tongues, the public ecstatic behaviour in 'prayer ministry' may have benefited the individual respondents, but it had no intelligible corporate role, other than affirming to the congregation that God was 'moving'.[162] The corporate dimension of the Spirit's ministry in constituting the body of Christ was thus chronically underdeveloped.

From a liturgical point of view the marginalization of the final dismissal compromises the whole sense of the 'prayer ministry' leading to a corporate engagement with God's mission in the world. The Spirit that Jesus received from the Father was fundamental to the fulfilment of his mission, and to the subsequent mission of the church (Luke 4:18,19 and Acts 1:8), but in 'prayer ministry' the connection with the public world appeared to have been suppressed.[163] The 'words of knowledge' are a further illustration of this for the knowledge imparted was always and only about individuals within the assembly, giving the impression that the worshipping community had become absorbed in its own self-knowledge, to the neglect of its public responsibility to the world it serves.[164] The Outside Observer's comment after the public 'prayer ministry' at St.C summarized this when he described it as "privately engaging, but publicly irrelevant".[165]

Conclusion

In the instinctive trinitarianism of the charismatic worship evident in case study worship, there were elements which reflected an orthodox

---

[161] Because tongues are unintelligible, so Paul argues, they are only of value in public worship when they are accompanied by an interpretation (1 Cor. 14:13).

[162] 'He who speaks in a tongue edifies himself, but he who prophesies edifies the church' (1 Cor. 14:4).

[163] For further discussion on the relationship between worship, mission and the Trinity, see Cocksworth's *Holy, Holy, Holy*, Ch.8: 'The Trinity, Worship and Mission'.

[164] In three and a half years of ministry at St. John's in Welling, I do not recall ever hearing a 'word of knowledge' which gave insight into the needs of the local or wider community.

[165] St.C, 6.00pm service, visit 1.

understanding of trinitarian worship. Praise and prayer was offered to each of the three persons of the Trinity. Worship reflected the economic doxology by being offered 'in the Spirit', reflecting what Allchin calls 'one of the great gifts of God to the church in the last quarter of a century' namely 'the discovery that the Church's life and worship is essentially *epicletic*, i.e. centred on the invocation of the Holy Spirit'.[166] However, much of what I found to be inadequate in the theology conveyed by the more charismatic elements of case study worship, the sung worship and 'prayer ministry', can be traced to a failure to locate this worship through the Son, to the Father. Tom Smail has consistently argued that one of the chief theological failings of Pentecostalism has been its tendency to construct a pneumatology in relation to the triumphant ascended Christ, to the neglect of the incarnate Christ.[167] A similar pattern has emerged in the above appraisal, in that two fundamental dynamics of the economy of the Son have been neglected. First, by neglecting the Christ who invites us into his worship of the Father, the sung worship tended to be self absorbed and individualistic, lacking a participation in the transcendent, and a genuine connection with the realities of creaturely existence. Secondly, by being dislocated from the Christ who invites us into his receiving of the Spirit from the Father, the 'prayer ministry' suffered from tendencies to compromise the divine freedom of the Spirit, and a failure to portray the life of worship as one of genuine responsiveness and moral obedience which is exercised corporately within the church, and in responsibility to the world in which the church is set. Thus, although case study worship was marked by trinitarian instincts, there were theological forces at work which prevented the charismatic worship observed developing a truly mature trinitarian character.

---

[166] A.M. Allchin, 'Walking in the Spirit: Freedom and Tradition in the Church's Life', in C. Craston (ed.), *Open to the Spirit*, 157 (italics original).

[167] For instance, his essay 'The Cross and the Spirit: Towards a Theology of Renewal' in T. Smail, A. Walker and N. Wright, *Charismatic Renewal*, 49-70.

Conclusion

The purpose of my research was to investigate forms of public worship propagated by the Charismatic Movement in the Church of England. Ever since its beginnings in the early 1960s, the Charismatic Movement has played a significant role in reshaping liturgical celebration in a variety of parishes across the Church of England. My decision to concentrate upon public worship arose not only on account of the Movement's widespread influence upon liturgical practice, but also from the conviction that public worship has been the primary medium through which the Movement's essential ecclesial features have been expressed and spread.

In reviewing the multi-disciplined approach of this work I am aware that it contains value for a variety of readers. Liturgists and those engaged in ritual studies will find a methodology and working example of how liturgical celebration can be explored and analysed. The six case study churches I visited between 1993 and 1995 provided the material for a detailed exploration of the reception and adaptation of elements of charismatic worship within a sample of Church of England parishes. This case study approach enabled me to focus my study on the concrete realities of worship as experienced and observed in these churches, and so provided a 'grounded' account of the ritual. As I have explained in Chapter 3, my sociological analysis embraced a *Verstehen* approach, using the ethnographic research methods of participant observation and interviews to gain information about the acts of worship and participant understanding of such activity. The analysis of the social reality of public worship, which, following Kelleher, I called the public horizon of worship, drew upon the social anthropologist Victor Turner's categorization of ritual into its ritual subjects, symbols and ritual process. I have also argued that the specificity of this case study approach need not compromise the relevance of its conclusions for the wider experience of charismatic worship.[1] Indeed, because of a high degree of relatability, my case study examples provide an analysis and interpretative framework that will create an informative

---

[1] See my opening remarks in Chapter 3.

dialogue with the wider instances of charismatic worship in the Church of England and probably other historic denominations as well. It would also be interesting to discover how and in what way the worship I have observed compares with the charismatic worship of the independent churches associated with the Restorationist or, as it now more commonly called, 'New Church' Movement.

The description and interpretation of worship that forms the central chapters of this work gives detailed examples of how the Pentecostal-Charismatic tradition has influenced liturgical celebration in the Church of England. For Anglicans this provides an important, and much overdue, chance to understand and review the 'grassroots' process of liturgical renewal that has accompanied the growth of Charismatic Renewal. My analysis of worship began by demonstrating the variety of ways in which the churches visited had developed forms of Sunday liturgy which were hospitable to charismatic expression. The differences between each church illustrated that the process of reception and integration of charismatic styles of worship was greatly dependent upon the tradition of each church and the liturgical, theological and pastoral convictions of the parish priest. However, this overview also demonstrated that along with the variety in liturgical practice there were two charismatic elements of worship shared by every case study: the distinctive style of sung worship, epitomized by the 'time of worship', and forms of 'prayer ministry'. The subsequent detailed description and analysis of these two ritual elements revealed the influence of Pentecostal-Charismatic traditions, most obviously in the contemporary influence of Vineyard conferences and Wimber, but also more classical and historic forms. These included expressions of Black Gospel music (transformation through sung worship) and an ethos of revivalism in patterns of eliciting congregational response ('prayer ministry').

Sociologists of religion and liturgists will be interested in the other main feature that emerges from these analytical chapters, namely the influence of contemporary cultural norms upon ritual expression. How much the growth and success of charismatic styles of worship has been due to their accommodation of the cultural values of late modernity is a question for further research, but its reality is significant, particularly within the context of discussions of the relationship between liturgy and contemporary culture. When liturgists began to seriously engage with the challenges of modern secularism in the 1960s there were a number who pointed to the deep gulf between the values of public worship and those of modern secular culture. At the World Council of Churches consultation in 1969, entitled 'Worship in a Secular Age', Charles Davis argued that there was an essential clash between corporate worship and modern secular culture that made it impossible for the recent reforms of worship to relate to culture.[2] In summarizing this point he said, 'Our faith and worship are not part of the modern secular world in which we live, not part of its socially shared and confirmed reality. As believers and worshippers we step outside the dominant secular culture as social deviants.'[3] The story of charismatic worship as evidenced in my case study work tells a somewhat different story to that anticipated by Davis. Far from fortifying itself in a 'ghetto' or reinventing itself in the 'desert' (the two types of deviant responses to secularism envisaged by Davis), it shows good evidence that it has assimilated aspects of contemporary culture as a means of expressing and heightening an authentic expression of 'worship in the Spirit'. It is a good example of what liturgists have called 'inculturation', the process by which pre-Christian rites have been adopted and given Christian meaning. In the 'time of worship' we have seen how popular discotheque culture and its romantic music styles have informed and shaped a ritual encounter based upon intimacy, a term that has strong resonance with a contemporary understanding of social relationship and now used by charismatic Christians to describe their worshipful relationship with God. Similarly in the ritual of 'prayer ministry' I have sought to demonstrate that the understanding of God's activity was embedded in the cultural values of popular live performance. By focusing on God's visibility, presence and spontaneity (values which had also been determinative of the style of music leadership in the 'time of worship'), the 'prayer ministry' became an arena in which the authentic 'live' presence of God was experienced. And further, as I have indicated, the benefits for participants were understood in ways that resonated strongly with the therapeutic sensibilities of late modern culture.

With regard to the process by which this liturgical inculturation has taken place there is very little evidence to suggest that it is the result of premeditated decisions by the influential in charismatic circles. As the liturgical scholar Aidan Kavanagh reminds us, inculturation has always happened, and continues to happen, with or without conscious reflection or planning on the part of worshipping communities.[4] For the members of the Church of England churches studied, and probably also the wider charismatic community, the suggestion that familiar styles of charismatic worship discussed in this book owe their form and expression to contemporary cultural norms will probably be met with both surprise and maybe also suspicion. But that would be a testimony to the successful and unconscious way in which such norms have been absorbed and now owned by partici-

---

[2] C. Davis, 'Ghetto or Desert: Liturgy in a Cultural Dilemma', *Studia Liturgica* 7 (1970), 2-3:10-27.
[3] Davis, 'Ghetto or Desert', 17.
[4] A. Kavanagh, 'Liturgical Inculturation: Looking to the Future', *Studia Liturgica* 20 (1990), 1:95-106.

pants as the authentic and God inspired way of charismatic liturgical
celebration.

The intriguing question that this raises is how has this liturgical style
defied Davis' predictions and overcome the seemingly unbridgeable gulf
between modern culture and Christian worship? The answer, I suggest, lies
in the evangelical character of Charismatic Renewal. By placing this study
within an historical context (Chapter 2) I have given an opportunity to view
the larger story of which the case studies are a part. This has particular
significance for the central concern of the series in which this book is
published, for the story of Charismatic Renewal in the Church of England is
predominantly an evangelical tale. The fact that it is not exclusively so is
made clear in my historical overview which highlights, for instance, the
involvement and influence of catholic Anglicans such as the Pulkinghams
and John Gunstone. However, one of the main themes to emerge from the
history is the way that evangelicals have consistently been at the forefront
of nurturing and propagating charismatic life within the Church of England.
One only needs to identify the parishes that have become well known
centres for Charismatic Renewal (St. Michael-le-Belfry in York, St. John's,
Harborne in Birmingham, St. Andrew's, Chorleywood, Holy Trinity,
Brompton and St. Thomas', Crookes in Sheffield) to be reminded of this
evangelical dominance. The significance of this observation for charismatic
worship and culture is understood when David Bebbington's seminal work
on the history of evangelicalism in modern Britain is recalled. In it he
challenges the common myth of evangelicalism as a movement that is
conservative and impervious to change.[5] He argues and demonstrates that
whilst holding to its core characteristics (conversionism, activism, biblicism
and crucicentrism), evangelicalism's capacity to be moulded and remoulded
by its cultural environment has been the most significant factor in its
continuing growth and development. Including the emerging Charismatic
Movement of the 1960s and 1970s in his survey, Bebbington argues that
one of the main reasons for the success of the Movement has been its ability
to create a Christian version of the 1960s counter-culture.[6] The charismatic
worship in my six case study churches indicates that this remoulding of
evangelicalism continues, as cultural norms of late modernity find fresh
expression in public worship.

It remains the case however that it is unlikely that charismatics would
wish to promote their style of worship on the basis of its resonance with
wider culture. Rather, the fire that lights the charismatic missionary
endeavour is the theological conviction that its worship gives expression to
an authentic worshipful relationship to God 'in the Spirit'. In the light of

---

[5]   D.W. Bebbington, *Evangelicalism in Modern Britain: A History from the 1730s to
the 1980s.*

[6]   Bebbington, *Evangelicalism*, Ch.7, 'The Spirit Poured Out'.

this claim it was essential that my sociological analysis of ritual be followed by a consideration of the adequacy of theology mediated by the worship I observed. Chapter 7 is thus offered as a theological critique and I hope that it will stimulate both charismatic and non-charismatic readers to a fresh critical consideration of the theological horizons mediated by charismatic worship. As we have seen, worship 'in the Spirit' expressed an instinctive trinitarianism, which led me to examine the adequacy of case study worship's trinitarian theology in relation to the historic orthodox trinitarian formulations, represented particularly by the trinitarian doxologies of Christian worship. I have argued that there were aspects of case study worship that affirmed an historic trinitarian understanding of worship in the Spirit, particularly by providing a corrective to established Western liturgical patterns that have underplayed the role of the Spirit. These aspects included a recovery of our God given vocation as liturgical beings to offer praise and thanksgiving within a communal context that sought to honour the divine personhood and freedom of the Spirit. However, the inherent problem with the worship observed was the relative poverty of expression given to worship that is 'in Christ'. The sung worship (most obviously in the 'time of worship') and public 'prayer ministry' betrayed a theology of the Spirit that had become dislocated from the economy of God's action in and through the Son, both in terms of participating in his offering of worship in the Spirit to the Father (sung worship), and in his receiving of the Spirit from the Father ('prayer ministry'). Thus, on the evidence presented, for charismatic worship truly to fulfill its desire to model worship 'in the Spirit' it needs to participate more fully in the new humanity revealed in Christ. Time will tell if this becomes a reality, and if it does then it can be truly said of the Charismatic Movement that it 'was at its most profound and also at its most influential as it worshipped.'[7]

---

[7] P. Ward, *Growing Up Evangelical: Youthwork and the Making of a Subculture*, 126.

Appendixes

Appendix A: Interview Questions for First Visit

Appendix A1: Congregational Interview (CI)

(* indicates question is specific to this category of informant)

1. How long have you been at St.Z? What made you choose to worship at St.Z?
2. (a) Which Sunday services do you attend?
   (b) Are there services you do not attend, and why?
3.* At the services you usually attend:
   (a) What service books/cards are used?
   (b) Describe what happens, using the following headings:
      Preparation for worship
      Confession of sin
      Praise
      Reading of Scripture
      Sermon (and response to the sermon)
      Creed
      Intercession
      Sharing of Peace
      Communion
      Ministry of prayer
      Ending of the service
   (c) Would the service include any testimonies? Regularly or occasionally?
4. Charismatic Christians have experienced charismatic gifts within worship.
   (a) Which of these gifts are evident in the service that you attend?
   (b) How frequently do they occur?
   (c) At what point(s) in the service are they usually exercised?
   (d) How does the leadership exercise control and testing of these gifts?
   (e) Is there public prayer for the coming of the Spirit?
5. What in your view is the high point of the service?
6. What do you find to be the most helpful aspects of the service you attend?
7. Are there any aspects of the service that you find unsatisfactory?
8. Which of the following would you is most happy to use as descriptions of the worship:
      Reverent, Biblical, Relevant, Anglican, Spontaneous, Orderly
      ... any other words you would add?
9. Would you describe the worship at St.Z as 'Spirit-led'?
10. What as far as you are aware have been the major changes in the worship at St.Z?

Appendix A2: Music Leader (ML1)

(* indicates question is specific to this category of informant)

1. How long have you been at St.Z? What made you choose to worship at St.Z?
2. (a) Which Sunday services do you attend?
   (b) Are there services you do not attend, and why?
3.* What musicians are used in worship?
4.* If there is a music group, what factors led to its formation?
5.* In which services and at what points in those services is the music group used?
6.* From what sources do you choose hymns and songs? Are any locally composed?
7.* Do traditional hymns have a place in your worship?
8.* Preparation:
   (a) Who chooses the hymns/songs for each service?
   (b) What principles control the choice of hymns/songs?
   (c) If songs are sung in succession at any point in the service (often called a 'time of worship'), what factors influence the order in which they are sung?
9.* During the service:
   (a) In the 'time of worship' which individual has leadership responsibility?
   (b) What is the role of the person with leadership responsibility?
   (c) What is the aim of the music group in the 'time of worship'?
10.* What qualities are important for a music leader to possess?
11. Charismatic Christians have experienced charismatic gifts within worship.
   (a) Which of these gifts are evident in the service that you attend?
   (b) How frequently do they occur?
   (c) At what point(s) in the service are they usually exercised?
   (d) How does the leadership exercise control and testing of these gifts?
   (e) Is there public prayer for the coming of the Spirit?
12. What in your view is the high point of the service?
13. What do you find to be the most helpful aspects of the service you attend?
14. Are there any aspects of the service that you find unsatisfactory?
15. Which of the following would you be most happy to use as descriptions of the worship:
       Reverent, Biblical, Relevant, Anglican, Spontaneous, Orderly
       .... any other words you would add?
16. Would you describe the worship at St.Z as 'Spirit-led'?
17. What as far as you are aware have been the major changes in the worship at St.Z?

Appendix A3: Church Leadership (LI)

(* indicates question is specific to this category of informant)

1. How long have you been at St.Z?
2.* What is the pattern of services and the thinking behind it?
3.* What liturgical forms are used for each service?
4.* Who's involved in leading worship?
5.* What vestments are worn by those who lead?
6.* Leading a service: Describe how you see your role in the following:
   Preparation for worship; your own and the congregation's.
   Confession of sin
   Praise
   Word: Scripture reading; sermon, and response to it; the use of testimony.
   Intercession
   Ministry of healing
   Communion
   Dismissal
7.* In what way has charismatic renewal influenced the way that you lead worship (you may find it helpful to use the framework above)?
8.* What qualities are important for a leader of worship to possess?
9.* What opportunity in church life at St.Z is given to teaching about worship?
10.*What part of the Anglican liturgical tradition has been enriched and developed at St.Z? Do you see St.Z in any way diverging from or in tension with Anglican liturgical tradition?
11.*What other worship traditions have influenced worship at St.Z?
12.*What is the aim of worship at St.Z?
13.*If there is a music group, what factors led to its formation?
14.*(a) Who chooses the hymns/songs for each service?
   (b) What principles control the choice of hymns/songs?
15. Charismatic Christians have experienced charismatic gifts within worship.
   (a) Which of these gifts are evident in the service that you attend?
   (b) How frequently do they occur?
   (c) At what point(s) in the service are they usually exercised?
   (d) How does the leadership exercise control and testing of these gifts?
   (e) Is there public prayer for the coming of the Spirit?
16. What in your view is the high point of the service?
17. What do you find to be the most helpful aspects of the service you attend?
18. Are there any aspects of the service that you find unsatisfactory?
19. Which of the following would you be most happy to use as descriptions of the worship: Reverent, Biblical, Relevant, Anglican, Spontaneous, Orderly
   .... any other words you would add?
20. Would you describe the worship at St.Z as 'Spirit-led'?
21. What as far as you are aware have been the major changes in the worship at St.Z?

Appendix A4: Outside Observer (OI)

1. Describe what happened using the following headings:
   Preparation for worship
   Confession of sin
   Praise
   Reading of Scripture
   Sermon (and response to the sermon)
   Creed
   Intercession
   Sharing of Peace
   Communion
   Ministry of prayer
   Ending of the service
2. What did the building and arrangement of furniture tell you about worship?
3. What expectations did you feel placed upon you, spoken or unspoken?
4. Would you use any of the following words to describe the worship:
   Reverent
   Biblical
   Relevant
   Anglican
   Spontaneous
   Orderly
   .... any other words you would add?
5. What impressed you about the worship?
6. What in your view were the less good features of the worship?
7. Do you have any questions that you would like to address to the church leadership?

Appendix B: Interview Questions for Second Visit

Appendix B1: Congregational Group (CGI)

1. What in the service did you find uplifting?
2. Was there anything that you found unhelpful, which perhaps made you frustrated or disappointed?
3. Was there anything unusual about this service?
4. When was God most present to you?
5. What could other churches learn from your worship here at St.Z?

Appendix B2: Leadership Group (LGI)

1. What went well in the service?
2. Were there any difficulties that arose?
3. Was there anything unusual about this service?
4. At what points in the service did you discern God to be present?
5. What is it about worship at St.Z that you most value and would want to share with other churches?

Appendix C: 'Words of Knowledge'

ST.C

The following were offered at the beginning of 'prayer ministry' at the 6.00pm service, visit 1:

- A picture of a zig-zag. I think what God is saying to someone is that that person would love to go straight but life is a minefield.
- A picture of a steam engine going down a track so fast - it hasn't got the time to stop at any stations to refuel or anything.
- A sailing boat that despite the high waves is still managing to go straight and keep its course.
- A teddy bear, and the words "trust me".
- A picture of fire and water; somebody in great conflict with somebody else.
- The first line of the chorus, 'How lovely on the mountains are the feet of him who brings good news', and then 'from him shall flow streams of living waters'.
- A man's name: Dr Goldman.
- Juggling floats
- I feel that there's someone here who's feeling a bit up in the air and doesn't quite know where to go.
- A bruised right thumb.
- A picture of black rings on a hook.
- A pineapple top
- A black patterned fan - a Spanish type, opened up wide.
- A beautiful brown pen.
- Flat tyres
- Headless chicken

ST.D

The following were offered in the 'prayer ministry' in the Mass on visit 2.

- Someone here with a problem with their toe, perhaps an in-growing toe-nail
- Someone with some kind of pain in their chest
- Someone with a pain in their right arm
- Someone has been made redundant, and they need to know God loves them
- Someone feeling weighed down under a burden of guilt about a situation.

ST.E

The following were offered at the 11.00am service, visit 2:

- Someone with a painful right big toe
- Someone with a painful and heavily bandaged left knee
- Someone dragging their feet with tiredness
- Jesus says he's got a lot of bread for the hungry, come and be filled

The following were offered at the 6.30pm service, visit 2:

- A person going for a brain scan
- Blocked sinuses
- "Relax, rest in my care"
- A lady suffering from panic attacks
- Pain in the right elbow
- Ache in the left arm and left wrist
- Pain in the lower left leg
- Pain in the lower ribs, right hand side

Bibliography

Abbott-Smith, G., *Manual Greek Lexicon of the New Testament* (Edinburgh: T&T Clark, 1981).

Albrecht, D., *Rites in the Spirit: A Ritual Approach to Pentecostal/Charismatic Spirituality* (Sheffield: Sheffield Academic Press, 1999).

Allchin, A.M., 'Walking in the Spirit: Freedom and Tradition in the Church's Life' in C.Craston (ed.), *Open to the Spirit: Anglicans and the Experience of Renewal* (London: Church House Publishing, 1987), 151-62.

Archimandrite Ephrem, 'The Trinity in Contemporary Eucharistic Liturgy' in A.I.C.Heron (ed.), *The Forgotten Trinity: 3. A Selection of Papers presented to the British Council of Churches Study Commission on Trinitarian Doctrine Today* (London: British Council of Churches/Council of Churches for Britain and Ireland, 1991), 47-61.

Augustine, *De Trinitate* in J. Burnaby (tr.), *Augustine: Later Works*, Library of Christian Classics, VIII, (London: SCM., 1955).

Basil of Caesarea, *St Basil the Great On the Holy Spirit*, (New York: St.Vladimir's Seminary Press, 1980).

Bax, J., *The Good Wine: Spiritual Renewal in the Church of England* (London: Church House Publishing, 1986).

Beall, P., and M. Keys Barker, *The Folk Arts in Renewal: Creativity in Worship, Teaching and Festivity as Developed by the Fisherfolk* (London: Hodder and Stoughton, 1980).

Bebbington, D.W., *Evangelicalism in Modern Britain: A History from the 1730s to the 1980s* (London: Unwin Hyman, 1989).

Becker, H.S., *Boys in White: Student Culture in Medical School* (Chicago: University of Chicago Press, 1961).

Begbie, J., 'The Spirituality of Renewal Music' in *Anvil: An Anglican Evangelical Journal for Theology and Mission* 8 (1991), 3:227-39.

Bell, J., T. Bush, A. Fox, J. Goodey, and S. Goulding, (eds.), *Conducting Small-Scale Investigations in Educational Management* (London: Open University 1984).

Booth, T.T., *We True Christians: The Church of the Cherubim and Seraphim*, University of Birmingham DPhil thesis (1984).

Buchanan, C.O., *Modern Anglican Liturgies 1958-1968* (Oxford: Oxford University Press, 1968).

— *Further Anglican Liturgies 1968-1975* (Nottingham: Grove Books, 1975).

— *Encountering Charismatic Worship* (Nottingham: Grove Books, 1977).

— 'The Pentecostal Implications' in *Authority and Freedom in Liturgy* (Nottingham: Grove Books, 1979), 21-28.

— *Latest Anglican Liturgies 1976-1984* (London: Alcuin Club/SPCK, 1985).

Burgess, R.G., *In the Field: An Introduction to Field Research* (London: Allen and Unwin, 1984).

Burnim, M., 'Black Gospel Music as Transformation' in M. Collins, D. Power, and M. Burnim (eds.), *Concilium 202: Music and the Experience of God*, (Edinburgh: T&T Clark, 1989), 52-61.

Chevreau, G., *Catch the Fire: The Toronto Blessing* (London: Marshall Pickering, 1994).

Cicourel, A.V., *Method and Measurement in Sociology* (New York: The Free Press, 1964).

Cocksworth, C., *Holy, Holy, Holy: Worshipping the Trinitarian God* (London: Darton, Longman and Todd, 1997).

— 'The Trinity Today: Opportunities and Challenges for Liturgical Study' in *Studia Liturgica* 27 (1997), 1:61-78.

Congar, Y.M.J., *I Believe in the Holy Spirit*, 3 volumes (London: Geoffrey Chapman, 1983).

Cox, H., *Fire From Heaven: The Rise of Pentecostal Spirituality and the Reshaping of Religion in the Twenty-first Century* (London: Cassell, 1996).

Craston, C. (ed.), *Open To The Spirit: Anglicans and the Experience of Renewal* (London: Church House Publishing, 1987).

Cray, G., 'Justice, Rock and the Renewal of Worship', in R. Sheldon (ed.), *In Spirit and in Truth: Exploring Directions in Music and Worship Today* (London: Hodder and Stoughton, 1989), 3-27.

Davis, C., 'Ghetto or Desert: Liturgy in a Cultural Dilemma', *Studia Liturgica* 7 (1970), 2-3:10-27.

DeVale, S.C., 'Power and Meaning in Musical Instruments' in *Concilium 202: Music and the Experience of God* (Edinburgh: T&T Clark, 1989), 94-110.

Dixon, P., *Signs of Revival* (Eastbourne: Kingsway, 1995).

Dunn, J.D.G., *Jesus and the Spirit: A Study of the Religious Charismatic Experience of Jesus and the First Christians as Reflected in the New Testament* (London: SCM, 1975).

Durran, M., *The Wind at the Door* (Eastbourne: Kingsway, 1986).

Ely, M., *Doing Qualitative Research: Circles within Circles* (London: The Falmer Press 1991).

Fenwick, J.R.K and B.D. Spinks, *Worship in Transition: the Twentieth Century Liturgical Movement* (Edinburgh: T&T Clark, 1995).

Flegg, C., *Gathered Under Apostles: A Study of the Catholic Apostolic Church* (London: Clarenden Press 1992).

Frye, N., *The Anatomy of Criticism* (Princeton, NJ: Princeton University Press, 1957).

Giddens, A., *Modernity and Self-Identity: Self and Society in the Late Modern Age* (Cambridge, Polity Press, 1991).

Glaser, B.G. and A.L. Strauss, *The Discovery of Grounded Theory: Strategies for Qualitative Research* (London: Weidenfeld and Nicolson, 1968).

Goldingay, J., 'Charismatic Spirituality: Some Theological Reflections', *Theology* XCIX (May/June 1996), 789:178-87.

Gunstone, J., *Greater Things Than These: A Personal Account of the Charismatic Movement* (Leighton Buzzard: Faith Press, 1974).

— *People for His Praise: Renewal and Congregational Life* (London: Hodder and Stoughton, 1978).

— *Pentecostal Anglicans* (London: Hodder and Stoughton, 1982).

— 'The Spirit's Freedom in the Spirit's Framework' in K. Stevenson (ed.), *Liturgy Reshaped* (London: SPCK 1982), 4-16.

— 'Preparing for Renewed Worship: 10 Years of *A.S.B.*', *Anglicans for Renewal* 41 (Summer 1990), 30.

— *Pentecost Comes to the Church: Sacraments and Spiritual Gifts* (London: DLT, 1994).

Gunton, C.E., 'The Spirit as Lord': Christianity, Modernity and Freedom' in A. Walker (ed.) *Different Gospels: Christian Orthodoxy and Modern Theologies* (London: Hodder and Stoughton, 1988), 169-82.

— *The Promise of Trinitarian Theology* (Edinburgh: T&T Clark, 1991).

— 'The Spirit in the Trinity' in A.I.C. Heron (ed.), *The Forgotten Trinity: 3. A Selection of Papers Presented to the BCC Study Commission on Trinitarian Doctrine Today* (London: British Council of Churches/Council of Churches for Britain and Ireland, 1991), 123-35.

— *The One, the Three and the Many: God, Creation and the Culture of Modernity* (Cambridge: Cambridge University Press, 1993).

Gunton, C.E. and D.W. Hardy (eds.), *On Being the Church: Essays on the Christian Community* (Edinburgh: T&T Clark, 1989).

Hammersley, M., and P. Atkinson, *Ethnography: Principles in Practice* (London: Tavistock Publications, 1983).

Hanson, R.P.C., *The Search for the Christian Doctrine of God: the Arian Controversy 318-381* (Edinburgh: T&T Clark, 1988).

Harper, M. (ed.), *As At The Beginning: The Twentieth Century Pentecostal Revival* (London: Hodder and Stoughton, 1965).

— *Walk in the Spirit* (London: Hodder and Stoughton, 1968).

— 'Principles of Congregational Worship', *One in Christ: A Catholic Ecumenical Review* 13 (1977) 1&2:36-39.

— *A New Canterbury Tale* (Nottingham: Grove Books, 1978).

Heron, A.I.C., *The Holy Spirit: The Holy Spirit in the Bible, in the History of Christian Thought and in Recent Theology* (London: Marshall, Morgan and Scott, 1983).

Hillyer, J.V., *Liturgical Change in Cambridge: Attitudes to Liturgy with Special Reference to Charismatic Gifts*, King's College London MPhil thesis (1977).

Hocken, P., *Streams of Renewal: The Origins and Early Development of the Charismatic Renewal in Great Britain* (Exeter: Paternoster Press, 1986).

— *The Glory and the Shame: Reflections on the 20th-Century Outpouring of the Holy Spirit* (Guildford: Eagle, 1994).

Hoffman, L.A., *Beyond the Text: A Holistic Approach to Liturgy* (Bloomington and Indianapolis: Indiana University Press 1987).

Hollenweger, W.J., *The Pentecostals* (London: SCM, 1972).

Hopewell, J.F., *Congregation: Stories and Structures* (Philadelphia: Fortress, 1987).

Howell, D., *Saints in Worship!* (Derby: Anglican Renewal Ministries, 1991).

Jasper, R.C.D. and P.F. Bradshaw, *A Companion to the Alternative Service Book*, (London: SPCK, 1986).

— *The Development of the Anglican Liturgy 1662-1980* (London: SPCK, 1989).

Jeremias, J., *The Prayers of Jesus* (London: SCM, 1967).

Jungmann, J.A., *The Place of Christ in Liturgical Prayer* (London: Geoffrey Chapman, 1965).

Kavanagh, A., 'Liturgical Inculturation: Looking to the Future', *Studia Liturgica* 20 (1990), 1:95-106.

Kelleher, M.M., 'Liturgical Theology: A Task and a Method', *Worship* 62 (January 1988), 1:2-25.

Lawson, F. and J. Finney, *Saints Alive!* (Derby: Anglican Renewal Ministries, 1982).

Leach, J., *Liturgy and Liberty: Combining the Best of the Old with the Best of the New in Worship* (Eastbourne: MARC, 1989).
— 'Hitting The Target', in *Christian Music* (Summer 1992), 2-4.
— *Hymns and Spiritual Songs: The Use of Traditional and Modern in Worship* (Nottingham: Grove Books, 1995).
Leat, D., 'Misunderstanding Verstehen' in *Sociological Review*, 20 (1972), 29-38.
Lewis, I.M., *Ecstatic Religion: An Anthropological Study of Spirit Possession and Shamanism* (London: Penguin, 1971).
Manning, B., *The Hymns of Wesley and Watts: Five Informal Papers* (London: Epworth Press, 1942).
Mannion, M.F., 'Liturgy and the Present Crisis of Culture', *Worship* 62 (March 1988) 2:98-123.
Maries, A., *One Heart, One Voice: The Rich and Varied Resource of Music in Worship* (London: Hodder and Stoughton, 1985).
Martin, B., *A Sociology of Contemporary Cultural Change* (Oxford: Blackwell, 1981).
Martin, D. and P. Mullen (eds.), *Strange Gifts: A Guide to Charismatic Renewal* (Oxford: Blackwell 1984).
McNeill, J.T. (ed.), *Calvin: Institutes of the Christian Religion* (Philadelphia: The Westminster Press, 1960), 1 and 2.
Mitton, M., *The Heart of Toronto: Exploring the Spirituality of the 'Toronto Blessing'* (Cambridge: Grove Books, 1995).
Moore, J., 'The Catholic Pentecostal Movement' in Michael Hill (ed.), *Sociological Yearbook of Religion* 6 (London: SCM, 1973), 73-90.
Neitz, M.J., *Charisma and Community: A Study of Religious Commitment within Charismatic Renewal* (New Brunswick, NJ: Transaction, 1987).
Otto, R., *The Idea of the Holy*, J.W. Harvey (tr.), (London: Penguin, 1959).
Percy, M., *Words, Wonders and Power: Understanding Contemporary Christian Fundamentalism and Revivalism* (London: SPCK, 1996).
— 'Sweet Rapture: Subliminal Eroticism in Contemporary Charismatic Worship', *Theology and Sexuality* 6 (1997), 71-106.
Pitts, W.F., *Old Ship of Zion: The Afro-Baptist Ritual in the African Diaspora* (Oxford: Oxford University Press, 1993).
Pulkingham, B., *Sing God a Simple Song* (London: Marshall Pickering, 1986).
Pulkingham, W.G., *Gathered for Power* (London: Hodder and Stoughton, 1972).
Ranaghan, K. and D. Ranaghan, *Catholic Pentecostals* (New York: Paulist Press, 1969).
Richter, P.J., 'God is not a Gentleman! The Sociology of the Toronto Blessing' in S.E. Porter and P.J. Richter (eds.), *The Toronto Blessing - Or Is It?* (London: Darton, Longman and Todd, 1995), 5-37.
Roberts, D., *The Toronto Blessing* (Eastbourne: Kingsway, 1994).
Robinson, D.W.B., 'Renewal from an Evangelical "Non-Charismatic" Viewpoint', in C. Craston (ed.), *Open To The Spirit: Anglicans and the Experience of Renewal* (London: Church House Publishing, 1987).
Roszak, T., *The Making of a Counter Culture: Reflections on the Technocratic Society and its Youthful Opposition* (London: Faber, 1970).
Runcorn, D., *Rumours of Life: Reflections on the Resurrection Appearances* (London: Darton, Longman and Todd, 1996).
Samarin, W.J., *Tongues of Men and of Angels: The Religious Language of Pentecostalism* (New York: Macmillan, 1972).

Saunders, T. and H. Sansom, *David Watson: A Biography* (London: Hodder and Stoughton, 1992).

Schmemann, A., *Introduction to Liturgical Theology* (Leighton Buzzard: The Faith Press, 1975[2]).

— *Of Water and The Spirit: A Liturgical Study of Baptism* (London: SPCK, 1976).

Schutz, A., 'Concepts, Constructs and Theory Formation', in M. Natanson (ed.), *Philosophy of the Social Sciences* (New York: Random House, 1963).

Scotland, N., *Charismatics and the Next Millennium: Do they have a future?* (London: Hodder and Stoughton, 1995).

Searle, M., 'The Notre Dame Study of Catholic Parish Life' in *Worship*, 60 (1986), 4:312-33.

Sennett, R., *The Fall of Public Man* (New York: Knopf, 1977).

Simpson, J. H., 'Religion and the Body: Sociological Themes and Prospects' in W.H. Swatos, *A Future for Religion? New Paradigms for Social Analysis* (London: Sage 1993), Ch. 9.

Sizer, S.S., *Gospel Hymns and Social Religion: The Rhetoric of Nineteenth-Century Revivalism* (Philadelphia: Temple University Press, 1978).

Smail, T.A., *Reflected Glory* (London: Hodder and Stoughton, 1975).

— *The Forgotten Father* (London: Hodder and Stoughton, 1980).

— *The Giving Gift: The Holy Spirit in Person* (London: Hodder and Stoughton, 1988).

Smail, T.A., A. Walker, and N.Wright, *Charismatic Renewal: The Search for a Theology* (London: SPCK, 1993).

Spinks, B.D., 'Trinitarian Theology and the Eucharistic Prayer', *Studia Liturgica* 26 (1996), 2:209-24.

Springer, K. (ed.), *Riding the Third Wave: What Comes After Renewal* (London: Marshall Pickering, 1987).

Steven, J.H.S., *Worship in the Restoration Movement* (Nottingham: Grove Books, 1989).

— 'Charismatic Hymnody in the Light of Early Methodist Hymnody', *Studia Liturgica* 27 (1997), 2:217-34.

Stibbe, M., *A Kingdom of Priests: Deeper into God in Prayer* (London: Darton, Longman and Todd, 1994).

Strauss, A.L. and J. Corbin, *Basics of Qualitative Research: Techniques and Procedures for Developing Grounded Theory* (London: Sage, 1990).

Stringer, M.D., 'Liturgy and Anthropology: The History of a Relationship' in *Worship*, 63 (November 1989), 6:503-19.

— *On the Perception of Worship: The ethnography of worship in four Christian congregations in Manchester* (Birmingham: Birmingham University Press, 1999).

Suurmond, J-J., *Word and Spirit at Play: Towards a Charismatic Theology* (London: SCM, 1994).

Swatos, W.H. (ed.), *A Future for Religion? New Paradigms for Social Analysis* (London: Sage, 1993).

Sykes, S.W., *Unashamed Anglicanism* (London: Darton, Longman and Todd, 1995).

Thornton, S., *Club Cultures: Music, Media and Subcultural Capital* (Cambridge: Polity Press, 1995).

Torrance, J. B., *Worship, Community and the Triune God of Grace* (Carlisle: Paternoster Press, 1997).

Torrance, T.F., *Theology in Reconstruction* (London: SCM, 1965).
— *Theology in Reconciliation: Essays towards Evangelical and Catholic Unity in East and West* (London: Chapman, 1975).
Turner, B.S., *The Body & Society: Explorations in Social Theory* (London: Sage, 1996[2]).
Turner, V., *The Forest of Symbols: Aspects of Ndembu Ritual* (Ithaca: Cornell University Press, 1967).
— 'Forms of Symbolic Action: Introduction', in *Forms of Symbolic Action: Proceedings of the 1969 Annual Meeting, American Ethnological Society* (Seattle: University of Washington Press, 1969).
— 'Ritual, Tribal, and Catholic', in *Worship* 50 (November 1976) 6:
Urquhart, C., *When the Spirit Comes* (London: Hodder and Stoughton, 1974).
Verghese, P., *The Joy of Freedom: Eastern Worship and Modern Man* (London: Lutterworth Press, 1967).
Wainwright, G., *Doxology: The Praise of God in Worship, Doctrine, and Life* (London: Epworth Press, 1980)
Wakefield, G., *The First Pentecostal Anglican: The Life and Legacy of Alexander Boddy* (Cambridge: Grove Books, 2001).
Walker, A., 'Sociological and Lay Accounts as Versions of Reality: Choosing Between Reports of the "Charismatic Renewal Movement" Amongst Roman Catholics', *Theory and Society*, 2 (1975), 211-33.
— 'Pentecostal Power: The "Charismatic Renewal Movement" and the Politics of Experience' in E. Barker (ed.), *Of Gods and Men: New Religious Movements in the West* (GA: Mercy University Press, 1984), 89-108.
— *Restoring the Kingdom: The Radical Christianity of the House Church Movement* (London: Hodder and Stoughton, 1988).
— 'Pentecostalism and Charismatic Christianity', in A.E. McGrath (ed.), *Encyclopedia of Modern Christian Thought* (Oxford: Blackwell, 1993), 428-34.
— *Telling the Story: Gospel, Mission and Culture* (London: SPCK 1996).
Walker, A. and J. Atherton, 'An Easter Pentecostal Convention: The Successful Management of a "Time of Blessing" ' in *Sociological Review* (August 1971), 367-87.
Walker, T., *Open to God: A Parish in Renewal* (Nottingham: Grove Books, 1975).
Ward, P., *Growing Up Evangelical: Youthwork and the Making of a Subculture* (London: SPCK, 1996).
Warren, R., *In the Crucible: The Testing and Growth of a Local Church* (Crowborough: Highland Books, 1989).
Weber, M., *Basic Concepts in Sociology*, tr. by H.P. Secher, (London: Peter Owen, 1962).
— *The Sociology of Religion* (London: Methuen, 1965[4]).
White, S.J., *Christian Worship and Technological Change* (Nashville: Abingdon Press, 1994).
Williams, C.G., *Tongues of the Spirit: A Study of Pentecostal Glossolalia and Related Phenomena* (Cardiff: University of Wales Press, 1981).
Williams, R., *Eucharistic Sacrifice: The Roots of a Metaphor* (Nottingham: Grove Books, 1982).
Wimber, J., *Power Evangelism: Signs and Wonders Today* (London: Hodder and Stoughton, 1985).

— *Power Healing* (London: Hodder and Stoughton, 1986).
— 'Intimacy with God' in *Worship* (Pevensey: Christian Music Association), 8 (Winter, 1988).
— *The Dynamics of Spiritual Growth* (London: Hodder and Stoughton, 1990)
Zizioulas, J.D., *Being as Communion: Studies in Personhood and the Church* (New York: St. Vladimir's Seminary Press, 1985).

CHURCH REPORTS

Cooper, J., *Music in Parish Worship*, (Statistics and Computer Department, Central Board of Finance of the Church of England, 1990).
General Synod *Report of Proceedings* 12, (London: CIO Publishing, 1981).
The Charismatic Movement in the Church of England (London: Church House Publishing, 1981).
The Church of England Yearbook (London: Church House Publishing, 1995).
The 'Toronto Blessing': Report to Conference 1996 by The Methodist Church Faith and Order Committee (Peterborough: Methodist Publishing House, 1996).
The Toronto Experience: An Exploration of the Issues, Board of Mission Occasional Paper No.7 (London: Church House Publishing, 1997).
We Believe in the Holy Spirit: A Report by The Doctrine Commission of the General Synod of Church of England (London: Church House Publishing, 1991).

PERIODICALS/NEWSPAPERS

Anglicans for Renewal (Vols. 31-41 entitled *ARM Link*)
News of Liturgy
Renewal
The Churchman
The Church of England Newspaper

HYMN BOOKS

Cry Hosanna! (London: Hodder and Stoughton, 1980).
Combined Sound of Living Waters and Fresh Sounds (London: Hodder and Stoughton, 1977).
Junior Praise (London: Marshall Pickering, 1986).
Mission Praise (London: Marshall Pickering, 1990).
New Mission Praise (London: Marshall Pickering, 1996).
Songs of Fellowship (Eastbourne: Kingsway, 1991).
Songs of Fellowship: Book 5 (Eastbourne: Kingsway, 1994).
New Wine '93 Songbook (Eastbourne: Kingsway, 1993).
Hymns and Psalms: A Methodist and Ecumenical Hymn Book (London: Methodist Publishing House, 1983).
A Collection of Hymns, For the Use of the People called Methodists 1780 (London: Wesleyan Conference Office).

LITURGIES

Alternative Service Book 1980 (London: Collins, 1980)
Enriching the Christian Year (London: SPCK/Alcuin Club, 1993)
The Book of Common Prayer (Cambridge: CUP)

General Index

Song Index

Jesus, we celebrate Your victory, 185, 193, 199
Jesus, we enthrone You, 109, 192
Jesus, You are changing me, 154
Jubilate, everybody, 106
Let there be love shared among us, 80
Lord Jesus, here I stand before You, 108
Lord, You are so precious to me, 197
Majesty, worship His Majesty, 107, 114
My heart is full of admiration, 106
O Father of the fatherless, 152, 176
O let the Son of God enfold you, 153, 159, 204
O Lord, You're beautiful, 121
One thing I ask, one thing I seek, 79
Purify my heart, 80, 136
Rejoice, rejoice! Christ is in you, 198
Rejoice, rejoice, rejoice!, 96
Save the last dance for me, 119
See where our great High Priest, 197
Shout for joy and sing, 105
Show me, dear Lord, how You see me in Your eyes, 152
So close to you, 122
Spirit of the living God…fill me anew, 176
Spirit of the living God…break me, melt me, 154
Through our God we shall do valiantly, 107
Time to make you mine, 124
To be in Your presence, 121-2, 197
We are all together, 105
We are here to praise You, 184
We see the Lord, 80, 129, 195
When I look into Your holiness, 130
When the Spirit of the Lord is within my heart, 117, 193
You are the Holy One, 129
You laid aside Your majesty, 107
You shall go out with joy, 81

Copyright Addresses

Big Life Music Ltd., 67-69 Chalton Street, London NW1 1HY.
Carlin Music Corp., 3 Bridge Approach, Chalk Farm, London NW1 8ED.
Christian Music Ministries, 325 Bromford Road, Hodge Hill, Birmingham, B36 8ET.
CopyCare, P.O. Box 77, Hailsham, East Sussex, BN27 3EF.
Make Way Music, P.O. Box 263, Croydon, Surrey, CR9 5AP.
MCA Music Ltd., 77 Fulham Palace Road, London, W6 8JA.
Perfect Songs Ltd., The Blue Building, 42-46 St. Luke's Mews, London W11 1DG.

Pete Sanchez, Jr., Gabriel Music Inc., 4723 Hickory Downs, Houston, TX 77084, U.S.A.
Polygram Music Publishing Ltd., 47 British Grove, London, W4 2NL.
Sovereign Lifestyle Music/ Music UK, P.O. Box 356, Leighton Buzzard, LU7 3WP.
Thankyou Music, 26-28 Lottbridge Drove, Eastbourne, BN23 6NT (Thankyou Music songs '*Adm. by worshiptogether.com songs excl. UK & Europe, adm. by Kingsway Music. tym@kingsway.co.uk. Used by permission').
Zomba Music Publishers Ltd., Unit 22-27, Quadrant Business Centre, 135 Salisbury Road, Queens Park, London, NW6 6RJ.

Studies in Evangelical History and Thought
(All titles uniform with this volume)
Dates in bold are of projected publication

Clyde Binfield
The Country a Little Thickened and Congested?
Nonconformity in Eastern England 1840–1885
Studies of Victorian religion and society often concentrate on cities, suburbs, and industrialisation. This study provides a contrast. Victorian Eastern England—Essex, Suffolk, Norfolk, Cambridgeshire, and Huntingdonshire—was rural, traditional, relatively unchanging. That is nonetheless a caricature which discounts the industry in Norwich and Ipswich (as well as in Haverhill, Stowmarket, and Leiston) and ignores the impact of London on Essex, of railways throughout the region, and of an ancient but changing university (Cambridge) on the county town which housed it. It also entirely ignores the political implications of such changes in a region noted for the variety of its religious Dissent since the seventeenth century. This book explores Victorian Eastern England and its Nonconformity. It brings to a wider readership a pioneering thesis which has made a major contribution to a fresh evolution of English religion and society.
2005 / 1-84227-216-0 / approx. 274pp

John Brencher
Martyn Lloyd-Jones (1899–1981) and Twentieth-Century Evangelicalism
This study critically demonstrates the significance of the life and ministry of Martyn Lloyd-Jones for post-war British evangelicalism and demonstrates that his preaching was his greatest influence on twentieth-century Christianity. The factors which shaped his view of the church are examined, as is the way his reformed evangelicalism led to a separatist ecclesiology which divided evangelicals.
2002 / 1-84227-051-6 / xvi + 268pp

Jonathan D. Burnham
A Story of Conflict
The Controversial Relationship between Benjamin Wills Newton and John Nelson Darby
Burnham explores the controversial relationship between the two principal leaders of the early Brethren movement. In many ways Newton and Darby were products of their times, and this study of their relationship provides insight not only into the dynamics of early Brethrenism, but also into the progress of nineteenth-century English and Irish evangelicalism.
2004 / 1-84227-191-1 / xxiv + 268pp

J.N. Ian Dickson
Beyond Religious Discourse
Sermons, Preaching and Evangelical Protestants in
Nineteenth-Century Irish Society
Drawing extensively on primary sources, this pioneer work in modern religious history explores the training of preachers, the construction of sermons and how Irish evangelicalism and the wider movement in Great Britain and the United States shaped the preaching event. Evangelical preaching and politics, sectarianism, denominations, education, class, social reform, gender, and revival are examined to advance the argument that evangelical sermons and preaching went significantly beyond religious discourse. The result is a book for those with interests in Irish history, culture and belief, popular religion and society, evangelicalism, preaching and communication.
2005 / 1-84227-217-9 / approx. 324pp

Neil T.R. Dickson
Brethren in Scotland 1838–2000
A Social Study of an Evangelical Movement
The Brethren were remarkably pervasive throughout Scottish society. This study of the Open Brethren in Scotland places them in their social context and examines their growth, development and relationship to society.
2003 / 1-84227-113-X / xxviii + 510pp

Crawford Gribben and Timothy C.F. Stunt (eds)
Prisoners of Hope?
Aspects of Evangelical Millennialism in Britain and Ireland, 1800–1880
This volume of essays offers a comprehensive account of the impact of evangelical millennialism in nineteenth-century Britain and Ireland.
2004 / 1-84227-224-1 / xiv + 208pp

Khim Harris
Evangelicals and Education
Evangelical Anglicans and Middle-Class Education
in Nineteenth-Century England
This ground breaking study investigates the history of English public schools founded by nineteenth-century Evangelicals. It documents the rise of middle-class education and Evangelical societies such as the influential Church Association, and includes a useful biographical survey of prominent Evangelicals of the period.
2004 / 1-84227-250-0 / xviii + 422pp

Mark Hopkins
Nonconformity's Romantic Generation
Evangelical and Liberal Theologies in Victorian England
A study of the theological development of key leaders of the Baptist and
Congregational denominations at their period of greatest influence, including
C.H. Spurgeon and R.W. Dale, and of the controversies in which those among
them who embraced and rejected the liberal transformation of their evangelical
heritage opposed each other.
2004 / 1-84227-150-4 / xvi + 284pp

Don Horrocks
Laws of the Spiritual Order
Innovation and Reconstruction in the Soteriology
of Thomas Erskine of Linlathen
Don Horrocks argues that Thomas Erskine's unique historical and theological
significance as a soteriological innovator has been neglected. This timely
reassessment reveals Erskine as a creative, radical theologian of central and
enduring importance in Scottish nineteenth-century theology, perhaps equivalent
in significance to that of S.T. Coleridge in England.
2004 / 1-84227-192-X / xx + 362pp

Kenneth S. Jeffrey
When the Lord Walked the Land
The 1858–62 Revival in the North East of Scotland
Previous studies of revivals have tended to approach religious movements from
either a broad, national or a strictly local level. This study of the multifaceted
nature of the 1859 revival as it appeared in three distinct social contexts within a
single region reveals the heterogeneous nature of simultaneous religious
movements in the same vicinity.
2002 / 1-84227-057-5 / xxiv + 304pp

John Kenneth Lander
Itinerant Temples
Tent Methodism, 1814–1832
Tent preaching began in 1814 and the Tent Methodist sect resulted from
disputes with Bristol Wesleyan Methodists in 1820. The movement spread to
parts of Gloucestershire, Wiltshire, London and Liverpool, among other places.
Its demise started in 1826 after which one leader returned to the Wesleyans and
others became ministers in the Congregational and Baptist denominations.
2003 / 1-84227-151-2 / xx + 268pp

Donald M. Lewis
Lighten Their Darkness
The Evangelical Mission to Working-Class London, 1828–1860
This is a comprehensive and compelling study of the Church and the complexities of nineteenth-century London. Challenging our understanding of the culture in working London at this time, Lewis presents a well-structured and illustrated work that contributes substantially to the study of evangelicalism and mission in nineteenth-century Britain.

2001 / 1-84227-074-5 / xviii + 372pp

Herbert McGonigle
'Sufficient Saving Grace'
John Wesley's Evangelical Arminianism
A thorough investigation of the theological roots of John Wesley's evangelical Arminianism and how these convictions were hammered out in controversies on predestination, limited atonement and the perseverance of the saints.

2001 / 1-84227-045-1 / xvi + 350pp

Lisa S. Nolland
A Victorian Feminist Christian
Josephine Butler, the Prostitutes and God
Josephine Butler was an unlikely candidate for taking up the cause of prostitutes, as she did, with a fierce and self-disregarding passion. This book explores the particular mix of perspectives and experiences that came together to envision and empower her remarkable achievements. It highlights the vital role of her spirituality and the tragic loss of her daughter.

2004 / 1-84227-225-X / approx. 360pp

Ian M. Randall
Evangelical Experiences
A Study in the Spirituality of English Evangelicalism 1918–1939
This book makes a detailed historical examination of evangelical spirituality between the First and Second World Wars. It shows how patterns of devotion led to tensions and divisions. In a wide-ranging study, Anglican, Wesleyan, Reformed and Pentecostal-charismatic spiritualities are analysed.

1999 / 0-85364-919-7 / xii + 310pp

Ian M. Randall
Spirituality and Social Change
The Contribution of F.B. Meyer (1847–1929)
This is a fresh appraisal of F.B. Meyer (1847–1929), a leading Free Church minister. Having been deeply affected by holiness spirituality, Meyer became the Keswick Convention's foremost international speaker. He combined spirituality with effective evangelism and socio-political activity. This study shows Meyer's significant contribution to spiritual renewal and social change.

2003 / 1-84227-195-4 / xx + 184pp

James Robinson
Pentecostal Origins (1907–c.1925): A Regional Study
Early Pentecostalism in Ulster within its British Context
Harvey Cox describes Pentecostalism as 'the fascinating spiritual child of our time' that has the potential, at the global scale, to contribute to the 'reshaping of religion in the twenty-first century'. This study grounds such sentiments by examining at the local scale the origin, development and nature of Pentecostalism in the north of Ireland in its first twenty years. Illustrative, in a paradigmatic way, of how Pentecostalism became established within one region of the British Isles, it sets the story within the wider context of formative influences emanating from America, Europe and, in particular, other parts of the British Isles. As a synoptic regional study in Pentecostal history it is the first survey of its kind.

2005 / 1-84227-329-9 / approx. 424pp

Geoffrey Robson
Dark Satanic Mills?
Religion and Irreligion in Birmingham and the Black Country
This book analyses and interprets the nature and extent of popular Christian belief and practice in Birmingham and the Black Country during the first half of the nineteenth century, with particular reference to the impact of cholera epidemics and evangelism on church extension programmes.

2002 / 1-84227-102-4 / xiv + 294pp

Roger Shuff
Searching for the True Church
Brethren and Evangelicals in Mid-Twentieth-Century England
Roger Shuff holds that the influence of the Brethren movement on wider
evangelical life in England in the twentieth century is often underrated. This
book records and accounts for the fact that Brethren reached the peak of their
strength at the time when evangelicalism was at it lowest ebb, immediately
before World War II. However, the movement then moved into persistent
decline as evangelicalism regained ground in the post war period.
Accompanying this downward trend has been a sharp accentuation of the
contrast between Brethren congregations who engage constructively with the
non-Brethren scene and, at the other end of the spectrum, the isolationist group
commonly referred to as 'Exclusive Brethren'.
2005 / 1-84227-254-3 / approx. 318pp

James H.S. Steven
Worship in the Spirit
Charismatic Worship in the Church of England
This book explores the nature and function of worship in six Church of England
churches influenced by the Charismatic Movement, focusing on congregational
singing and public prayer ministry. The theological adequacy of such ritual is
discussed in relation to pneumatological and christological understandings in
Christian worship.
2002 / 1-84227-103-2 / xvi + 238pp

Peter K. Stevenson
God in Our Nature
The Incarnational Theology of John McLeod Campbell
This radical reassessment of Campbell's thought arises from a comprehensive
study of his preaching and theology. Previous accounts have overlooked both
his sermons and his Christology. This study examines the distinctive Christology
evident in his sermons and shows that it sheds new light on Campbell's much
debated views about atonement.
2004 / 1-84227-218-7 / xxiv + 458pp

Martin Wellings
Evangelicals Embattled
Responses of Evangelicals in the Church of England to Ritualism,
Darwinism and Theological Liberalism 1890–1930
In the closing years of the nineteenth century and the first decades of the
twentieth century Anglican Evangelicals faced a series of challenges. In
responding to Anglo-Catholicism, liberal theology, Darwinism and biblical
criticism, the unity and identity of the Evangelical school were severely tested.
2003 / 1-84227-049-4 / xviii + 352pp

James Whisenant
A Fragile Unity
Anti-Ritualism and the Division of Anglican Evangelicalism
in the Nineteenth Century
This book deals with the ritualist controversy (approximately 1850–1900) from the perspective of its evangelical participants and considers the divisive effects it had on the party.
2003 / 1-84227-105-9 / xvi + 530pp

Haddon Willmer
Evangelicalism 1785–1835: An Essay (1962) and Reflections (2004)
Awarded the Hulsean Prize in the University of Cambridge in 1962, this interpretation of a classic period of English Evangelicalism, by a young church historian, is now supplemented by reflections on Evangelicalism from the vantage point of a retired Professor of Theology.
2005 / 1-84227-219-5

Linda Wilson
Constrained by Zeal
Female Spirituality amongst Nonconformists 1825–1875
Constrained by Zeal investigates the neglected area of Nonconformist female spirituality. Against the background of separate spheres, it analyses the experience of women from four denominations, and argues that the churches provided a 'third sphere' in which they could find opportunities for participation.
2000 / 0-85364-972-3 / xvi + 294pp

Paternoster
9 Holdom Avenue
Bletchley
Milton Keynes MK1 1QR
United Kingdom

Web: www.authenticmedia.co.uk/paternoster